MW01010191

THE TROUBLE WITH CITY PLANNING

The Trouble with City Planning

What New Orleans Can Teach Us

KRISTINA FORD

Yale UNIVERSITY PRESS

New Haven and London

Published with assistance from the Louis Stern
Memorial Fund.

Designed by Sonia L. Shannon.
Set in Adobe Minion type by Duke & Company,
Devon, Pennsylvania.
Printed in the United States of America at
Sheridan Books, Inc.

Library of Congress Cataloging-in-Publication Data
Ford, Kristina
The trouble with city planning : what New Orleans
can teach us / Kristina Ford.
p.   cm.
Includes bibliographical references and index.
ISBN 978-0-300-12735-5 (alk. paper)
1. City planning—United States—Case studies.
2. Land use—United States—Case studies. I. Title.
HT167.F674 2010
307.1'2160973—dc22   2010018736

A catalogue record for this book is available from
the British Library.

This paper meets the requirements of ANSI/NISO
Z39.48–1992 (Permanence of Paper).

10   9   8   7   6   5   4   3   2   1

For Richard

CONTENTS

INTRODUCTION

After Hurricane Katrina came late in August 2005, news reporters covering the devastation began calling me, seeking to understand what had happened in New Orleans. Why. What would happen next. I had been the city's director of planning from 1992 to 2000 and was by this time living far away in Maine. Journalists could reach me, but they could not reach the city's usual on-site planners, who like everyone else had sought refuge, and their cell phones didn't work in the storm's aftermath.

Few of the reporters who called had ever actually seen New Orleans. And those who had seemed to know only what tourists see—the French Quarter and the Garden District, the St. Charles streetcars, the historic restaurants. But now, because helicopters carrying television crews endlessly criss-crossed the city's skies, these reporters could see all parts of New Orleans—a living map. Their perspective was skewed, though, since what could be seen were not streets with intersections and pedestrians and traffic flowing, but miles of rooftops—some with people holding up SOS banners—barely surfaced above an oil-streaked plane of water. Everywhere was undifferentiated destruction (Figure 1).

Although one vast section of the city proved easy to identify. Bounded by the river, the Industrial Canal, and the Intracoastal Waterway, here the destruction seemed not just vividly evident but especially thorough in its scope and breadth. This was the Lower Ninth Ward. From the air, reporters could see the red grain-carrying barge that had calamitously broken through the canal's wall on the day of the storm, coming to rest atop a yellow school bus. They could see houses pushed akimbo, off their pilings and into one another. Wooden buildings were masses of soaked rubble. Cars and boats rested on rooftops, power poles teetered at unaccustomed angles—held up only by the strength of their wires. Small motorboats trafficked

FIGURE 1: Canal Street in New Orleans after Hurricane Katrina (Chris E. Mickal, NOFD Photo Unit. Courtesy The Historic New Orleans Collection.)

through the poisoned water, rescuing citizens from tiny islands of high ground, and Coast Guard helicopters airlifted children to safety. A reporter, so it seemed, could portray the whole catastrophe of Hurricane Katrina just by using the Lower Ninth Ward as its emblem. It was a diorama for all aspects of the city's tragedy.

On August 30, the first day after the storm, as the news spread across the world many reporters from newspapers, television, and radio suddenly wanted to know even *more* about New Orleans. One journalist asked me, "All of you knew this could happen. Do you look back now and think you should have done something different?"

I had been watching the same coverage she was watching—the forlorn people awaiting help at the Convention Center, the stranded rooftop survivors, the waders through what had been streets. I saw the dead. And even though I didn't recognize the individuals, I knew the people. I answered, "Yes. Much should have been done differently."

It was the only creditable answer. City officials entrusted with the care of New Orleans' citizens should've prepared for their safety. No one should've stayed and ridden out the storm. Citizens should've had jobs that paid enough for cars and for escape. Hospital generators shouldn't have been placed on ground floors; city documents shouldn't have been stored in basements. Pumps should've worked. Officialdom should've ensured the strength of levees. FEMA should've come sooner.

The bill of particulars could as well have included not ever founding a city *here*. But here it *was* established in 1721, as close to the mouth of the Mississippi River as possible, and it is now one of America's largest ports. Commodities—wheat, grain, beans—harvested in states stretching from Montana to Ohio, and with a low value-to-weight ratio, were (and are) barged to New Orleans for the simple, important reason that other conveyance is too costly. A port on the river and near the Gulf of Mexico is necessary, and any such site would be vulnerable to hurricanes.

But sensing the reporter's profounder question and addressing it as a planner for whom hindsight can be galling, I went on. "Yes, we could have used New Orleans' land better. We could've *not* built the Lower Ninth Ward on reclaimed swampland; we *could've* clustered families on higher ground. We could've refused to allow subdivisions on the city's outskirts, and instead guided developers to the ample vacant land downtown. We could've used our highest ground—historically invulnerable to flooding—for something better than surface parking lots."

And there was more. New Orleans had long paid insufficient attention to the consequences of its land-use decisions and seemed to make an ongoing civic project out of making them badly. I could've explained that bad prior municipal decisions are the normal working context for all planners, whose job in any city is to make the most of land-use choices already on the books. Because planning is by nature reactive to what already exists and to what is proposed as change, planners are almost always forced to wait—for a new political regime, for a fatter economy to make feasible renovating a derelict bus terminal or tearing down a dilapidated strip mall. And in perpetually stagnant economies—New Orleans' for example—values don't increase, blight worsens, and city planning has a hard time improving the city.

Although I didn't perceive it while talking to the reporter so soon after the hurricane, I began to think in the following days that the city awash in flood and its own bad decisions might actually be experiencing a rare opportunity. For in one terrible night and day, a new recourse for correcting old mistakes had become thinkable. In the face of this destruction, rebuilding and reuniting the city's absent population were now unarguably necessary. By this disastrous stroke, city planners were given an opportunity to do the jobs they were trained to do—to devise how to use the city's lands more to the city's betterment.

I've kept an image from the early days of October 2005. It's a photograph that accompanied a news story written a month after the storm. Only it is an image not of New Orleans, but of Oklahoma—a picture taken from inside the entryway to a simple house, looking onto a front porch where several people are sitting on folding metal chairs. A little girl in pigtails leans against a man. They all stare forlornly out at the pretty autumn landscape. The freshly harvested Oklahoma veldt stretches a hundred yards toward a small drying barn with a red corrugated aluminum roof. Beyond are thick woods, where only a few leaves have started to turn color. These "Oklahomans" were displaced New Orleanians, some from the Lower Ninth Ward—survivors who'd been sent north after their failed attempt to ride out the storm. Their houses were destroyed and now these citizens had little to do but wait and hope that government would imagine a plan to bring them home and provide for them there.

True, the mayor of New Orleans had formed a commission and charged it with writing a plan for recovery. But what the promisingly named body— the Bring New Orleans Back Commission—had in mind was less promising to these citizens in Oklahoma. The commissioners, prominent men from New Orleans, had already informed the *Wall Street Journal* that "New Orleans Brought Back" had to be something very different from the city of the past. The commission's scheme would have better services and fewer poor people. New Orleans had to be rebuilt, but in a completely new way—a way more in tune with the city's desired demographics, geography, and politics. The world should know, the commissioners said, that the city wouldn't get back the citizens who hadn't had the resources to evacuate the city, because they wouldn't have the resources to return. "That's just a fact," one commissioner concluded.

As it happened, even while the Bring New Orleans Back Commission was explaining the new urban practicalities, many citizens were already returning to their homes in the well-to-do French Quarter, the Garden District, or Esplanade Ridge. These neighborhoods—built centuries earlier on the city's high ground—hadn't even flooded, and therefore potable water was soon made available and electricity was restored, allowing displaced residents to return and set about repairing what was damaged. Difficult as resuming ordinary life was, it did not require a new plan for the city. Quickly, restaurants reopened and Bourbon Street was again filled with returned residents, journalists, relief workers, and insurance adjusters out on the town. Tourists arrived, wanting to see for themselves what had happened, and by December 2005—three months after Katrina—the newspaper's society pages reported debutante balls.

However, those people who'd lived in the flooded neighborhoods, people like the refugees in Oklahoma, truly needed a new plan for restoring the city before they could come back. And between then and now, I've come to see their somber plight as signifying the plight of all New Orleans' citizens whom city planning has always failed. Although the specific refugees of this specific catastrophe can be seen to stand persuasively for all citizens around America who've been let down, thwarted, or otherwise dissatisfied by city planning wherever it's a part of government. Displeased citizens constitute a much more diverse group than storm refugees or discrete survivors, but they are in fact regular citizens in every American city. Its members might indeed be surprised to think that they constitute a group at all, since their individual dissatisfactions manifest themselves so divergently: they might be developers in Dallas who can't build a subdivision because planners require an expensive common sewerage system; or they might be environmentalists in Chicago who learn that subdivision development— unchecked by city planners—has wrecked natural bird habitats. They might be minimum-wage workers in Omaha living in downtown flophouses that city planners have approved for expensive modernization by developers after an upscale clientele; or they might be preservationists who oppose modernizing the flophouses because they're significant parts of the city's history.

Examples of similar disappointments are well distributed around us, dutifully reported in every newspaper in America. Contradictory complaints, to be sure; different constituencies. Yet all share a comparable dissatisfaction with planning that eventuates in a comparable doubt that planning could ever serve them better.

Inspired by New Orleans' forlorn citizenry and by all who lack confidence in city planning—including planners who've found their knowledge unwelcome—I've imagined this book to propose answers to critical questions that all these complainants might frame: Why has city planning ignored vulnerable citizens? Why does it thwart economic development? Why hasn't it saved natural habitats? Why don't elected leaders take planners' advice? Why indeed is city planning even necessary? What good does it do? These questions are so familiar and so commonplace that one can only think that there must be some trouble with how city planning is practiced.

Fixing the trouble is essential because city planners perform the most important tasks of government—looking to the future, advising on issues regarding a city's physical development, thinking how to use every asset of a city not just to prevent bad things from happening, but to bring about good things. City planners seek to make life better in cities that are thriving, and better in cities trying to recover from a storm.

One doesn't have to love cities—or even live in one—to recognize that city planning is worthwhile. One has only to consider the magnitude of what must be built *next* in America to accommodate its projected growth. In the next thirty years America's population will increase by a third and will require nearly half again as many dwellings as now stand. Americans will construct nearly twice as much commercial space as already exists. If all this building were to occur on land not currently developed, the nation would lose 40 million acres of farmland, fields, and forests to development.[1] Therefore, making cities better becomes an attractive and necessary alternative to growth into undeveloped land; better cities can preserve the rural character of small communities and can also reduce the nation's reliance on oil.

By looking closely at planning activities in several New Orleans neighborhoods—including the Lower Ninth Ward—this book engages the most fundamental aspects of planning practice. Every American city has its own versions of the neighborhoods discussed here. Every American city has areas like the Lower Ninth Ward, which was inadvertently created when a large shipping canal was built for the sake of increasing business at the Port of New Orleans. Other cities create equivalently vulnerable neighborhoods—and relegate to them citizens with comparably few political and economic resources. This happens when freeways are built for the sake of attracting more industry, but increase air pollution for the residents nearby. Blighted areas get created when a municipal airport adds a runway to entice tourists, irrespective of the noise and risk of disaster to adjacent subdivisions. When speculators "discover" a potentially trendy neighborhood downtown, the out-priced residents—usually poor people—have little choice but to relocate in isolated low-income housing districts, which then are the subject of local news exposés about civic pathologies: drug wars, teenage pregnancy, truancy. Throughout America these are all places that suffer in the putative win-win equation of urban development.

City planners in New Orleans deal with the same problems planners anywhere in America face. The city has sections built long before city planning was a part of government, as well as neighborhoods built only with the approval of city planners. Today New Orleanians still agreeably participate in a romance that their town is unique. But in terms of city development, city decisions, and city problems New Orleans isn't so unique. Many other American cities, for instance, are vulnerable to natural disasters: hurricanes, earthquakes, volcanoes, flooding. Many other American cities have blighted downtown neighborhoods, declining tax revenues, homeless people, and undermaintained infrastructure—streets, sewerage, bridges. And in terms of planning, New Orleans most certainly is like other places: it has ignored citizens who were displaced by single-minded economic development schemes; it has failed to prevent wasteful residential and commercial development, and it has allowed nuisance land uses to elbow into quiet neighborhoods.

How a city uses its land enshrines its citizens' hopes, its laws, its procedures, and its failures to pay attention. I recognize that my planner's bias is to suppose a city can correct old mistakes. Still, I think it's important to determine how New Orleans—and any other city—can make better land-use decisions, even if in fact it can't correct what's been done before. In the post-Katrina desolation, New Orleans reveals many troubles with contemporary planning practice in America. I'll use what the tragedy in New Orleans inadvertently disclosed to suggest what's wrong, what's right, and what can make city planning better—wherever it's practiced. Sometimes it seems the problems and the solutions are plain. But as Jasper Johns said, "sometimes things are so well-known they're not well seen." A hurricane made me see what this book can make clear. Would that this clarity had been achieved more simply.

PART ONE

The Practice of American City Planning

ONE

Cities as Planners See Them

In the aftermath of Hurricane Katrina, the world was eager for news of New Orleans. Photographers filed images from every devastated part of the city and reporters told stories of the victims who'd lived there—how old they were, where they came from, how they made a living. Their race. In its devastation, the city became "interesting," but for reasons other than the usual ones—the totemic tourist attractions, the music, the food, the "culture," and the worn-out characterizations visitors liked: The Big Easy, Laissez Le Bon Temps Rouler, the City that Care Forgot. The new subject of interest about New Orleans was how it had so quickly become a city of tragedy and sufferers, and this required much more fundamental explanations than what had sufficed for sightseers before the storm.

As more was reported about what parts of town had suffered the most damage, even native New Orleanians became aware of places and people they'd never taken much notice of. Their lack of knowledge wouldn't be particularly unusual anywhere, since citizens know about their cities primarily in local terms—staying close to home and traveling mostly to and from the discrete parts of town where they live and like to shop, where they work and where their children go to school. Thousands of people who grew up in Brooklyn or Queens have never been to Manhattan—and vice versa; countless Watts residents have never seen Pasadena. I knew people from New Orleans' Garden District whose only experience with the Lower Ninth Ward had been to drive past it on their way to duck blinds in St. Bernard Parish, or who'd never seen the Vietnamese neighborhoods in New Orleans

East, or who didn't know that their gardeners kept axes in their attics at home in case overwhelming flood waters forced them to find safety by chopping through the roof.

City planners, on the other hand, must essentially know everything about a city and be its students. They must learn what's already been built, then become familiar with who lives where and under what circumstances. They must know where jobs are and how people get to them. They must notice vacant land, and observe where children attend school and where they can play. Planners must take note of the spatial arrangement of different land uses—notice that a pool hall is next to a high school, or that apartment buildings are situated far away from public parks. Planners must know the routes citizens can take to evacuate when catastrophe threatens.

Planners' greatest strength is what they necessarily know about cities, including geography and prior civic leaders' plans and choices for developing land within a municipality. City planners in New Orleans would necessarily know the city's high points, its inundatable lows; they would know why the oldest and richest parts of New Orleans, for instance, would never be badly flooded, whereas they also know that neighborhoods built in twentieth-century New Orleans would necessarily lie under several feet of water were a flood to occur. In addition, city planners have learned the professional theories that attempt to comprehend and make coherent the natural and human factors that shape a landscape.

Inasmuch as this book has a conjoined purpose—to detail the specific problems with planning endeavors in pre- and post-Katrina New Orleans, and to use New Orleans as a case in point for illuminating both the strengths and the larger troubles with city planning—it seems in order early on to take the reader on a short excursion through the city's complex geography. New Orleans' geographical peculiarities would be known (and definitely were known) by city planners before and after the flood, just as planners in any city would know its geographical peculiarities and plan in accordance with them. Several maps are provided in the following pages to assist comprehension of the decidedly unusual series of geographic factors, human choices, and assorted schemes and plans that together established New Orleans as a port on the Mississippi River and subsequently contributed to the tragic destruction by Hurricane Katrina.

Like all major rivers, the Mississippi has over the course of thousands of years created natural levees along its banks as annual spring floods overflowed the river's channel, then receded, to leave behind sediment carried in the water. In prehistoric New Orleans, the coarsest sand and silt settled first, closest by the river banks, creating high ground. Less coarse sediment traveled farther away from the river. And the eventual result of this sedimentation was the creation of a pair of ridges parallel to the river's course on both sides, ridges that were highest—between five and ten feet—at its banks. These are what geographers call the *natural levees* in New Orleans. Perhaps surprisingly, each levee is between one and two miles wide—widest along the convex arcs of the river's meanders where the channel bears forcefully into the bank, slows, and leaves the most sediment before flowing to the next turn. The narrowest natural levees, accordingly, lie where the river's course is straightest. The natural levees in New Orleans slope gradually down and away from the channel's banks for a mile or two, with a fall of about one vertical foot per five hundred feet of horizontal distance—and end where the floodwaters stopped at the low-lying swamps that surrounded the city. (Figure 2 depicts the Mississippi River's course from above New Orleans to the Gulf of Mexico.)

These natural levees are not what a layman might believe a levee to be, and are not perceptible except to a trained observer, since they slope so very gradually away from the banks of the river. Man-made levees—the narrow and high mounds of grass-covered earth that have been constructed all along the edges of the Mississippi—are the levees of conventional lore that protect the city, but simultaneously they mark where *natural* levees begin at their highest point beside the river.

The French government founded New Orleans on a bank of the Mississippi, where the river's ninety-degree turn to the south creates a wide and high natural levee sloping toward Lake Pontchartrain. The city's original location on a crescent meander of the Mississippi River is now the Vieux Carré, or French Quarter, where in 1721 a street network was laid out in the grid pattern a visitor can still see today. (This original layout of the Vieux Carré is included on the historical map shown as Figure 3.) The simple design, now sanctified by local archivists as New Orleans' first plan, was drawn up and followed by French military engineers to defend the fledgling city from its enemies. Confident of being fortified against attack, the French

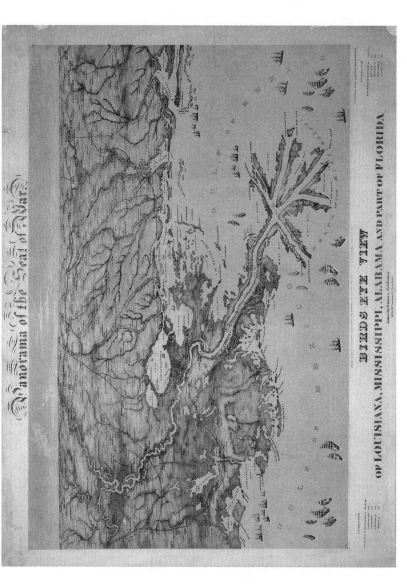

FIGURE 2: Bird's-eye View of the Mississippi River, 1861. In this panoramic image of the Mississippi River drainage through Louisiana, New Orleans appears roughly in the middle—illustrating how far upstream the port lies from the Gulf of Mexico, which is about a hundred miles away. This depiction includes a dramatic rendering of what geographers call the "bird's foot" configuration of the river's delta, caused when a river composed of heavy sediment flows into a slow-moving body of water like the Gulf of Mexico. (The Historic New Orleans Collection, accession number 1956.50)

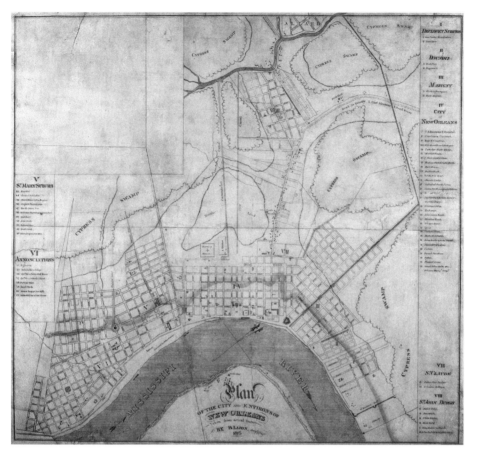

FIGURE 3: Plan of the City and Environs of New Orleans, 1816. French surveyor Barthélémy Lafon mapped the city's earliest settlement as eight sections indicated with roman numerals. Section IV is the French Quarter. (The Historic New Orleans Collection, accession number 1945.3)

set about realizing the commercial rewards of their new port by authorizing Jean-Baptiste Le Moyne Bienville—who along with his brother, Pierre Le Moyne Iberville, had founded the city—to govern the colony. Bienville began governing by giving land to French citizens, including himself and his brother (naturally enough), in return for the recipients' efforts to establish plantations upstream and down from the tiny city, and to import colonists who would produce commodities intended for a world market.

This quid-pro-quo method of developing the new colony surely attracted schemers, and from time to time the French Crown had to correct the most grievous land grabs and giveaways. But gradually, the land on the natural levees was apportioned into long pencil-like plantations with narrow frontages to the river and with cropland sloping "back" toward the cypress swamps that extended all the way to Lake Pontchartrain. The unusual shape of these original plantations took optimum advantage of the city's geographic circumstances: each owner had access to the river for selling crops, and could live on his own high ground. Even when spring floods topped the levees' highest points at the river bank, water drained toward the swamp and dried quickly.

Prior to 1865, slaves of course lived on the city's high ground with their wealthy owners, but other early inhabitants found few advantages from the geography. Poorer residents—including un-enslaved black people—settled beyond the "back" boundaries of the plantations (farthest from the river, that is), where the land was lower. Spring floods brought the most water here, and it receded only slowly. This area formed the back boundary of all neighborhoods built on the natural levees and was referred to collectively as "back of town," where to this day many of the city's poorest black citizens reside.

As the Port of New Orleans thrived and more people were drawn to the city, the old dedicated plantations, upstream and down, were gradually subdivided and individual lots parceled off. No plan—not even one as simple as a prospective street layout—oversaw such transactions, and as a consequence New Orleans grew according to where individual buyers found property available at an agreeable price for their new enterprises. Unsurprisingly, though, the original French owners kept the best of the high ground for themselves, their families, and their slaves. In time, these former plantation owners passed into the power structure of the growing city, and resided in neighborhoods along what became St. Charles Avenue—the land they'd originally settled and were familiar with. Here today, rich whites— many bearing the names of the original French planters—reside near the black descendants of domestic slaves whose owners had provided them housing before and then after emancipation, in order that they continue working in the mansions and gardens of their former owners. This is "uptown" New Orleans, a designation taken from the area's location upstream of the French Quarter.

Much of the city's geography and its development history became dramatized and re-revealed immediately after Hurricane Katrina. Floodwaters simply didn't reach houses built on the natural levees. Even "back of town," the lowest of the natural high ground, was relatively undamaged, because all residential design before 1900 was put in place with the probability of flooding known. On the highest ground, houses on heavy foundations were raised on pillars high enough to allow water to stream beneath without drowning inhabitants—and without causing much structural damage. In the distant lower sections of the natural levee, back-of-town craftsmen had devised a method of raising houses by using light balloon frames that sat atop stone piers. The frames were two-by-four joists made of cypress wood taken from the local swamps, and could satisfactorily survive prolonged periods of standing in floodwater. On all the natural levees, modest bungalows as well as elegant mansions were sited on small lots, thus effectively clustering New Orleans' population into the safest areas.

This original pattern of urban development in New Orleans, depicted in Figure 4, stayed in place for nearly two hundred years, though not because of any prudence on the part of government. As described, the natural levees of New Orleans ended at cypress swamps, which the city owned and whose use for two centuries had been limited to fishing and harvesting wood. City leaders, however, longed to make something more of these swamps—to drain them, to recover the land and put it to a more profitable use: sell it, develop it, collect taxes. It might seem to be the standard passion of American city leaders in any age.

To realize this tantalizing end, in the early 1800s the city of New Orleans sponsored construction of canals meant to drain the swamps and force the drained water into Lake Pontchartrain. But these public projects were unsuccessful until 1899, when New Orleans engineer Baldwin Wood invented a heavy-duty pump capable of lifting great quantities of water and moving it to the lake—no matter that this water contained tree trunks and other large debris, as the water from the cypress swamps surely did. Encouraged by the prospect of new saleable land, the city set about draining its swamps, using Wood's pumps as well as the existing drainage canals. As one might expect, however, the land that gradually emerged was low and also required protection from future flooding. The city then paid to

FIGURE 4: Topographical and Drainage Map, 1878. Surveyor Thomas Hardee's map shows late-nineteenth-century development amid the cypress swamps. (The Historic New Orleans Collection, accession number 00.34a,b)

construct man-made levees along the drainage canals—thus fortifying the newly emerged land—and by the late 1920s much of the area between the Mississippi River and Lake Pontchartrain (the area usually thought of as modern-day New Orleans) was ready for development. On Figure 5, a map of contemporary New Orleans, land created from cypress swamps in the early twentieth century can be identified.

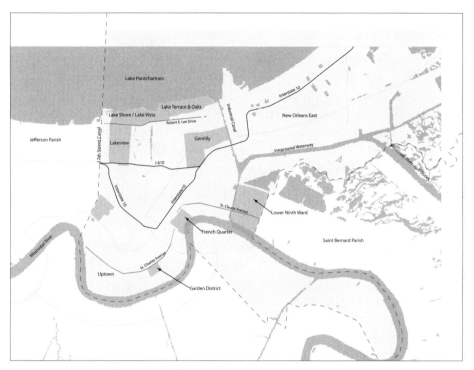

FIGURE 5: Modern New Orleans. This map shows the city as it was developed after 1900, when the Wood pump made it possible to drain the cypress swamps that limited the city's physical expansion. Among the historic neighborhoods that were settled on the Mississippi River's natural levees are the French Quarter, the Garden District, and Uptown. Neighborhoods built on drained swamp and other man-made land include Lakeview, Lake Terrace, Gentilly, and New Orleans East. (Images rendered by Natalie Yates. GIS data distributed by "Atlas: The Louisiana Statewide GIS," Louisiana State University CADGIS Research Laboratory, Baton Rouge [http://atlas.lsu.edu], and by Louisiana State University Information Clearinghouse, Baton Rouge [www.katrina.lsu.edu].)

As if brought into existence solely to continue land creation and development, the city's new planning commission in 1927 trumpeted the news that land once uninhabitable was now drained and ready for housing. As the *Times-Picayune* reported, the commission believed that in twenty or so years, as many as 1.4 million people would live in New Orleans.

As it happened, New Orleans never attained more than 600,000 residents (in 1960), and the actual development of the land drained in the 1920s didn't start until twenty years after the planning commission's proud proclamation—not until after World War II. That first planning commission didn't—and in its behalf, couldn't—foresee that in New Orleans, as in every other city in America, residential construction would stall during the period beginning with the stock market crash of 1929, and then remain stagnant through the Great Depression and the long war. For nearly twenty years, demand for housing was critically unmet throughout America—including New Orleans. The end of World War II finally set in motion immense population shifts as soldiers returned home, and developers across the country built millions of single-family houses that the federal government's newly enacted mortgage guarantees had ensured a market for.

By the early 1950s, ready buyers were suddenly in great supply, many of them returned GIs who were assisted financially not only by federal loan guarantees, but also by new income tax regulations that made interest payments and property taxes on houses deductible. Between 1947 and 1964, there were more than 1.2 million new houses built in America *per year*—whereas in the preceding twenty years only a few thousand had been constructed annually.[1] In New Orleans after World War II, the previously drained swamplands were finally—and quickly—developed all along the old drainage canals, where man-made levees shored up residents' confidence that the land they were living on was safe.

The neighborhoods built on New Orleans' drained land looked dramatically different from the original parts of the eighteenth-century city. For one thing, because new ground seemed plentiful, houses were no longer clustered, and most of them weren't raised above ground level, since flooding seemed "impossible." Rather, and according to the fashion of American postwar suburbs, developers built ranch-style homes on concrete slabs, and surrounded each house with ample yards. Building materials were no longer chosen for their resistance to water in the manner of the old cypress construction. And all the residents of these new homes were white, a result of restrictions contained in the very deeds the owners signed.

This brief history describes the provenance of Lakeview, which appears on Figure 5 as a settlement of subdivisions built on land created from swamps and set alongside one of the original nineteenth-century drainage canals—the Seventeenth Street Canal—where modern houses on large lots made it look more like any 1950s American suburb than like the New Orleans of the French Quarter and St. Charles Avenue. New postwar homeowners in Lakeview felt as safe as those who lived on the city's oldest high ground or in any of the city's safest precincts. The geography that had once imposed severe constraints on human settlement seemed to have been overcome.

Designs on New Orleans' natural landscape reached beyond transforming its swamps into buildable land. Ever since the city had been founded, the volume of commerce going through its port had necessarily been limited by the location and capacity of navigable waterways. The Dock Board—a group of officials commissioned by Louisiana's governor to manage the Port of New Orleans—made two significant changes to shipping routes in the twentieth century, both of which supposed that the city's geography could be enhanced so as to increase trade, and both of which ultimately contributed to city planning's ongoing dilemma of coping with a difficult landscape.

First, the Dock Board oversaw completion of the Industrial Canal in 1923. More formally known as the Inner Harbor Navigational Canal, this waterway allowed ships to pass between the Mississippi River and Lake Pontchartrain. Such a connection between the river and the lake had been desired for as long as the city had existed, but it became possible only with twentieth-century mechanics.[2] A newly invented lock system was installed to accommodate, first, the fact of the lake's water level being ten feet higher than the river, and second, the twenty-foot range in water level that the river experiences over the course of a year—highest, as you would imagine, at spring runoff, lowest late in the summer.

The Dock Board believed the site it had chosen for the Industrial Canal was economically optimal. The canal was planned where the lake and the river were closest to each other, so the cost of construction would be less than at any other location. Furthermore, because the city owned most of the land where the canal was to be built, the cost of acquiring the necessary right-of-way would undoubtedly be cheaper than any other choice. Unsurprisingly, New Orleans' elected leaders concurred with the Dock Board's plans, not only because the canal's construction promised the usual array of economic benefits—tax revenues, jobs, and so on—but also because the canal would lie inside New Orleans' municipal boundary and therefore profits earned by the lock's operations wouldn't be shared with other local jurisdictions such as St. Bernard Parish.

Construction of the second significant alteration to New Orleans' waterways began in 1958, when the U.S. Army Corps of Engineers undertook an extension of Louisiana's Intracoastal Waterway.[3] This extension was to begin at the Industrial Canal and stretch all the way to the Gulf of Mexico, thereby offering shippers a much shorter—and safer—route between the gulf and the Port of New Orleans. The map in Figure 6 clearly shows why shippers would prefer such a route. Rather than entering the mouth of the Mississippi River and then following its hundred-mile route through the meanders and shifting sandbars of the lower Mississippi to reach New Orleans, boats could sail from the Gulf of Mexico into the dredged waterway, continue on this route all the way to the Industrial Canal—and enter the Mississippi River precisely at the Port of New Orleans. By following this relatively straight route in either direction the transit was made 25 percent shorter.

The Industrial Canal was an engineering triumph, and when the extended Intracoastal Waterway was joined to it city leaders anticipated increased commerce for the maritime industry and improved municipal revenues. But even though it didn't seem ominous at the time, construction of the canal portended that any part of the city lying downstream of its course would hereafter be reached only by crossing bridges. Thus the Industrial Canal literally divided the area of New Orleans into two halves. Subsequently, the Intracoastal Waterway further divided the lower half of New Orleans, beyond the Industrial Canal. One division lay to the north of the Intracoastal Waterway, extending to Lake Pontchartrain, and the other to the south, between the waterway and the Mississippi River. The newly cut-off part of New Orleans below the Industrial Canal and south of the Intracoastal Waterway included the area that became known as the Lower Ninth Ward.

Parenthetically, it should be noted that other cities routinely create similar cut-off sections of town like the Lower Ninth Ward when they widen roadways through existing neighborhoods, making it difficult—or dangerous—for residents to walk to their usual destinations, or when they build grandiose sports arenas that disrupt old street patterns and sever local residents' sense of connection with the rest of their city. The results of cutting off the Lower Ninth Ward came to appear extreme and dire in

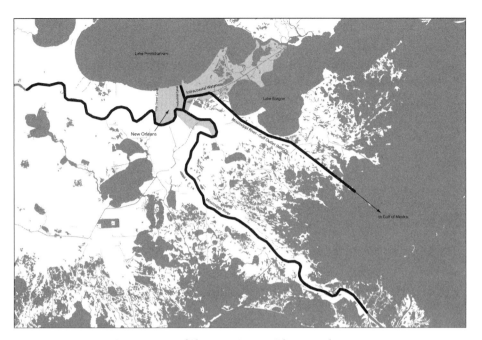

FIGURE 6: A Comparison of Shipping Routes. This map shows two routes
shippers could take to the Port of New Orleans: the Mississippi River or the
Mississippi River–Gulf Outlet. The MRGO route reduced the distance 25 percent
and avoided navigating through the river's many meanders. (Images rendered
by Natalie Yates. GIS data distributed by "Atlas: The Louisiana Statewide GIS,"
Louisiana State University CADGIS Research Laboratory [http://atlas.lsu.edu],
and by Louisiana State University Information Clearinghouse [www.katrina
.lsu.edu].)

the days after Katrina, although the process by which this part of town was
made separate is not unusual in any American city.

For all the promise that the Intracoastal Waterway had seemed to offer the
shipping industry, very few shippers used it because the channel was relatively shallow and also because the sediment carried in the water—water
from the sediment-laden Mississippi River—was continuously falling to the
bottom of the waterway, making its depth unreliable. As a consequence,
the state of Louisiana and the federal government appropriated money to

improve the Intracoastal Waterway—to widen it, deepen it, and keep its channel at a consistent depth by constantly dredging the bottom to clear sediment away (i.e., send it downstream). In addition, man-made levees were constructed all along the widened intracoastal route to protect adjacent land from flooding. When these public works were completed in 1968, the section of the Intracoastal Waterway that began at the Industrial Canal was renamed in honor of its purpose—the Mississippi River–Gulf Outlet (MRGO, pronounced locally as "Mister Go"). The theory underlying plans for the massive MRGO project had it that shippers would prefer its route because they could avoid the Mississippi River. Trade at the Port of New Orleans was sure to increase.

As it happened, shippers made much less use of MRGO than anticipated. The tonnage and number of ships in the channel peaked in 1982, and then declined steadily—partly because the congressional appropriations necessary for dredging the channel to keep it at a consistent depth were inadequate to the task, and shippers returned to the Mississippi River. After 1998, so few ships used MRGO that the annual appropriation for its maintenance was insufficient to dredge the channel to the dimensions necessary for most vessels. Still, the channel remained officially open, a vestige of hopes to increase trade at the Port of New Orleans.[4]

The Mississippi River, the new Industrial Canal, and the section of the Intracoastal Waterway known as MRGO were not only significant features of New Orleans' recent geography; they also had a profound effect on the Lower Ninth Ward, so named because it was the Ninth Ward's downstream section, which became physically separate from the rest of the city when the Industrial Canal was opened in 1923. Only two bridges connected the Lower Ninth Ward with the rest of New Orleans when the canal was completed.

Before 1900, and as in the rest of the city, development in the then undivided Lower Ninth Ward was near the Mississippi River and on the natural levee that sloped gently toward cypress swamps and the lake. St. Claude Avenue in today's Lower Ninth Ward follows the approximate boundary of that natural levee, and it was between the avenue and the river that most residents of the Lower Ninth Ward lived before 1950. But after that year, as the postwar population of New Orleans grew, city services were extended into the drained swamps that lay between St. Claude and the Intracoastal

Waterway. Soon houses were built there. These residences were smaller than those in Lakeview because builders in the Lower Ninth Ward targeted lower-income prospective home buyers. But these postwar houses were similarly constructed: down-market suburban homes on concrete slabs at grade.

As I detail New Orleans' peculiar geography in a way that illuminates its challenges for city planners and ultimately likens its problems to those of many American cities, let me refer briefly again to the maps shown in Figures 5 and 6, where you can find the location of another large extension of buildable land inside the New Orleans city limits—an extension that occurred in the quadrant of the city that was partitioned by the Industrial Canal and the Intracoastal Waterway (by then known as MRGO). This area lies between Lake Pontchartrain and the Intracoastal Waterway, a portion of land now known as New Orleans East, where the city authorized the subdivision of fifty square miles of low-lying ground in the 1970s, thereby transforming another cut-off area into a neighborhood. Development of this former swampland had a different champion from Lakeview, where city leaders had themselves given assistance to draining and building on the swamps. In New Orleans East, the champions of development were private speculators who realized the opportunities they'd been afforded by the federal government's program to build highways.[5]

In the 1950s, construction of a network of highways began throughout the United States, inaugurating what became the Interstate Highway System. In Louisiana, Interstate 10 (completed in the mid-1960s) was built to connect New Orleans to the Gulf Coast—both east and west. The design of all controlled-access federal interstate highways mandates exits that provide access to local towns, and it was accordingly at the sites of these exits that most new post–World War II suburban housing was built. In New Orleans, much of Interstate 10's eastern route—the section beyond the city's center and the Industrial Canal—was still within municipal boundaries. In this section of the interstate, the required exits dead-ended at uninhabited swamps. But from prior experience, New Orleans' speculators knew that such swamps could become solid land and that home buyers would be attracted to new subdivisions built there.

The city's planners approved development in what became New Orleans

East just as they had in Lakeview and in all the city's other neighborhoods built on drained swamplands. And as speculators predicted, many people bought homes in this new, eastern section of New Orleans. Everybody involved in the development of New Orleans East—city planners, speculative builders, and new residents—was confident the levees that protected the rest of the city also protected this land from Lake Pontchartrain and the Mississippi River's flood plain.

A topographic map of New Orleans' various elevations above sea level delineates the areas that were still inundated by Katrina's floodwaters on August 31, 2005—two days after the great storm. This map, shown as Figure 7, dramatizes how false—and tragic—was the feeling of safety among people who lived in neighborhoods built on land reclaimed from the swamps after 1900. Most of the flooded areas were low-elevation neighborhoods that after the hurricane were several feet underwater, whereas those areas built earlier—those atop the natural levees—suffered little flood damage. The uptown Garden District and the French Quarter were already dry by August 31, while Lakeview, built on reclaimed swamp, still stood in the ten-foot-deep water that had flooded through the breached Seventeenth Street Canal. New Orleans East remained completely flooded for days, although Interstate 10—built on higher ground—was as dry as it had been the day it opened to traffic.

In the Lower Ninth Ward, the high ground was mostly dry on the natural levee between the river and St. Claude Avenue. But between St. Claude and MRGO—the former low-lying land undeveloped before 1950—the wreckage of houses shoved off their slab foundations lay under several feet of water that had either spilled from the breached Industrial Canal or been pushed up over the levees along MRGO by the flood surge. Here in the Lower Ninth Ward is where CNN showed fishing boats on rooftops, tires thrown high in trees, and upright utility poles listing at forty-five-degree angles. The destruction went on and on, to the Orleans Parish line—and beyond it into St. Bernard Parish, where the land, sadly, is even lower.

In purely historical terms, *any* street that appeared on a map of New Orleans drawn in the nineteenth century—such as the map shown in Figure 4 —probably did not flood. Correspondingly, the most devastated areas were those built on low land, and notably built *after* a planning commission had been installed in New Orleans city government. One could justly say that

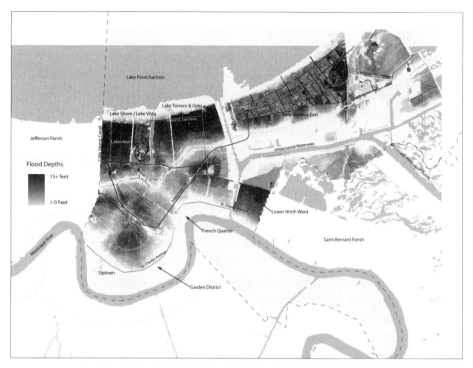

FIGURE 7: Topographic Map of New Orleans, August 31, 2005. This image shows the depth of water still standing in the city two days after Hurricane Katrina. The land was dry on the natural levees—and on some of the man-made land along Lake Pontchartrain. But most of the neighborhoods built on the drained cypress swamps were flooded with as much as fifteen feet of water, which stood for several days before it was possible to pump it back into the lake and the river. (Images rendered by Natalie Yates. GIS data distributed by "Atlas: The Louisiana Statewide GIS," Louisiana State University CADGIS Research Laboratory [http://atlas.lsu.edu], and by Louisiana State University Information Clearinghouse [www.katrina.lsu.edu].)

building the original New Orleans had been a project constrained by the primal facts of its flood-prone site, while building the *new* New Orleans was a different kind of animal—one built on the certainty that technology could overcome those primal facts and free planners to concentrate on schemes for increasing commerce and for housing new residents.

*   *   *

This geographical excursus through the history of development in New Orleans suggests that in the aftermath of Hurricane Katrina, asking what city planning should have done differently in New Orleans was, and is, not an idle question at all. This question is a good one wherever foreseeable tragedy destroys what mankind builds. Two years after Hurricane Katrina, subdivisions in Southern California were destroyed in wildfires spread by Santa Ana winds. A planner for one scorched county explained to a reporter that his office had no duty to slow development on lands subject to wildfires, but only to ensure people's safety when fires happened. His office had a reliable evacuation plan, he said, and had been directed by the county's elected leadership to devise safety rules for future construction. Planners were thinking of requiring one hundred feet of open space around each new house, where nothing could catch fire, and were investigating new building codes that would ensure residents' survival even if their homes burned to the ground around them. This planner's answers bespeak a municipal conviction that a different plan—one that might prevent more subdivisions from being built along the well-known route of Santa Ana winds—wouldn't be useful, and that what might be done differently is a matter of inventive construction methods that effectively overcome local geography.

Hurricane Katrina bared New Orleans' tragic reliance on plans and development schemes being able to "overcome" local geography. Having suffered through that storm and its disastrous aftermath, city leaders were convinced that they required a new plan. And indeed, New Orleans has undergone a flurry of planning since the hurricane, conducted by experts of national repute who brought to their task the most widely regarded approaches of their profession. Five years later, however, rebuilding has proceeded so randomly among the devastated neighborhoods that *no* plan seems at work. It is fair to say that planning to rebuild New Orleans has been a fiasco, although a review of plans devised after the great storm makes it possible to discern what the planning profession itself might do differently—and better.

TWO

Intimations of Trouble
Plans After Hurricane Katrina

The annual meeting of the Louisiana Chapter of the American Planning Association was scheduled to convene the first week in October 2005—little more than a month following Hurricane Katrina, as it happened—and was to be held in Shreveport, a city far north of the Gulf Coast. Those in charge of staging these yearly conventions always sought a conference title that would bring some new and attractive focus to the event, thereby drawing city planners and planning consultants from around the state. In 2005 the organization settled on "Planning for Prosperity," which was a new angle in Louisiana, where prosperity had been elusive since the 1984 oil bust. Then there was the hurricane, and the title of the 2005 planning convention was quickly edited to be "Planning for Prosperity: Opportunities in a Post-Katrina World."

In the immediate aftermath of the storm, this title might've seemed a wide and hopeful view of how Louisiana's planners could assist in rebuilding the state's Gulf Coast and improve the economy there. But as time has passed, events have made the title seem to encapsulate how planning consultants and architectural firms from around the United States viewed devastated New Orleans: as a place where they could win contracts to write plans for recovery from the disaster based more on their pet planning theories than on what they knew about the city. Several important but importantly inadequate planning efforts took place in New Orleans during the years after Hurricane Katrina, and summarizing those efforts can highlight much that is usually invisible about plans and planning.

The first plan for rebuilding New Orleans was prepared by expert consultants—planners, developers, and bankers hired by Mayor Ray Nagin's Bring New Orleans Back Commission—and was unveiled in January 2006 to a very large audience gathered at a downtown hotel ballroom.[1] The people there were ordinary citizens, elected representatives, local and national news media, and they all expected to hear logistical details of steps that would bring displaced residents home and also support the scattered individual rebuilding efforts already under way. This seemed to be what a recovery plan would logically provide so that life in New Orleans could gradually return to a condition that resembled life as it had been.

Instead, the attendees were shown a large map of the city, on which the locations of open space were depicted in a future New Orleans, newly configured to be safe from floods. On the map, shown as Figure 8, six areas were encircled by dashed green lines, and those six circled areas covered much of the city's land that Hurricane Katrina had ruined—including most of the Lower Ninth Ward. The plan's draftsman announced that the green-circled areas represented new parkland, where any future floodwaters—even as deep as those brought by Hurricane Katrina—would naturally flow without causing harm to any resident.

The large audience included some displaced New Orleanians who'd made considerable effort to attend, and those citizens audibly wondered—politely, at first—what would happen to people whose houses had stood in the, as it were, "green zones." Where would they eventually live? And where could they stay while the city was reconfigured as the plan foresaw? Those were details to be worked out later, the Bring New Orleans Back Commission answered. Other people in the audience, citizens who lived on the city's high ground, also wondered—a little less politely—if the people from the flooded areas were going to be forced into existing and newly reviving neighborhoods uptown. Newcomers—even though they were New Orleanians—wouldn't be welcome where they might disrupt ordinary neighborhood life, one speaker from the high ground said. Others at the meeting—many from the also badly flooded Lakeview district—were pleased to find that their neighborhoods weren't circled with green dashes. Yet those Lakeview residents who'd already started rebuilding tartly asked when they could expect to receive city services. So far, they pointed out, only neighborhoods where tourists went and where the richest New Or-

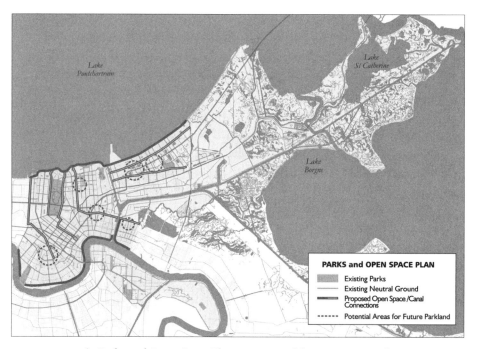

FIGURE 8: Parks and Open Space Plan, a section of the Bring New Orleans Back Action Plan presented on January 11, 2006. The dotted circles mark locations for future parkland, but the plan did not explain what would happen to the residents of these areas—or their property. (Prepared by Wallace Roberts & Todd for the Bring New Orleans Back Commission)

leanians lived had been provided with electricity and water and working sewers. Unfortunately, the answers to what became increasingly strident questions lay in details yet to be worked out by the commission's esteemed experts.

I attended this fractious meeting, and like others there I had come with hopeful expectations for what would be presented. After all, immediately following Hurricane Katrina, urbanists from around the world had offered equable advice for rebuilding New Orleans, most commonly recommending that the devastated city reduce its physical extent and cluster its citizens on the higher ground of natural levees.[2] Such an idea, sympathetic scholars said, might return the city to its historical dimensions, house all its residents in safer neighborhoods, and simultaneously reduce the extent and cost of municipal services. In the early days after the storm, it seemed that this advice—crafted as a rational plan for redevelopment by the mayor's commission and its renowned consultants—could make New Orleans better for everyone who'd lived in the city before the storm. But that wasn't how the audience saw the plan.

Instead, the audience saw that working out the commission's stated "vision" for a "New Orleans Brought Back" would result in something very different from the city before Hurricane Katrina.[3] As seemingly distinct and even conflicting as individual reactions were to the commission's plan for what that very different city would be, everyone in the audience—including myself—could agree about what the plan omitted. Sure enough, space had been provided for the flow of future floodwaters, but no plan was being made for people who'd once lived in those ceded spaces. Nor was there a plan for people independently rebuilding their now flood-devastated houses—who only asked that necessary city services be provided. Everyone in the room that afternoon saw that the planners speaking to them had only *imagined* what New Orleans could eventually become, and had created what one might call an end-state plan: long on vision, but short on time frame and specific details.

Of course, any plan for any city should ideally unite its citizens. But the Bring New Orleans Back Commission's plan quickly divided its listener-residents, and allowed individual fears about the real, immediate future to feed already divisive fears among neighborhoods. While the plan was being written, New Orleanians had started reading and hearing two memorable phrases that members of the commission employed to explain the plan's intentions—that it would "shrink the city's footprint" and "increase residential density on the natural levees." Both phrases immediately alienated the citizens who heard them. "Shrink" seemed to mean that some neighborhoods would not be rebuilt, which implied that individual homeowners would lose their equity—even though many of their houses were now ruined or no longer standing. And "density," as applied to the previously sprawling, low-scale, low-density city, portended high-rise development on the natural levees, meaning Le Corbusier-inspired housing towers like those found in Chicago.

The plan presented by the commission portended the bad results citizens feared that "shrink" and "density" implied. The unfortunate Bring

New Orleans Back meeting ended when the audience booed the poorly detailed plan, and literally shouted it down for ignoring what the city's suffering citizens needed right away. The audience felt insulted by what it'd been offered—a childish colored-in map of an envisioned city that these citizens either didn't want or thought could be achieved only by causing them even greater personal harm and loss. Mayor Nagin, sitting with the commission he'd empaneled, announced at this point that he was "uncomfortable" with the plan. Whereupon it was shelved and the well-intentioned experts went home.

This disputed plan by the Bring New Orleans Back Commission failed a city already fearful of its future, and split New Orleans in two—into one set of neighborhoods located safely on the natural levees and a second set located on the unsafe low-lying and imperiled land. Moreover, citizens living on the high ground were afraid of the changes that "density" might bring in the safe neighborhoods they'd returned to. For their part, citizens of the low-lying neighborhoods—most of whom hadn't been able to return and were in essence homeless—were afraid that a "shrinking" city would mean they'd never find the economic means to come back. Worst of all, with its citizens so clearly seeking the unifying direction a plan could provide, the city abandoned the idea of a truly large-scale redevelopment plan that would provide for all the citizens who had lived in New Orleans before Hurricane Katrina.

Instead, according to a press release from the mayor's office, in view of the Bring New Orleans Back Commission's failure to articulate a good vision for a recovered city, New Orleans would hereafter be rebuilt according to what individual property owners decided to do. If "enough" residents returned to rebuild their houses, the press release stated, then city services would be extended to them. The mayor—who'd been elected on the platform of running government like a business—said that the "market" would suffice for a plan. The "market"—which referred (by implication, never by definition) to how many people actually returned to specific neighborhoods and started reconstruction—would determine how the city would "come back." But this laissez-faire plan failed to state any criteria for determining what "enough" residents meant when it came to deciding who would receive city services—which left citizens in even graver uncertainty. Furthermore, citizens were now uncertain that they could obtain insurance for rebuilt houses without an official plan to rebuild the areas that had flooded.

Simultaneous to abandoning the plan proposed by his Bring New Orleans Back Commission, the mayor cited budget concerns and laid off most of the planning staff working in city hall. Those still on the job were consumed with squabbles among property owners who'd returned to un-flooded, high-ground neighborhoods: whether a ruined restaurant from a flooded area could reopen in a vacant storefront uptown; whether the abandoned structure where hot sauce had been manufactured could be renovated for low-income housing. Trying to settle disagreements among neighbors about the appropriate uses of specific pieces of property al-ways occupies the day-to-day work of city planners—even when civic life is normal. But after the storm, such normality was achieved only in the high-ground, unflooded sections of town. Yet remarkably New Orleans city planners were not put to work on a plan for recovery.[4]

A month passed after the Bring New Orleans Back Commission re-vealed its color-coded map. Mardi Gras krewes paraded in February 2006, six months after the hurricane, and the city's annual mystery of who was King of Carnival and who his Queen was solved once again. On Ash Wednesday the mayor issued airy press releases boasting of the number of visitors who'd attended Mardi Gras and how much money they'd spent. This was civic life as usual, he said, which explained his administration's focus on providing services in the French Quarter and the Garden District. To the mayor it seemed a rational choice for focusing the city's devastated assets. Good for us all.

In March, only a few weeks after Mardi Gras, the mayor issued an-other press release—this time encouraging the devastated neighborhoods (Lakeview, the Lower Ninth Ward) to begin to plan for themselves. He again promised that if "enough" (still not defined) former residents returned to their old homes (or where their old homes had once been), the city would take responsibility for extending services. Water, sewerage, police protec-tion would resume. Precisely where these displaced but returning citizens might live while the putative rebuilding went on, he did not explain, nor did he explain when the money promised by President Bush to rebuild New Orleans might arrive. Although only a small number of businesses in the city had reopened, the mayor didn't suggest a likely source of employment to tide citizens over while their houses were being repaired, nor did he say what would happen to private citizens' investments in their houses if "enough" residents ultimately did *not* return to a particular neighborhood.[5] Needless to say, these vital concerns were issues a citizen might expect to hear addressed by a plan for rebuilding, and they were the concerns home-owners using their insurance proceeds to rebuild would wonder about. And yet, with no other prospects before them, some neighborhood groups set about planning for recovery as the mayor suggested by trying to find former residents and enlisting them to return to the city.

Not much happened. Very few homeowners received the rebuilding funds they thought had been pledged by the nation's president.[6] A few people who'd received insurance proceeds parked trailers in their front yards, moved in, and lived in them while repairing their damaged houses. Many more trailers were supposedly on their way to New Orleans, pro-vided by the Federal Emergency Management Agency to house citizens who wanted to come back and find work, and to shelter those who either hadn't owned their homes or hadn't yet received insurance reimbursements. But very few of these promised FEMA trailers ever arrived—partly because the city's elected leaders couldn't agree about where to put a large expanse of unsightly temporary housing that was reviled by many of their constituents who already had returned. Most of the devastated neighborhoods remained dark and empty.

Meanwhile, nobody *could* return to the city's several public housing projects, although most of the buildings there hadn't been damaged by the storm. These structures had provided housing for more than five thousand families before the hurricane, but they were boarded up after their residents, like all other New Orleanians, were ordered by the National Guard to leave the city. Three years after the storm, these buildings were still boarded up, although the city had by then scheduled their demolition to make way for new housing designed to attract a mixture of poor and middle-income rent-ers. Demolishing the city's public housing projects had been a desire of New Orleans' elected officials for many years, partly because these developments had become increasingly the location of drug dealing and murder, and partly because some of the projects were on valuable downtown real estate that developers thought could be used more profitably. The city's leaders found in the aftermath of the hurricane a plausible pretext for removing these buildings, whether or not they were damaged. No plans were made for the families who'd lived in them.

Nor were there plans for giving assistance to owners of rental property, although before the storm more than half of the city's population rented their homes. But eighteen months passed before owners of apartment buildings destroyed by Hurricane Katrina were even provided applications to receive their share of federal rebuilding funds, and during that time no plans were made for replacing rental property. As a consequence the average monthly rents in the small number of undamaged apartments were multiples of what they had been before the storm. Most of the city's former renter-residents could not afford the going price, though insurance companies paid it to house claims adjusters sent to New Orleans.[7]

Still, the mayor's office released no more press releases on the subject of a plan, and none on the subject of extending city services. Government—at every level—seemed to have no plan for the future. No plan to bring New Orleanians back home.

After a few months of this uneasy state of no-plans-in-the-offing, the New Orleans city council decided to bypass the mayor's office, and in late spring 2006 it hired expert planning consultants to develop plans for fifty neighborhoods known to have flooded.[8] More months then went by, during which citizens attended public meetings convened by the council's planning consultants, answered questions about what they hoped the future city would look like, and trusted these newly arrived professionals to create a feasible plan for rebuilding.

But before the council's new planners could finish their commissioned work, the mayor announced that an entirely new and different planning effort would commence in the late summer of 2006, this to result in a plan that included all neighborhoods—not just the ones that had flooded. Nagin, who'd never held public office before being elected mayor, said he had just learned that without such a citywide plan, the federal government would not release the authorized rebuilding funds to New Orleans.[9] And so, with a grant secured from the Rockefeller Foundation, the mayor hired five teams of independent planning consultants whose work would include all seventy-two neighborhoods that make up the city. Each neighborhood, according to the mayor, could choose which of the five teams it preferred to work with. Thereafter, consultants would convene public meetings and conduct surveys, and somehow what the five teams suggested for their assigned neighborhoods would be "woven into" a citywide plan within six months.

The consultants themselves explained that their "sprawling planning effort" would result in a document two thousand pages long. The mayor said that when this document, already named the Unified New Orleans Plan, was complete, reconstruction could begin in an orderly way.

Glossed over was the fate of the city council's plans for the fifty flooded neighborhoods. They'd be "taken into account" or "folded in," according to the mayor's office. Many specifics of the mayor's Unified New Orleans Plan were equally vague, such as how the consultants would "use modern telecommunications" to interact with neighborhoods where no residents had returned. Nonetheless, when the Unified Plan meetings got under way a little more than a year after Hurricane Katrina, citizens once again met with the mayor's new consulting planners to answer questions about the city's future. Some people, particularly those from the flooded neighborhoods, complained about "planning fatigue," saying that they'd answered these same questions for former consultants and resented their precious time being wasted in answering them again.

The Unified Plan consultants responded by encouraging citizens to think big—to imagine all manner of civic improvements they would like to see. Such practical matters as how much these "big" improvements might cost could be ignored in behalf of finding a glorious vision of what New Orleans could become, the consultants said. Thus encouraged, citizens suggested bike paths, sidewalks, and rebuilt schools throughout the city; they imagined revitalized retail districts. Later, the consultants were forced to delete these visionary items from the Unified Plan when federal officials reminded them that the plan had to be limited to what the government was actually willing to pay for. The Unified Plan, federal authorities said, should include only what was required to "recover" the city from its devastated condition.

Citizens again groused about their time being wasted—on this occasion because consultants had directed them to imagine "big" improvements. But for reasons of pure enervated pragmatism, even the complaining New Orleanians supported the completion of the Unified Plan, knowing it would at least bring them the money they'd long been promised for rebuilding their city. Citizens doggedly returned to more planning meetings.

Meanwhile, just as the Unified Plan initiative was getting going, and just as fatigued citizens were again answering planning consultants' questions about what they wanted from the city in the future, the mayor (it can only be said) suddenly announced a new "out of the box" planning initiative. He again sought expert consultants—planners and internationally renowned "starchitects"—to create dazzling plans to transform neighborhoods along four and a half miles of the Mississippi River into a "vibrant, sustainable world-class waterfront" that would attract wealthy newcomers.[10] There would now be more meetings for citizens to attend.

While all *this* planning was going forward, the mayor also hired a recovery director—a former professor of planning at the University of California at Berkeley who'd helped the city of Oakland, California, rebuild after a disastrous earthquake in 1989 and who was now living in Australia—and put this man to work in January 2007. The widely traveled professor set about making plans for New Orleans based on his theory that if commercial centers were built, people would inevitably follow, and promised there would be more meetings to discuss his choice of seventeen strategic locations where the city would invest in reconstruction.

Urban planning professors in New Orleans—knowledgeable about both the city planning profession and the city itself—could not understand how a creditable plan could result from this blizzard of planning. They pointed out that the city's own planning commission, though composed of people long dedicated to deliberating planning matters in New Orleans, was only marginally involved, having been directed by the mayor to limit its work to approving what consultants presented. Citizens themselves were even more bewildered, particularly those who'd made time for all the meetings despite the everyday rigors of post-Katrina New Orleans—gutting mold-infested houses, dragging toxic refrigerators to the curb, buying overpriced materials for repair, finding schools for their children, and arguing with insurance adjusters about whether floodwaters or wind had caused the damage that was ostensibly covered by their policies. All of this, of course, was the enterprise of citizens going it alone, those who only wanted a plan that relieved them of worries regarding the big picture of their city's future.

Citizens who hadn't been able to return and were far away in Oklahoma and Wisconsin—but close to their own fears and divinings—began to suspect that secret plans were in the making. They saw a chaos of misguided ventures and little evidence of improvement. Reports from the city told of worsening poverty, murder, thieving, and despair. It all fostered a mood of hard-to-contain and hard-to-rebut suspicion among displaced New Orleanians that plans were being made actually to prevent the city's poorer residents from coming back: plans that would ensure public housing was torn down; plans that would prevent rebuilding of rental properties; plans that would allow complete demolition of houses that were only partially damaged without notifying their displaced owners. So little progress was made in the Lower Ninth Ward that its former residents returned to an old fear fostered by events in the infamous 1927 flood—that the levees along the Industrial Canal had been deliberately breached to wash the poor folks away and allow white speculators to grab their land.[11]

But consultants continued working on the Unified Plan amid all this tumultuous activity and suspicion about their actual purpose. Finally, in July 2007, they presented a document that satisfied federal requirements for a plan. When completed, the Unified Plan was seen to envision New Orleans rebuilt as it had been prior to August 29, 2005. In this plan, all former land-use decisions—good and bad—were reified. People could rebuild on the low-lying, drained swamplands in Lakeview, the Lower Ninth Ward, and New Orleans East, and nobody had to be concerned any longer about the frightening notions of densification and a shrunken city. This new plan was gratefully received by most citizens, who by now seemed to care less about the plan's "vision" than about its fundamental effect: that reconstruction might finally be funded, and city services might again be provided everywhere.

In less than two short years, the attempted planning for recovery in New Orleans after Hurricane Katrina went through a handful of divergent approaches. First was the Bring Back New Orleans plan, which had in mind a different physical city—one that provided safe catchment areas for floodwaters. The second effort was less a planning initiative than a planning lacuna, when the mayor would have "the market decide" the city's future form. A third phase, sponsored by the city council, planned for only two-thirds of the city, and was subsumed by a fourth phase that successfully crafted a Unified Plan for all of New Orleans' neighborhoods and resulted in federal reconstruction money finally coming to the city.

Despite all this planning, the eventual form the city will take is anyone's guess. In the two years it took for the Unified Plan to be put in place, citizens made their own individual plans—many of which unfortunately didn't and don't include returning to, or staying in, New Orleans. For one thing, the cost of insurance in the city remains volatile, as is the issue of whether adequate city services can even be provided wherever they're needed. And as is widely acknowledged, the strength of the old protective levee system is an ongoing subject of consternation.

The extent of what remains unknown about New Orleans' future motivated what I term a fifth phase of planning in the devastated city. In this most recent phase, the mayor sought an "out of the box" plan to transform the city's riverfront (not its flooded land) into an architectural showcase; the city's professorial recovery director concentrated on plans to rebuild shopping centers; and the City Planning Commission of New Orleans hired consultants to develop yet another plan—a Master Plan, the commission calls it. Apparently, the future of New Orleans remained in such consequential flux that more plans had to be made.

For a city with New Orleans' spotty record of planning—which had allowed so much development on low-lying, drained ground—and for a city *so* devastated by *such* a calamity, much of the confusion about planning for recovery should be viewed sympathetically and without shock. I have recounted this complicated post-Katrina chronology not to find fault, but rather because in the phases of planning in New Orleans I see several important details that are both crucial to the performance of city planning and yet also usually hidden.

The first such detail was that the mayor had little grasp of what a city's plan should be, even a plan he inaugurated with so much expert planners' advice and with the self-explanatory purpose of "rebuilding" his wrecked city. Of course, he wasn't alone in misconceiving the purpose of a plan for rebuilding, as demonstrated when the federal government had to inform planning consultants at work on the Unified Plan to drop the "big" ideas they'd solicited from citizens. A second noteworthy detail is that neither the city council nor the mayor included the city planning commission in any of the several efforts to develop recovery plans. Instead, the planning commission's contribution was confined to approving what consultants proposed. These two details from the planning efforts that followed the hurricane reveal quite starkly what I know is a usual and critical failure of elected leaders to know—or use—what city planners have to offer.

Another detail a reader may have taken curious note of is the succeeding waves of planning consultants who arrived—and continue to arrive—in New Orleans. The use of consulting planners, however, is not unusual. Municipal plans are meant to last for twenty or twenty-five years, and keeping an in-house staff large enough to mount such infrequent planning efforts would not make sound fiscal sense. Even what might seem wasteful in the post-Katrina planning flurry—the money spent time and again to hire consultants, only to send them home—constituted a trivial proportion of the $13 billion the Unified Plan estimated reconstruction would cost.

Furthermore, as most cities have found, much is gained by the practice of hiring planning consultants to write plans. Consulting firms can—and often do—bring new ideas with them, and can work out new approaches to planning problems unconstrained by what's usually been acceptable in political terms in an individual municipality. Typically, the important role of a city's own planners in creating a new plan is to set out its intention and to calculate whether what the consultants propose will work, or at least calculate how their ideas might be modified to work, and then to determine how to make the new plan appealing to the local jurisdiction. When this method of consultancy works well, innovation is tempered by the cultural particulars of individual cities, and a new plan brings about local improvements. When this method of consultancy does not work well, as it surely did not in New Orleans, where consultants worked outside the city's ordinary planning processes, new plans are found lacking.

What's most noteworthy in the five-phase chronology isn't the large number of consultants who came to town, or how much money they contracted to be paid, not even how little the city planning commission was involved in the consultants' work. Rather, what's noteworthy is that not one of these successive planning contractors took advantage of what the immediately previous planners had proposed. This odd fact was unexpectedly revealed in citizens' complaints of "planning fatigue." Also remarkable in this regard is that while the questions and answers gathered by different consultants may have been the same—as fatigued many citizens—the plans that resulted were materially *different*. This means that it's worth looking closely at what planners ask as they conceive of plans for cities, at what planners actually do with the answers they elicit, and also *why* new consultants would start over, rather than begin with what previous planners had found.

Perhaps the most unusual element of this saga of New Orleans' efforts to fashion a recovery plan is how much attention so many citizens paid to these various initiatives—and how many elected leaders tried to take a hand in them. Neither is usual in local government plan-making, and its incidence here and now of course can be explained by the shocking extent of devastation caused by Hurricane Katrina. Most everybody—and especially those who'd become refugees—could see the necessity of a plan for bringing this destroyed city back to its feet. Roads had to be rebuilt, as did sewerage and water systems; commercial activities had to resume so that jobs would become available again; housing had to be constructed; schools, churches, and libraries had to be repaired. All of that activity— and much more like it—counted on New Orleans' protective levees being made resistant to storms and flood surges at least as strong as those that came with Hurricane Katrina. The extent of what was at stake meant that consultants making plans to rebuild New Orleans enjoyed a rarely seen level of participation by interested citizens.

Precisely because so many people took part in planning efforts after Hurricane Katrina, it's possible to discern from their public statements several assumptions that typically mystify citizens about plans and planners in any city. Intuitively, people assume city planners are charged to devise a plan based on what citizens want from the future. Yet when New Orleanians gave the same answers to the same questions about the future that different consultants posed, the plans that resulted were bafflingly unalike.

Another intuitive assumption citizens make is that because planning is a part of city government—as anyone knows—the nature of a city plan should be guided by the city's elected leaders. But as the tumult of events in post-Katrina New Orleans showed, elected leaders didn't have confidence in most of the plans they were shown, and they only supported the Unified Plan in order to receive federal reconstruction funds.

Finally, citizens suppose that once a plan is approved, the city will be built in conformance with it. Yet, as mentioned, what New Orleans will look like in its rebuilt future—ostensibly in accordance with the Unified Plan—is anyone's guess because individual New Orleanians have already made important and diverse decisions about how or even whether they'll continue living there. These decisions have been largely unaffected by the adopted Unified Plan.

In other words, important details from the five-phase planning process in New Orleans after Hurricane Katrina show that almost no part of our usual understanding of and vocabulary for the phrase "city planning" is as accurate—or as obvious—as it might seem: not "the plan" itself, not what city planners do, not who plans are made for, not even how one determines what citizens want from the future. And, most important, not how the plan affects what gets built in a city. Much that's taken for granted by citizens and by planners themselves can't be.

Which means that to answer the very appropriate question of what city planning in New Orleans should have done differently—or what might all city planners do differently in the future—one first has to understand the documents that make up a "city plan" and the activities that "city planning" comprises.

THREE

What Are City Plans?

Another bright October day in New Orleans, six rainless weeks after Hurricane Katrina. Tree-shaded State Street, in uptown, looked as it had in the days before the storm—blooming flowers encircled the mansions, no fallen tree limbs blocked the sidewalks. A homeowner stood in his driveway spraying herbicide onto the weeds growing between the flagstones, his thoughts casting toward evening. It was an ordinary autumn weekend in New Orleans.

But life was far from ordinary in the not-so-distant neighborhoods of Lakeview and the Lower Ninth Ward. In Lakeview, weeks of standing floodwater had killed every plant and most every tree. In the Lower Ninth Ward, wrecked houses still leaned into one another at perilous angles, and the National Guard was preventing people from visiting what had been their homes. This dismaying triptych offers a glimpse of the radically different human circumstances found in New Orleans after Hurricane Katrina, circumstances that a plan for recovery would need to comprehend and address in order that the plan itself be coherent.

This exaggerated set of contrasting human circumstances from the early days following Katrina is at heart no different from the complex human circumstances that ordinarily face planners who must draft a plan in any city. There are in fact profound similarities, although individual plans always contain unique and idiosyncratic details that make uniformity impossible. Best then to establish a set of first principles.

Although it is so ordinary a word as to seem to require no definition, a city's "plan" turns out to be an elusive entity. To a layman, the word implies a document that presents an inspiring vision of how the city *should* or *might* look in the near future, and includes handsome renderings of the envisioned townscape to come. Early in the profession's history, planners agreed with this layman's understanding—not surprisingly, since planners themselves conceived such tantalizing plans and presented them to citizens. But city planning has evolved from these original conceptions. To a modern city planner the word "plan" implies a compendium of mostly unillustrated documents that act together to predict and oversee the process of urban development. Such documents include economic studies and projections, demographic descriptions of local citizenry, and many technical reports and individual plans for various aspects of urban life.[1]

Most citizens' conception of a plan dates from the late nineteenth century, the period in American history when reform-minded citizens took a sharpened interest in what Industrial Age cities had become—squalid neighborhoods crowded with immigrants, fetid tenements, and air dense with pollution. Historians refer to this period as the Progressive Era, and the forward-thinking efforts of the era's progressives led, among other outcomes, to the creation of three public service professions in cities. A goodly portion of the reformers of the time concentrated on improving the health of individuals who lived in the filthy industrial cities, and their work gave rise to the public health profession. Other civic-minded citizens concentrated on problems of immigrants arriving to American cities for factory work. These were immigrants from abroad and from America's small towns, most of whom lacked sufficient personal resources to adjust by themselves to how society was changing from its rural origins. The work of these reformers eventually resulted in the social work profession. Still others took up the cause of improving life in squalid Industrial Age cities by redesigning the cities themselves. These reformers' ideas provided the foundation of the American city planning profession.

The seminal ideas of American city planning were first worked out and put on display in Chicago, on the midway of the Columbian Exposition in 1893, an extravaganza whose theme was to show the world how it could live better. Organizers of this early World's Fair commissioned the construction of a group of white Beaux Arts buildings situated around a formally landscaped lagoon. Called the White City, this installation was intended as a shocking contrast to the smoke-blackened ugliness of the host city, and was also meant to suggest that cities could—and *should*—be beautiful, rather than being jerry-built improvisations erected around factories, railroads, slaughterhouses, and sweatshops.

This fantastical White City at once entered the imagination of exposition-goers and, more to the point, of early urban planning enthusiasts, who became engrossed by imagining ways to replace antiquated, sooty, and congested "ugly" parts of cities with noble architect-designed expanses of bright new buildings and parks. The working postulate of these particular progressives was that urban immigrants who lived in orderly surroundings would "naturally" become better citizens, and through the process of adopting the desirable norms of the middle class would leave their previous cultures behind and assume the newly available better ones.[2] In particular, immigrants would leave behind the languages or dialects they spoke and the customs they observed. Life would be better all around—though as the urbanist Lewis Mumford later described it, life would only be better because workers who lived in slums had been compensated by having places to watch civic parades.[3]

Most laymen anticipate that their city's plan will be like the first one based on the White City installation at the Columbian Exposition. The iconic Plan of Chicago was co-written in 1909 by one of the White City's designers, the architect Daniel Burnham, who'd been hired by prominent businessmen and industrialists in the city's well-to-do Commercial Club to imagine their city's physical future.[4] In this plan, Burnham focused largely on public improvements—majestic parks and boulevards along Lake Michigan, as well as streets, railroads, and harbors newly engineered to serve and facilitate the moneymaking operations of downtown enterprise. Freight facilities were consolidated with passenger railroads; harbors were expanded where the Chicago and Calumet Rivers emptied into Lake Michigan; industrial activities were removed from the lakeshore. Every aspect of Burnham's plan was so artfully rendered that it's been reprinted ever since, and can often be found in the anteroom of architects' offices around the world. This handsome plan—which implicitly promised to make the mockup White City an actual city—inaugurated what's come to be popularly known as the City Beautiful movement in urban planning.

The problem was that the beautiful Plan of Chicago strikingly ignored what the Commercial Club apparently hadn't wanted to think about—housing and neighborhoods where working-class Chicagoans would actually live. Perhaps this was a subject too complicated and resistant to an architect's solution, as well as being too costly for the members of the club to contemplate. Yet the issue of squalid neighborhoods wouldn't go away. Burnham, however, had a soothing explanation for what his plan didn't include. He convinced his client that inasmuch as an orderly and dignified city would inspire citizens to lead noble and productive lives, their quotidian needs for better housing and healthier environs didn't actually need to be planned for. Instead, improvements to the poor districts of town would be the naturally occurring side effects of the grand building efforts he foresaw. Burnham's advice to his client, in other words, was to ignore the problem. But the upshot has been that because of what is grossly left out of City Beautiful plans, the planning profession eventually left this movement behind, and modern planners today fault Burnham's trickle-down notion of neighborhood improvement as mandarin.

Most people who page through Burnham's handsome renderings don't notice that he has omitted working-class neighborhoods in his Plan of Chicago. Laymen, even those sophisticated about civic affairs, still imagine their city's plan will provide some incarnation of what Burnham drew. And possibly because his vision appears so seamless, Burnham is still one of America's most venerated planners, although among planners themselves he's primarily remembered for the advice he gave them: "Make no little plans; they have no magic to stir men's blood and probably won't be adopted. Make big plans; aim high in hope and work."[5] These stirring words have had a grip on planners' imaginations ever since, although modern planners are less concerned with creating beautiful drawings and more concerned with embracing every aspect of urban life, including the lives led by cities' poorer residents.

In the context of the very different geographical areas that constitute any city, and the very different economic and cultural characteristics of the citizens who live there, a modern plan envisions the future by specifically expressing a citizenry's desires for change in all components of a city—components such as streets, parks, and methods of fire protection, individual neighborhoods, land-use regulations, public utilities, flood protection measures, evacuation procedures, and virtually all other vital urban concerns. Ideally in a plan nothing important about a city is left out. For that reason planners refer to the document they create as a *comprehensive* plan. Planners also call such plans *master* plans or *general* plans, although mostly they're referred to simply as plans.

Irrespective of what it's called, a modern comprehensive plan contains within itself several individual plans written for each component of a city—subentities that planners refer to as "elements" of the comprehensive plan. The Housing Element, for example, discusses the quantity of different types of new housing (low-income apartments, individual houses, condominiums, and so on) that are likely to be needed in the future. The Transportation Element of a comprehensive plan takes up a city's roadway and highway systems and discusses improvements—including mass transit—that must be completed to accommodate a population expected to increase or to serve projected new commercial enterprise. Other elements have a similarly obvious affiliation with identifiable components of a city. Each element has as its primary responsibility to describe what new land uses are projected for that component—how many units of housing must be built, where new streets will be constructed, the number of new parks to be provided, for example.[6]

Although the notion of a comprehensive plan and its component elements might seem a confusingly complicated conception, it is a conception that seeks to ensure that different elements of the entire plan can be coordinated. To assist with coordination, planners write another element—the Land-Use Plan—for inclusion in the comprehensive plan. The Land-Use Plan summarizes the individual projections about future uses of land found in each of the other component elements. In formal planning jargon, the land-use plan thus becomes the principal component element of comprehensive plans. Because most citizens are primarily interested in how particular areas of the city will be developed in the future—as commerce, as industry, as public facilities—they take a special interest in land-use plans because the contents describe how *all* the land within municipal boundaries is used and is to be used in the future. Thus, citizens who actually use the plan can easily find the areas of greatest interest to them. Singularly among all different elements that compose a comprehensive plan, the land-use plan is the element most often referenced by laymen.

A city's land-use plan contains forecasts written by planners describing where a city will grow or how it will shrink. To write these forecasts, planners identify what already exists in a city—buildings, streets, parks—and then they use population and economic projections to estimate how much more housing, how much additional commercial and industrial space a city is likely to require over predetermined periods of time. Planners then match these projections to the views citizens have expressed about what they want the city to become. These views, which planners refer to as constituting a plan's *vision* of the future, are solicited from citizens during public meetings convened for this very purpose. Finally, planners illustrate the text of the land-use plan with maps of what already exists in the city, on which are detailed precisely where—according to the plan's stated vision of the future—families will live in projected new houses and apartment complexes, where new stores will be permitted, where industrial plants can operate, where libraries, swimming pools, and other public facilities can be sited, as well as the routes that roadways and public transportation will follow.[7] A planner's final task is to take all that has been gathered and expressed—forecasts, citizens' views about a desirable future, maps showing how land will be used—and write a coherent document that is the land-use plan.

As I've said, the land-use plan is the element citizens are most familiar with in their city's comprehensive plan. This is largely because the written descriptions of future development and the land uses themselves are readily understandable by laymen. Planners usually consider the land-use plan as central to the city's comprehensive plan, and in fact often refer to the land-use plan as the "city plan," or even as the "master plan." But because the discussion in the remainder of this book will focus principally on land-use plans, use of the word "plan" by itself will always refer to the land-use plan. For the sake of clarity, when I subsequently address important connections between a comprehensive plan and its land-use plan element, I will clearly distinguish between the two.

Comprehensive plans—and all their elements, including land-use plans—of course must serve the specific setting and character of a subject city. And it would seem evident that planning operates in its most identifiable and "easy" ways on undeveloped tracts of land owned by single individuals. Plans for such cities as Irvine, California, and Celebration, Florida, start with unimproved land (pastures, fields, orchards) on which the owner envisions a community *to-be-built,* one where marketing surveys have targeted home buyers and calculated their prospective wants—the preservation of a natural environment, assurance of privacy and security, manageable distance to a commuter railway. All is doable if no one's living there yet.

In these startup situations, residents—whose lives are being planned for—are typically a stratum of citizens who will choose to live in a community based largely on how much property costs there and on how the community is planned. If the plan doesn't attract them, or provides housing they don't like or can't afford, they may look elsewhere.

In this relatively simplified clean-slate, planned-community paradigm, the plan foresees and essays to avoid and resolve conflicts among land uses *before* they're engaged. For planners who make these plans, the most significant variables in creating the desired future are the accuracy of their demographic projections and their estimation of what prospective buyers want from where they live, plus of course the timetable for completion, which depends on mortgage rates, the financial climate, workforce availability, and the speed of population growth. Under this planning model, a city becomes (initially, at least) what its plan has portrayed.

But when a city already exists—when it comes equipped with a complex history and an existing population with active and established desires for the future—then planning grows eminently more complicated. Here, prior development has left a mixture of old uses that may radically conflict with what the contemporary city believes it needs. As well, land is owned by not one person but by many persons—and by citizens of diverse means with different ideas for using their land. Some residents have no desire except to live on their own property, undisturbed, whereas others wish to make money from what they own by renting out an apartment over their garage, or opening a beauty salon in an unused bedroom. Other owners may want to make a living by purchasing vacant fields, subdividing them, and selling off individual lots. Still others may choose to buy dilapidated downtown factories and transform them into first-class hotels.

As well, what individuals seek to do to profit from their land may obviously impede their neighbors' enjoyment of their own property. Some neighbors may have previously enjoyed the serenity of a vacant field that its owner now wants to subdivide. Other neighbors may fear that increased traffic to a new beauty salon will reduce their own serenity. In a still different case, neighbors may think a dilapidated factory should be preserved for its architectural significance instead of being transformed into a destination resort.

Because individual decisions about the use of property constitute one important engine that causes a city to change over time, planners and planning itself must imagine integrated city plans that address the difficulties posed by these competing ideas, so that change occurs for the city's betterment. Furthermore, one must also know that difficulties always arise because the city's economy—perhaps the largest determinant of how and when change occurs—depends on national and international market forces that are beyond the power of a city to influence, thereby making the other factors more difficult, complicated, and politically contentious.

From this brief comparison of planning new cities and planning old cities, one can discern logical components that would constitute good plans for existing cities. In practical terms, the plan ideally accounts for why a city was built where and as it was—and from these sources traces the course of problems the city faces. Planners writing a new plan in an existing city will always, for example, find that a neighborhood has been constructed alongside a noisy cement plant that operates twenty-four hours a day; or that carcinogenic waste created by an old, but now closed, chemical factory has polluted the ground where an elementary school now stands; or that people are living today in areas that have flooded for centuries. Beyond that, planners writing a plan for an already-existing city are challenged to represent the competing, sometimes conflicting sets of desires of a current citizenry. And finally, a plan ought to portray an envisioned future so that people, planners included, can readily grasp its complex substance as a clear depiction of how the city would develop if it were in accord with what citizens want. While one might call this almost an aesthetic prerequisite—people, after all, easily respond to artful drawings—what I mean with regard to "portray" is how well a plan marshals all its contents into a coherent and useful document. This might not require drawings at all.

The plans to recover New Orleans after Hurricane Katrina described in the previous chapter didn't do well at satisfying any of these ideal prerequisites. I can make this point clearly by discussing the first plan that was made public (the Bring New Orleans Back plan), as well as the plan that sufficiently satisfied the federal government to cause it to release reconstruction funds to the city (the Unified Plan).

The Bring New Orleans Back plan, which proposed to transform ruined, hurricane-wrecked neighborhoods where people once lived into parkland where future floodwaters could flow, failed to acknowledge the historical reasons that people would ever live on inundatable ground in the first place. Neither did the plan solve the obvious problem of where those same people *should* live—safely—in a rebuilt city of the future. This plan also neither acknowledged nor tried to accommodate the more diverse interests of citizens of the ruined city. Inarguably, many citizens displaced by the hurricane wanted badly to return to New Orleans. But citizens who had already returned home didn't want their neighborhoods "densified"— their pejorative word—by construction of new housing for displaced New Orleanians.

These were the plan's most glaring flaws. Yet it was the manner by which the Bring New Orleans Back plan portrayed its primary recommendations that ultimately doomed it. The map—with its green-dash circles wherein flooded neighborhoods were designated as parkland—portrayed, one might say *graphically,* what the plan failed to provide. There were in fact no circled areas assigned to distinguish areas where the flooded-out citizens might live in a rebuilt city. In short, the plan did not visually portray a future the citizenry wanted. Nor, as described, did New Orleanians want to hear more about it.

On the other hand, the Unified Plan—whose adoption resulted in federal reconstruction money finally being released to New Orleans—might in fact be said to have satisfied all the ideal prerequisites of city plans, although one could also argue that its success was won by default. First, the consultants who wrote the Unified Plan might indeed have understood how land in New Orleans had been used in the past—and even why. But they proposed nothing that would change the preexisting development patterns that had so dramatically contributed to the city's great loss of neighborhoods built on floodable land. Instead, the Unified Plan promised that the city would be rebuilt *as it had been* before the hurricane, thus affirming all previous land-use decisions made by the city and ignoring the disastrous consequences to low-lying residences. Second, although planners encouraged citizens to envision "big" ideas for the future, the federal government promptly declared that such grand notions could not be included in the plan, whereupon the consultants fell back on a simple "unifying" vision: that the citizenry wished to return to a New Orleans that was as it had been. In effect, the consultants dispensed with the task of finding—for a diverse citizenry—a consensus vision. And the Unified Plan was adopted.

Citizens' own confession of "planning fatigue" suggests how bewildered they were by the series of different planning efforts mounted to create a plan to restore New Orleans after Hurricane Katrina. One purpose of this book is to demystify plans—and city planning itself—by explaining why planners end up writing plans that confuse and alienate citizens. And the book's purpose is also to describe how to formulate a plan that is *un*-confusing.

It is, however, important to say that the phrase "city plan" might imply that a single document exists, one written by city planners which describes all that interested citizens need to know about how their city is likely to change in the future. But a "city plan" is only one among several documents that describe a city's future. In New Orleans—a typical example—many city departments prepared plans that affected the use of the city's land, and these plans were formulated without consulting city planners. In one instance, the mayor's Office of Housing independently wrote plans that allowed the city to qualify for federal funds to build low-income apartment buildings. Entities that operated well outside the authority of the City of New Orleans, and its planning department, made their own plans: the city's universities (including Tulane and Xavier) had plans drawn up, as did the governing authorities of City Park and the Audubon Zoo (among others). Louisiana, as you might expect, had long ago established a Dock Board with commissioners to govern the prosperous port, and this agency also made plans for how it would operate, grow, and develop. Even the Levee Board, whose jurisdiction included the extended protective levees along the Mississippi River, Lake Pontchartrain, and the various drainage canals within city limits, made plans—all done without consulting the city planning commission.

Newly hired planners (as well as veterans) were themselves confused by this uncoordinated welter of plans. Citizens, it must be said, were noticeably less confused by all these plans since they were either unaware of them—and of who made them—or they genially assumed city planners had a hand in them all and so could be blamed for everything. Planners had and have difficulty defending themselves since most people—even those who routinely attend planners' public meetings—find the duties of planners to be as mysterious as the plans they prepare. Elected officials share their constituents' mystification. It's thus sensible to take up the subject of What City Planners Do.

FOUR

What City Planners Do and
Why They Do It That Way

When I was first made planning director in New Orleans, thirteen years before Hurricane Katrina, the *vision* of the city's diverse citizenry included, as you might imagine, many competing and sometimes conflicting imperatives. This vision included retaining the city's historic character while attracting new industry that brought with it new, well-paying jobs. It included revitalizing run-down neighborhoods and reducing the social and economic isolation of the poor. It included providing parks and recreational areas in every neighborhood. Plus much more. To my mind, as the new planning director, this was all good. But it was definitely a complex set of forces from which a government was to forge a mutually agreeable strategy for guiding future development.

In addition, New Orleans was experiencing several significant constraints on how, precisely, the several aspirations of its citizens could be realized. In 1984, the price of oil fell so low in world markets that old oil-and-gas corporations operating in the city transferred their white-collar workers back to Texas and closed downtown offices in New Orleans. This precipitate departure relegated New Orleans to its old dependence on a fragile tourism-based economy, an economy with a long history of slow growth due to high local taxes, an inexpert workforce, and unreliable elected officials. These growth factors became even more significant and constraining when investors compared the potential profits from doing business in various cities, and chose against New Orleans.

There was a second significant inhibitor to the city's ability to respond to its citizens' desires. New Orleans' population had declined in every census since 1960. And those who'd departed were well-educated young people and such talented citizens as the city's famed jazz musicians—many of whom had realized there were better jobs, better living circumstances, and more opportunities for work in other places.[1] As a consequence, the city was left with an unusually large concentration of poor, undereducated citizens living in what had become increasingly blighted neighborhoods as more and more residents left New Orleans and abandoned their homes. Twenty percent of the city's housing units stood vacant in 1990, which was at least twice the vacancy rate found that year in cities of similar size—Cleveland, Baltimore, Memphis, and Pittsburgh. Abandoned houses were in every neighborhood of New Orleans, and their broken windows and sagging rooflines were bleak reminders of the city's unpromising economic prospects.

Finally, there were significant problems of municipal finance in New Orleans that stood in the way of what citizens envisioned for the future. Cities deliver services such as police and fire protection, snow removal, and garbage collection, and they build public works such as streets and water and sewerage systems. All are paid for primarily by the taxes levied on the value of land that individuals and businesses own. In 1960, the population in New Orleans was at its all-time peak of 600,000 residents. But as citizens found better jobs elsewhere and the population declined, tax revenues went down in lockstep. Further, when oil companies relocated their New Orleans operations back to Texas, the city lost the tax revenue from this lucrative industry, as well as tax revenue collected from companies that had served the old industry's many ancillary needs—accounting firms, lawyers, suppliers, and so on. By 1992, when I came to work at city hall in New Orleans, taxes collected from business enterprises were greatly reduced from pre-1984 years, and only 485,000 people lived in the city. This meant that, compared with 1960, there were many fewer businesses and 20 percent fewer residents to pay for fixing potholes and providing fire protection and police services to an urban area that had once held 600,000 citizens and many more industrial and commercial firms. One could've said the city was living beyond its means.

Given this set of rigorous constraints, I thought the City Planning Commission of New Orleans, along with the whole concept of planning in that city, faced grave challenges. The planning commission, which I directed from 1992 through 2000, saw that a better future depended not on opportunistic rapid change but on the slow evolution of what already existed. New Orleans could be improved—incrementally—by an individual opening a boutique hotel in the old International Trade Mart downtown, or by someone renovating an abandoned house in Gentilly to be a music studio. These were the sort of urban developments the New Orleans City Planning Commission oversaw. And they were changes that only gradually bring jobs to more people, only gradually increase the city's tax collections and allow civic improvements—only gradually fulfill a diverse citizenry's expressed vision.

I'd been given the job of writing a new plan for the city. And I knew I needed to see how the city's challenges affected citizens' lives in different neighborhoods. One might describe this as looking at New Orleans clear-eyed—seeing what happened to all that had previously been built, which included abandoned houses, rich neighborhoods, playgrounds, street patterns, strip commercial development, and dilapidated factories—and discerning the messy, unpredictable and disorganized processes that fuse into the experience of living in any city. A good plan would obviously be based, I thought, on the city's present economy and labor force, and it would understand how the city had been built over time and why it looked as it did. And yet the plan would simultaneously appreciate the various and contradictory aspirations coexisting there. A good plan would enable citizens to live and work under conditions as favorable to their well-being and happiness as they could afford—as Frederick Law Olmsted, Jr., observed in the early years of the planning profession.[2] To me, his words mean that paying attention to the here-and-now of a city and the day-to-day lives of people living there was as important as developing a vision for how citizens might someday live in the city that a plan foretold.

I consider this version of a plan to be hopefully large and wide because it comprehends underlying history and geography, and in addition accepts all that goes on in a community, all its citizens and what they do. This notion of a plan also takes into account citizens' desires for the future and then assesses how it might be possible to achieve those desires, given local economic, budgetary, and demographic constraints. In this way, a good plan requires and makes good use of all that city planners are trained to understand. Such a plan is also *useful,* because it is more than a pretty picture of the future—rather, it is a practical guide to achieving that future. City plans could be characterized (and admired, to my mind) as making the best with what planners have to work with.

What I've referred to as a good plan might seem plodding and undesirable to citizens who only expect from a plan an inspiring vision of how the city *should* or *might* be. And of course my version of a plan will read as unnecessarily complicated to citizens who only want assurance that what they like won't change—except for the better. In addition, this model may even seem irrelevant to people who don't see how a plan can make any difference to their immediate needs to pay the rent or find a job. I encountered all these adverse reactions—and many more—while I was planning director in New Orleans before Hurricane Katrina. And I surely saw them again when the Bring New Orleans Back Commission presented its plan for recovery, a plan that concentrated on a vision of the future without contemplating and including what was necessary to achieve that vision. To me, however, the Bring Back plan had seemed irrelevant to and disdainful of real-life circumstances of citizens of New Orleans, and as well, it seemed not useful as a guide.

I know something about how city plans can *not* be useful. When I was hired as planning director in 1992, New Orleans was operating according to a series of plans and land-use regulations the city had adopted throughout the previous twenty years. The oldest of these planning documents—dating from 1970—couldn't possibly have taken into account several important and recent transformations in the city. Extensive white flight to adjoining Jefferson and St. Tammany Parishes had not been envisioned; neither had black flight from the inner city to New Orleans East. Indeed, the very existence of New Orleans East had not been foreseen in many planning documents my office employed. More recent plans, of course, hadn't foreseen the departure of oil companies and their white-collar employees following 1984—events that dramatically changed the nature of the city's economy and its workforce, and eventually opened the way for legalized gambling in Louisiana in 1992.

The old land-use regulations also predated most effects of racial integration, which meant that new housing and new commercial enterprises were guided by ordinances written when whites were the city's majority population, and adopted when only whites sat on the city council. Conversely, by the time I went to work in city hall, two-thirds of the city's citizens were African-American, as were the great majority of elected leaders. In terms of planning, New Orleans was making decisions for a city that in many ways didn't exist anymore.

However, the planning commission that hired me in 1992 knew very well that it was working with a greatly changed city. In the months before I came to work the commission had adopted a plan titled *New Century, New Orleans*—a listing of policy proposals stating in broad terms how all the city's planning documents and land-use regulations should reflect the new economic, political, and racial circumstances of contemporary New Orleans. My job, the planning commissioners said, was to use the policies outlined in *New Century, New Orleans* to bring city planning up to date— which meant to revise and make useful the various documents that guided development of land within the city's limits.

The commission's directive and the responsibilities it anticipated would certainly not seem simple on their face, but they were much more complex than they might even appear. To begin, I determined to compare all the plans previously adopted by the city planning commission—including plans that were still in effect—with the policies articulated in *New Century, New Orleans*. My office reviewed its own documents to learn what was out of date, what needed more study, what might require further comment by citizens. We also reviewed a twenty-year-old land-use plan for the entire city, as well as plans specific to individual districts in the city—neighborhoods along the riverfront and the downtown business district along Canal Street. As anyone might expect, we found many internal contradictions in this work as well as many suggestions that were no longer pertinent. The entire process, however, brought to my notice that successive plans very rarely build upon, or even refer back to, what had been *planned* before. This was something I would have to rectify so that a sense of continuity would exist between the new plan I was hired to write and the plans written previously.

On the day I was introduced to the city council as the new planning director in New Orleans, each member of the council praised my credentials and dutifully promised to work with me. And then the council's president spoke. "This has all been very nice today, Dr. Ford," she said ruefully, "but the next time you come here you best wear a suit of armor." Her warning was an unsubtle

reminder that it is the city council—not the planning director—that determines how landowners can use their land in New Orleans, and any
advice I might give based on the city's plan and my advanced professional
degree would be only one factor in the council's decisions. Other factors,
needless to say, would come into play—the city's budget, changes in the
city's economic circumstances, politics—any of which might override the
persuasive power of a plan.

The council president was rather coldly warning me that city planning
could expect conflict, and that my first task of bringing planning documents up to date could just as easily be a case in point. I knew the council
president's welcome, bracing though it was, only intended to remind me
of where the action is in city hall. A plan is one thing. But executing a plan
is quite another. This—and it's important to say so—is perhaps the least
understood aspect of city planning's assumed logical simplicity and efficacy.
Typically, people (citizens, observers, laymen, and politicians) think a city
adopts a plan that puts on display how citizens want land in the city to be
used, and that the city then adopts regulations to *channel* uses of property
into consistency with the plan, and that, finally, development occurs in accordance with the "vision" the plan has articulated. Under this paradigmatic
(and fantastical) process, the town-as-planned becomes the town-as-built.

Plans are customarily written to be reliable for twenty or so years—the
length of time the planning profession long ago determined future land
uses could be both foreseen and also regulated by ordinances enacted by
city councils to help guide the use of land in accordance with a plan's vision. This is the desirable end of writing a plan. But during the twenty-year
period plans are in effect, the regulations—usually drafted by city planners—that city councils adopt are always subject to change by action of
the city councils themselves. A council member may initiate a change because regulations apply to individual landowners who present a compelling
reason not to follow them. Unforeseen economic events might occur—a
state could legalize gambling, for example; the federal government could
close a military base inside city limits. These events can alter both a plan's
original basis and the regulations meant to carry it out. The discretion city
councils have because they possess the power to deviate from a city's plan
gives flexibility to the plan, thereby allowing it to remain useful even when
fundamental circumstances shift.

But the flexibility city councils enjoy also occasionally allows them to ignore and even subvert plans. A case in New Orleans is an apt example. During a period of economic stagnation, a prospective tavern owner petitioned to renovate a vacant commercial building into a bar near Tulane University—even though the city's adopted plan and land-use regulations envisioned a more tranquil residential neighborhood for undergraduate students. The property owner argued before the city council that his bar would provide jobs and tax revenues. The city council agreed with him, thus going against the plan and city regulations.

Such minor planning matters obviously constitute the standard operating procedures of most cities, and they involve balancing the desires of landowners with the aspirations of a larger community as expressed in its plan. City planners, whose job is to advise the council and then ensure that its decision is carried out, are specifically trained for this important balancing act, which requires knowledge of everything within the scope of city government that affects how land is used—capital improvements, building codes, municipal finance, taxation policy, and public safety—all of which are crucial elements in the way citizens live together in a city. A modern city planner's expertise is to recognize the relative importance of any land-use decision, large or small, and to attempt to inform the city council's decisions so that the council's flexibility and responsiveness to the citizenry do not mean losing sight of the common aspirations of that same citizenry—as expressed in the city plan.

But planners also recognize other significant factors a city council must take into account—factors that have a clear connection to how land is used. States create local governments, in part, to finance and provide ordinary urban services—a list of which includes city planning.[3] The more revenue a local council can collect without raising taxes, the greater versatility it will have to provide services. Of course, providing services while also keeping tax rates low is the principal way elected officials stay in office. And while cities raise some of their budget from sales or income taxes, their principal source of revenue is the property tax, which imposes levies based on the value of land and buildings. In other words, cities have a clear fiscal interest in how much tax revenue will be created through the use of real estate within their borders. When the New Orleans city council allowed a bar to replace a derelict storefront near Tulane, it foresaw collecting more tax receipts than in the past. In addition, the council also knew that new jobs would be created to construct and then to operate the bar, and the income from these newly created jobs would be taxed. The plan mattered less when faced with these more compelling fiscal considerations.

Back to my welcome to the city council in New Orleans. The aftermath of the council president's brisk warning about what I could expect as planning director—conflict, out-of-the-box rough n' tumble give and take you don't find in classrooms or textbooks—was that while working with these very city council members over the next years, I found in fact a considerable diversity of attitudes toward planning. Some members made choices that took the city's plan to heart and into account. Others voted for the most publicly popular course of action irrespective of the plan. Still others never deviated from thinking that anyone who would invest in New Orleans was to be coddled, not subjected to governmental regulation. And there were some who made decisions for unexplained reasons, even admitting, "I have no vision of what the future should be," while never turning to the city's plan for guidance.

On reflection, however, the oddest part of my early encounter with the city council was not that the council president suggested a suit of armor. That was just a glimpse into her larger view of the world—a world of combat. Much odder was that I would enter my job long before I ever met the city council, even though the council itself would play the preeminent role in what I could accomplish using the city's plan.

The body that hired me to be planning director was the New Orleans City Planning Commission, an agency of city government that operates—in New Orleans, at least—independently of the mayor and the city council. How this important independence is achieved, and its effect on city planning, are subjects of a later chapter. For now it's only necessary to know the reasons for and the functions of city planning commissions.

The reasons that there *are* planning commissions originate in the late nineteenth century, when the corrupt machine politics of America's industrialized cities led reformers to conclude that city planners needed to be protected from the political pressure they would endure if they worked under the authority of elected officials. Most proponents of planning at the time didn't believe it could ever be a popular city function among property-owner citizens, because plans characteristically restrict the use of land to activities that the town as a whole considers suitable. However, individual property owners invariably have their own ideas for how to put their land to use, and those ideas frequently conflict with the community's ideas. As a consequence, nineteenth-century proponents of planning could foresee that individual constituents—many with money and power—would undoubtedly pressure local politicians to change a plan or interpret its stipulations in biased ways, or might get rid of planners altogether. One purpose of independent planning commissions, then, was to prevent these unwanted outcomes.

After 1926—when the United States Supreme Court decided it was constitutional for municipalities to regulate how individuals could use their property if such regulation was based on considerations of an entire community's welfare—planning commissions assumed a purpose in addition to protecting city planners. This purpose was to inspire citizens' support for the entire endeavor of city planning. Commissions throughout America argued in public that good planning could improve the value of all landowners' properties, inasmuch as a well-planned town would be attractive as a place to do business. Early planning commissioners were typically prominent businessmen—often they were realtors—chosen for their abilities to convince peers that all this was true. Later, as planning became a more accepted and active part of local government, and as land-use regulations survived intense judicial scrutiny, independent commissions found another reason for their own existence. Planning commissions became entities whose self-appointed task was to temper the professional planning staff's advice, using the commission's common sense about such matters as how a community should change, what sound land-use decisions should look like, what was fair, and finally what was politically practicable.

The way planning commissions operate within local government was— and is still—defined by state law, which delineates a commission's formal duties. Planning commissions were and are convened to adopt city plans and to take public testimony on planning and land-use matters. And they are charged with hiring a planning director who oversees the work of a planning staff as it performs such daily planning chores as issuing building permits to contractors, explaining land-use regulations to citizens, listening to complaints about land uses and controls, or interpreting the comprehensive plan when neighborhood organizations ask whether the plan would help them prevent a new development they oppose.

On land-use matters that require decisions by local governing bodies—zoning changes and subdivision approvals, for example—the commission is also required to take formal notice of how the planning staff has analyzed an issue, to hear public testimony on the matter, and then to make a nonbinding recommendation for action to the ultimate decision maker. Usually, this decision maker is a city council, whose members read the planning staff's report and the transcribed testimony from hearings conducted by the planning commission, and then consider the commission's recommendation for disposing of the land-use matter at hand. The council then conducts its own public hearing before reaching a final conclusion. In this process, the advice of city planners can be modified by either the planning commission or the city council, or both. Or it may be modified not at all. This is called a two-hearing process for reaching land-use decisions and it is typical of how such decisions are made throughout America.

This, then, is the administrative structure through which planning advice passes to elected leaders who ultimately decide land-use matters. Elaborating this structure doesn't really *explain* why I was so long meeting the city council where I was told to put on my suit of armor. But it does demonstrate the degree to which a city's planning director and its chief legislative council are institutionally buffered from each other to assure that each can function independently and do the city's business in ways that best serve the citizenry.

This brief rehearsal of what city planners do and why and how they do it offers a glimpse at the disjointure between a city's plan and how it's used. Yet this description also begins to open a keyhole view onto why city planners often encounter a difficult time finding an audience with those policy makers who must decide how land can be used. With this disjunct in mind, I contend that several standard procedures by which planners go about their duties should be changed. But to understand why changes are necessary (and a good idea), the reader must understand how these procedures are evident in practice—in particular to understand who makes use of city plans, how plans are created and executed, and how planners interact with elected leaders. These consequential subjects can best be illuminated by describing instances of how planning actually operates, and by describing these operations in contradistinction to how textbooks explain it.

Planning in New Orleans after the great storm of 2005 dramatizes much about the usual way city planning has been practiced in America. But the catastrophe of Hurricane Katrina brought a hot light of expectation, frustration, suspicion, and individual tragedy to that practice, and in so doing revealed its flaws. This book means not to concentrate on how individual parts of New Orleans have "come back" after all the planning that's gone on since the storm. Rebuilding is finally proceeding throughout the city—albeit in a nonorganized way—and any such specific description would be quickly out of date and ultimately offer little help to a broader understanding of the more generalized troubles with city planning. While the specifics of the ongoing rebuilding process in New Orleans might be engrossing to one such as I who loves the city, my concern is with matters fundamental to the planning profession itself.

What follows then is a description of how city planning was conducted in New Orleans before—and after—Hurricane Katrina, and relies on incidents that reveal the larger discipline of city planning no matter where it's practiced. These are notably not tales of success (although some narratives have reached more or less successful outcomes). Rather, I've chosen to recount incidents that illuminate the ferment of unforeseen, unaccountable, and even disappointing events that play out as city planners go about their tasks.

It should be noted that I have taken some license in describing many incidents that follow. I've foreshortened and simplified, even occasionally changed the actual locations, of many complicated intrigues, barely understandable double-crosses, endless misinterpretations, inscrutable personal agendas, overbearing egos, threats, delays, and insults that lie behind any issue city planners routinely confront. I'm not presenting gossip, but instead am relying on real incidents to explain how city planning accommodates the vagaries of human nature and personality with the ultimate intention of transcending the specific and provisional, and putting on display what good planning entails. In New Orleans—regarding the city's future—the points of view expressed by citizens of the Lower Ninth Ward seem little different from those I heard expressed in the rich Garden District, which in turn were quite typical of those in other historically significant sections of town. And these, in all likelihood, are little different in substance from points of view expressed by citizens of any city in America.

The incidents I've chosen to recount disclose the fundamental trouble with my profession—which is that although planners understand much about cities and how to improve them, what we know is only spottily, inadequately, often wastefully used. After reading the following accounts, a reader should acquire sufficient understanding of city planning to understand how the variety of changes I'll later suggest can make the profession more usefully persuasive wherever it's practiced.

FIVE

How Planners Interact with Citizens

Shortly after my introduction to the New Orleans city council in 1992, a citizen who lived on the city's West Bank called me.[1] He said he was from Algiers, referring to the New Orleans neighborhood across the river from the French Quarter. He lived near the locally famous firm that manufactures Mardi Gras floats, and was worried about rumors that Mardi Gras World, as the business is known, intended to expand its operations by purchasing adjacent houses—the ones that he and his neighbors happened to live in. He informed me he had organized a neighborhood association and wanted me to speak at their next meeting.

"We want to know what you have planned for us," were his precise words.

This resident's view was that much of the circumstances of citizens' lives is determined by an elite group of public officials who are in league with powerful economic interests in the city. This power elite, it's commonly believed, can't easily be influenced by ordinary people. If Mardi Gras World—a great money machine—wanted to expand into poor residential sections of Algiers, the citizens living there knew the city's leaders wouldn't oppose it. But the assumptions embedded in the request by this citizen from Algiers were more interesting—and unusual—for their intertwined fears and hopes: he clearly feared (and assumed) that city planners had made a plan consonant with what the power elite imagined, but he also hoped that those same city planners might be planning something else, something better for him and his neighbors than forcing them to move.

Understanding these assumptions—and then going to the meeting he'd asked me to attend—let me know how much and how widely I was going to have to explain city planning to the community if my office was to accomplish what I'd been hired to do. In the instance of my caller from Algiers, I had to reassure fearful citizens that as a matter of professional practice, planners *don't* draw up plans without including residents, as this new organization suspected. I knew Mardi Gras World had no plans for expansion at the time, though because that could change—as the neighborhood organization and I were both aware—it was important that these West Bank citizens participate in all the efforts city planners were just then commencing to revise out-of-date plans and land-use regulations so that they matched how the city *was* in 1992, including who lived there, who was in office, what the economy provided in terms of job opportunities, and what urban services the city's budget had to support.

The speech I made at the meeting of a few residents from Algiers typified the efforts planners on my staff made throughout the city to give citizens confidence that their ideas would become part of revised, up-to-date city planning documents. Without that confidence, we knew, an important prerequisite of a good plan (including a good *revised* plan)—how well it represents the aspirations of a diverse citizenry—cannot be achieved.

Over the next five or so years, city planners in New Orleans worked with citizens on many occasions like this one as we set about revising the planning commission's documents. In some instances, we were simply trying to put regulations into more easily understood English—rather than planners' or lawyers' jargon—so that an interested layman could understand them. In other efforts, we had the much larger intention of completely rewriting a plan because it didn't take into account how the city had developed in the previous twenty years. It's fair to say that citizens took heart from the consistent efforts city planners made to involve them, and after a time we received an informal reward when the city council president told me we were "doing a fine job."

The formal payoff of our efforts to explain city planning to citizens and involve them in our work of revising out-of-date planning documents came five years after I became planning director. In 1997 the planning commission felt ready to take on the largest task imagined in *New Century, New Orleans*—which was to revise the city's twenty-year-old land-use plan. This is the single most important part of any city's comprehensive plan because it brings together subordinate plans for the various components of a city, combining them to determine how all of a city's land should be used in the future. We felt ready because it seemed New Orleans' citizens were finally confident our purpose was to provide for them all, and therefore they would agree to work with us.

Accordingly, and with money allocated by the city council, late in 1997 the planning commission hired planning consultants that my office was to oversee, and we set them to the task of revising the land-use plan by convening public meetings, which I chaired, accompanied by members of my staff. Working with the consultants, we had prepared a large-scale map of the city, and we brought it wherever we went so that citizens could point out where they thought new land uses should go as the city grew. In each particular neighborhood where a meeting was held, we asked the assembled residents to identify on the map the uses they personally preferred in their own neighborhood—and also what they didn't want there. In enlisting these citizens' responses, we were working through the list of daily experiences, frustrations, and pleasures that contribute to a citizen's palpable sense of urban life—and we were also asking the standard questions any planner would ask.

To reach the entire citizenry we held meetings about the new land-use plan throughout the city, attended by a wide cross-section of lay and official types, community activist groups, governmental agencies, and historic preservationists. The planning consultants we'd hired to help formulate a new land-use plan kept notes of all that was said during the meetings. Sometimes we were joined by a representative of the Bureau of Governmental Research—an organization of mostly wealthy and well-educated conservatives from uptown neighborhoods. The bureau was held in high regard in New Orleans and periodically issued useful reports detailing some aspect of what went on in City Hall that it found faulty.

The first meeting was in a community center in the Lower Nine—as New Orleanians refer to the Lower Ninth Ward—the largely African-American, largely poor neighborhood whose origins were so closely tied to how New Orleans had once changed the use of land within its civic boundaries. At our meeting, held on a night of thunderstorms and with a member of the Bureau of Governmental Research present, I asked the dozen residents who were present to tell us what they liked—or didn't—about the Lower Nine. My question was an icebreaker in behalf of getting citizens to speak freely both about troublesome land uses in the district and about what new uses they'd like to see in the future.

The first speaker was a nurse's aide who worked at Charity Hospital—a long bus ride away from the Lower Ninth Ward, and a journey often made longer when the drawbridge across the Industrial Canal was raised to let a barge pass through. But what this nurse's aide didn't like, she said, were the vacant and dilapidated houses that blighted the neighborhood near her home. Some of these structures, she told us, had official notices nailed to them, warning of dangerous conditions within and prohibiting entry. Crack cocaine businesses operated there now, and the area was a dangerous nuisance. Around any of these houses, the nurse's aide said, weeds grew as high as her waist and hid feral dogs who lived there in packs. She was frightened, she said, when she walked past to catch her bus. Basically, she wanted the city to do something about these crack houses. She said she'd like to move, only she knew she wouldn't be able to sell her house.

Another respondent, a city bus driver, spoke about the potholes on his street—so deep, he said, that the noise of cars hitting them woke his ailing grandmother at night. A second-grade teacher complained that a liquor store operated next to her school twenty-four hours a day, and her young students on their way to class had to pass by foul-mouthed drunks.

The representative of the Bureau of Governmental Research who was attending the meeting took me aside while she put her raincoat back on— she was leaving early—and told me peevishly that the meeting was a waste of time because so few people had attended and because I'd allowed speakers to get off the subject of future land-use matters. Citizens, she argued, should make the complaints we'd heard that evening to the city council—or to the police department—since the problems they described were matters of enforcement. The city council, she pointed out, had passed ordinances that required weeds to be mowed, prohibited bars from operating within five hundred feet of schools, and charged the animal control officer with capturing stray dogs. These were not issues for city planning, which she believed should focus on the future. Then she left.

I knew what the woman from the bureau's leaving was about, as most city planners would—because we have seen it before and in all cities. She simply didn't want to think that poor conditions in a poor neighborhood could be a preliminary consideration to creating a plan for the future. The bureau—a self-described good-government watchdog—had recently become preoccupied with the notion of a master plan, which its members thought would specify every detail and aspect of the city in an ideal future state, and would ensure that every change to land uses in the city would be consistent with those specifications. That's what the bureau thought planning *was*. It was *not* listening to people talk about their lives. The belief that a plan can be so entirely comprehensive and flawless in its scope is a common one, whose source lies in the nineteenth century's White City and Daniel Burnham's Plan of Chicago. When this representative from the bureau criticized the meeting in the Lower Ninth Ward for not making attendees stick to the subject of the physical form the city of New Orleans should take in the future, she was restating Burnham's advice to make only "big plans."

But contemporary planners, even those set on writing "big plans," must (and most do) take into account all aspects of life in a city, which means necessarily including where its working classes live, and involving these citizens—as I was attempting in my meeting in the Lower Ninth Ward—in developing plans by discussing with them those contact points where a plan will actually come into their lives. Which gratefully means that the practice of planning has evolved since Burnham's day, to take a more democratic view that plans should be based not on what architects—or master planners—want, but on what citizens want. And need. Planners today know that citizens who live in neighborhoods like the Lower Ninth Ward are at least as vitally interested in solving problems such as potholes, crack houses, feral dogs hiding in uncontrolled weeds, and bars next to elementary schools as they are in imagining what form a wondrous city of the future might take.

How a master plan portraying New Orleans in an ideal future state could solve the problems of the speakers from the Lower Ninth Ward was particularly hard for me to see—at that moment. The nurse's aide, the bus driver, and the schoolteacher had few options for what they could do differently—while the *other,* beautiful future state was somehow being planned and achieved. Apparently, they were just meant to suffer along and endure. They certainly couldn't sell their houses and move to a better neighborhood, as the nurse's aide said. The dilapidated structures around her house were vestiges of neighbors who hadn't sold their homes either, and had finally abandoned them to New Orleans' forces of blight: a fiercely humid climate, Formosan termites, vandals, and people whose trade was illegal drugs.

In any neighborhood where economic growth is unlikely, new land uses are equally unlikely and therefore city planning has to be less concerned with imagining a far-off future than with figuring out what will improve citizens' lives while they're living them. Such a custodial vision requires planners to seek out accounts of life in neighborhoods from their residents and devise solutions accordingly. A new land-use plan might include recommendations that the city amend how it regulates particular uses—new churches might be required to provide additional off-street parking, for example, so that parishioners don't block neighbors' driveways on Sunday mornings. Or the new plan might recommend prohibiting commercial kennels—and their barking dogs—from residential areas.

And for problems with less obvious solutions, planners can rely on their national peers to suggest measures taken in other cities to solve such commonplace annoyances as high weeds growing around vacant houses in poor neighborhoods. Very, very few problems occur only in one city. Because other places might have addressed the same or similar situations, solutions can be sought there, modified to suit a particular city's geographic, economic, and cultural circumstances, and included in its land-use plan. In their critical custodial role, city planners complement and ground the visionary role the world mostly associates with planning. While the future envisioned in any city's plan is gradually achieved, planners can include a vision of measures that attempt to fix problems in the here and now.

But back to the 1997 meeting in the Lower Ninth Ward.

I've always thought it was unfortunate that the Bureau of Governmental Research's representative left out of impatience with the meeting that night, too bad she didn't see what happened when I turned the discussion to the future, the subject she'd wanted me to insist on. For if she'd stayed, she would've heard a similar impatience with the meeting expressed by an elderly New Orleans woman who'd dutifully worked with the other attendees to agree that a grocery store was a land use needed in the Lower Nine. This woman's group even identified the best location for a grocery—where two city bus routes crossed and where there was ample land for parking.

But then this woman said to me, "Kristina, why waste our time figuring out where a grocery store should go when we know it won't ever come here?" She went on to describe the economic and demographic dynamics of the Lower Ninth Ward: ever since public schools were integrated in 1963, white citizens had moved farther out St. Claude Avenue into St. Bernard Parish; local merchants had followed them and their buying power. Grocery stores, drugstores, dry cleaners—these were now gone. And left behind were seedy stores on street corners that sold out-of-date products at high prices, and bars where unemployed men passed the day—the classic commercial profile of a declining area. No grocery store would foresee any profits here, she said. Doesn't city planning know that?

Of course we did, but I chose to answer her question with professional dogma about how a planner goes about discovering what a diverse citizenry considers a mutually agreeable vision of their city's future—what I have previously called a prerequisite for a good plan. A grocery store only seemed unlikely *now,* I said; but a planner's duty is to plan for what citizens want when the city's economy improves. Economic prosperity, I went on to say, is of course the chief source of optimism for any city official, no matter how unlikely it is. I explained that if we designated on a plan where citizens wanted a grocery store, a developer intent on building one could be steered to that location. This was a thumbnail sketch, I concluded, of why we asked the questions we did.

I understood from the perplexed look on her face that this woman was unconvinced, though she nodded at my answer and politely let the subject drop. I saw that she'd probably agree with the bureau's representative that this meeting had been a waste of time, and that any plan that resulted from it wouldn't be useful. The reasons for each woman's dissatisfaction were clearly different—one wanted the meeting to result in a vision of an ideal city, the other thought plans only portrayed unattainable dreams. Both women thought the other's view about planning was a waste of time. What I knew from this seeming stalemate was that I had to write a plan that overcame both perceptions.

The land-use plan that we wrote—one based on the series of meetings that began with this one in the Lower Ninth Ward—went on to win a special award in 1999 from the Louisiana Association of Planners. And we were cited in part for the methods used to involve citizens in its preparation.

That outcome seemed very unlikely on the stormy night in 1997, when the bureau's representative had left precisely because of the flaws she saw in our methods, and the elderly lady who lived in the Lower Ninth Ward nodded at my answer but asked no further questions. At the time, I regretted my inadequate answer about why we'd talk about a grocery store that wouldn't ever come, though as later chapters describe, this incident gave rise to suggestions I'll come to make for changing the ways that planners engage citizens.

As to the other fault the Bureau of Governmental Research's representative found that night—that only a dozen citizens attended—I also had a standard professional excuse and explanation for that. I'd been pleased to see as many as twelve people attend our meeting since the Lower Nine was a neighborhood of economic decline. This wasn't a section of town that had endured the changes in land use that growth brings—and that usually draw citizens to planning meetings. Therefore, these citizens' attendance implied a certain hopefulness that a good plan could result. But my standard planner's optimism overlooked the fact that these citizens had previous—and bad—experiences with plans. This neighborhood had been created decades earlier by plans made by, and carried out by, the Dock Board when it built the Industrial Canal and when the Army Corps of Engineers built the Intracoastal Waterway. The neighborhood had no part in making these plans, and the planning commissions of the day had no complaint about them since they encouraged shippers to travel from docks on the Industrial Canal to the Gulf of Mexico using a shortcut that avoided the river's time-consuming meanders. The city would undoubtedly profit. Neither plan recognized that it simultaneously increased the Lower Nine's vulnerability to floods.

The twelve residents who came that night, therefore, had good reason to come, though it was different from *my* optimistic explanation for their attendance: they were suspicious about anyone involved with planning. And of course the extent to which their suspicions were accurate became tragic in 2005, when Hurricane Katrina pushed a huge volume of water up the Mississippi River–Gulf Outlet into the Industrial Canal, overtopping levees along the way and forcing a barge through the canal's floodwall, drowning the Lower Ninth Ward. Plans had rendered them helpless.

* * *

There's a useful connection to be forged between the meeting conducted in 1997 in the Lower Ninth Ward—years before Hurricane Katrina—and all the meetings that were held to develop a recovery plan *after* the hurricane. In all instances—before and after the storm—what New Orleanians wanted was simple reassurance that their needs would finally be addressed. Even after the hurricane, citizens were realistic about how long that might take. They knew firsthand the extravagant and appalling extent of their city's tragedy, and were willing to concede that all couldn't be put right at once.

The Bring New Orleans Back Commission's plan—with its green dotted-line circles—focused attention solely on the physical form of the city as it might appear at some point in an unspecified future. As everyone in the commission's audience realized, there was no plan imagined for what would happen while that presumably safe—and ideal—future was being achieved. As they first looked at this drawing, most people in the audience must have thought exactly what the elderly lady at my meeting in the Lower Ninth Ward had said eight years earlier: why was their time being wasted on a far-off vision of the future when so much of ordinary life needed specific and immediate attention? The audience knew everything about the city was at stake—particularly their future in it.

The commission wasn't allowed a chance to deal with the hostile disagreement its presentation of the map confronted. This was unfortunate because, having read the entire report—which included much more than the trivializing map—I knew there were many wise and useful aspects to it, such as a well-thought-through and thorough list of what was required for rebuilding New Orleans. But the commission had lost its audience and the political support of the mayor, who had no appetite for persevering with a plan that had been so badly received.

I believe the commission's planners could have persevered past the contumely and chaos their plan provoked, just as my office eight years earlier had gone on to write a land-use plan despite the opposing thoughts expressed at our meeting in the Lower Ninth Ward. But instead, the Bring New Orleans Back Commission was disbanded, and a confusing sequence of planning efforts began during which citizens attended multiple meetings and answered repetitive questions posed by many different planning consultants—but without understanding how a workable plan would result. And it took nearly two years for a post-Katrina rebuilding plan to be approved for New Orleans, and that finally acceptable plan envisioned nothing more than recreating the city as it had been before the storm. It's tempting to enter into a digression about what plan *should* have been made after the hurricane; but it's more useful to look at what the experience in devastated New Orleans reveals about the difference between what citizens expect from plans and what plans actually provide in ordinary times as well as during catastrophic periods.

The incidents described from New Orleans both before and after the hurricane demonstrate at a very fundamental level how difficult it is both to explain a plan's purpose and also to create a plan that citizens can see as something other than a waste of time. These difficulties begin to suggest why elected leaders who make final decisions about land uses in cities don't readily seek advice from their city's plan. Put in the simplest terms, all the planning efforts that transpired in New Orleans—before and then after Hurricane Katrina—dramatize how obscure the logic of city planning is to anyone but a planner.

One reason for this is that most city plans are formulated by superimposing previous planning models—such as the iconic plan created by Daniel Burnham for Chicago—on a contemporary city without taking into account the circumstances there. But there's more to it, which has to do with how planners engage citizens even as they are trying to take into account their situation. To understand how planners and citizens so often misunderstand one another requires a little more discussion of the plans they ostensibly work on together. A short history of the evolution of plans in America can help explain how my profession has gotten so out of touch with its audience.

SIX

The American Evolution of Plans

Several important twentieth-century American plans had a different audience and a different theory of urban betterment from Daniel Burnham's Plan of Chicago. Burnham's plan was written for a group of wealthy businessmen and concentrated on imagining grandiose public improvements as a method of transforming the city into something ideal. But other important twentieth-century plans were sponsored by governments, rather than by private entities such as Chicago's Commercial Club, and took an interest in improving the lives of citizens directly, rather than relying on trickle-down effects of public spending as Burnham's plan had. Furthermore, these other twentieth-century plans became models for plans adopted in most cities in America—including New Orleans. However, there were several flaws contained in the frequently replicated plans—flaws as serious as the Plan of Chicago's omission of housing for working-class Chicagoans.

The 1909 Plan of Chicago was the first modern American iconic plan—although because most of Burnham's grand designs were simply too expensive for Chicago to undertake, they never materialized. Even the large public parks along the city's lakefront that exist to this day were but a small part of Burnham's grand plan. In spite of Chicago's not building the plan as was originally proposed, however, the beauty of parks along Lake Michigan and the elegance of the plan's drawings of an idealized city still seize the imagination of laymen—who fervently hope their city's plan will offer them a vision similar to the one the Plan of Chicago portrayed. In New Orleans, a vision of an idealized city was what the Bureau of Governmental

Research expected from our planning meeting in the Lower Ninth Ward in 1997. And in 2006, it was such a vision that the Bring New Orleans Back Commission thought it was presenting for rebuilding the devastated city.

But other important American plans have had a greater effect on development in American cities, including New Orleans, than the Plan of Chicago did, and simultaneously have shaped how planners view their responsibilities in local government.

As we've seen (most graphically in Figure 7), the French Quarter, the Garden District, and other neighborhoods built along the natural levees near the river were not submerged under floodwaters on August 31, 2005, two days after Hurricane Katrina. But another large expanse of the city was also surprisingly unflooded after the storm. This part of New Orleans lies along the shore of Lake Pontchartrain at the city's northern boundary and stretches from a mile east of the breached Seventeenth Street Canal farther eastward all the way past the ruined channel of the Industrial Canal—a distance of more than five miles. Think of a band of dry ground all along Lake Pontchartrain's southern shore.

This dry terrain clearly represented more of the city's high ground, but it was not elevated land that lay atop the previously discussed natural river levees. This dry land was man-made land, and on it were neighborhoods called Lake Shore, Lake Vista, Lake Terrace, Lake Oaks—wishful names a subdivision developer might've employed despite the fact that Lake Pontchartrain was invisible from any of the homes built there. The developer, as it happened, had been the Board of Levee Commissioners of the Orleans Levee District (Levee Board, informally), a powerful satellite of the Louisiana state government whose members oversee all activities that occur on the levees within the district—although the structural integrity of the levees remains the responsibility of the Army Corps of Engineers. The Levee Board makes sure the grass on the levees is mowed; it employs a police force to patrol the levees; it provides recreational facilities such as walkways and picnic tables for the public. And it seeks opportunities for economic development. In the early 1920s, the Levee Board persuaded the Louisiana legislature to finance a modernization scheme for the lakefront, promising that improvements would generate enough cash to repay the state. From this finagling, subdivisions were born.

The Levee Board had in mind no small plan in 1925. It would build a seawall on the bed of Lake Pontchartrain, three thousand feet from the then existing shoreline; this seawall would be fashioned as concrete steps facing north to the lake—the steps are there today—and would parallel the shore for nearly five and a half miles. The lake bottom outward from the new concrete seawall steps would be dredged, and the former lake-bottom material then used to fill the area between the new wall and the old shoreline, elevating new ground to a height of five to ten feet above the surface of the lake. More dredged lake-bottom soil would also be used to construct flood levees parallel to the newly created shoreline, protecting the man-made high ground from storms that might force water from Lake Pontchartrain over the seawall. This "new" city land bordered a street to be named Robert E. Lee Boulevard, a wide roadway that roughly traced the location of the old lakeshore and simultaneously defined the inland border of the new lakefront neighborhoods. As one might imagine, such a large project took considerable time to complete, and though begun in 1925 it wasn't finished until the late 1930s. Furthermore, it was so expensive that the Levee Board ran out of the money it had borrowed from the state, and the depression-era Works Progress Administration helped construct many of the planned improvements.

However, and pertinent to the topographical map from 2005, the Levee Board's modernizations—purposefully or not—created one of the highest parts of the city of New Orleans, along with inventing two thousand new acres of saleable land. To raise money for repaying the state's loan for this project, the Levee Board leased some of the new land for a municipal airport at the lakefront, and leased a bit more for an amusement park at the whites-only beach. The board likewise had the good sense to keep its creditor—the state—inside the tent, so it donated a large tract to Louisiana State University for a New Orleans campus at the lake, which is thriving today. But mostly the Levee Board repaid the state by selling the property it had created. In 1939, the board commissioned a plan for developing this prime real estate, and once that plan was complete, began selling parcels at pretty prices to individual buyers and contractors.

These lakeshore developments in New Orleans epitomize one view of what might be called "good" city planning. The Levee Board's elaborate plan for its property was designed in the English garden city tradition first made popular in 1927 in America at Radburn, New Jersey, wherein that town's sylvan, low-density residential neighborhoods—kept separate from commercial enterprise by landscaped buffers—were designed to evoke a garden. The Radburn-derived design in New Orleans had extensive public parks along the lakefront between the protective levees and the seawall where to this day citizens hold cookouts and family reunions at sheltered picnic tables, or sit on the concrete steps of the seawall and catch soft-shell crabs. Farther inland and safely behind the levees, single-family houses were arranged on large lots along dead-end internal streets, a pattern chosen to inhibit traffic and afford safety for children playing outdoors. All the streets were given the tranquilizing names of gemstones and flowers—Topaz, Crystal, Turquoise; Larkspur and Petunia. One neighborhood even includes a bird sanctuary, and its streets take the names of indigenous species. Throughout these planned communities are several well-landscaped and well-maintained commons for residents who can walk to them via a series of rambling pedestrian ways. Grocery stores, movie theaters, drugstores, and other commercial destinations are concentrated in small shopping centers unreachable via the interior roadways, so that again traffic isn't a nuisance. In some eyes, these neighborhoods are in-town suburban dreams.

Developers have long since tired of the old slogan "garden city" in their up-to-date efforts to market well-planned neighborhoods like those along Lake Pontchartrain, and each new year brings new "concepts" to describe such projects, though the connecting thread of these slogans through the years and through the country is that they express what people believe is the purpose of city planning: pretty and peaceful residential life. A recently popular slogan is "smart growth." One journalist described a smart-growth development in Mercer County, New Jersey, for his paper's real estate section, choosing words that vividly recall Radburn's design from nearly eighty-five years ago: "The neighborhoods here seem plucked from an urban planner's catalog: trimmed lawns, picket fences and freshly minted homes. . . . A greenbelt wraps the town like a bow."[1] Garden-city plans, and the towns and neighborhoods developed according to them, are durable icons of what constitutes "good planning" as perceived by developers and their customers—as well as by journalists.

To me, the developments on New Orleans' lakefront and those in suburban New Jersey are flawed models for plans because they reflect "good planning" only in a highly rarefied and circumscribed sense. The very prettiness of these neighborhoods suggests why Peirce Lewis, one of New Orleans' most ardent yet objectively cold-eyed scholars, calls them "ornaments." Planning Lake Vista, Lake Oaks, and the other neighborhoods was little more than a matter of working out a design for domestic tranquility where nothing had been built before and where residents would be of the same economic class—the middle class—who could afford to live in such planned communities, could afford the expensive maintenance the landscaping required and who had cars and leisure to enjoy it all.

The flaws of ornamental garden-city plans have been noted since they were first conceived early in the twentieth century. Critics have vigorously faulted the profession all along for devoting its talents principally to the bourgeoisie and to such developments as Lake Vista. And truly, the design problems of planning a new suburb didn't, and don't, include making sense of old buildings and old street layouts, nor do these plans have to navigate among rivalrous expectations of citizens who already live in the area—and who like it just how it is. These, as discussed, are the thorny issues in any existing city, issues that its plan must comprehend. But garden-city plans are best suited to developments that will occupy undeveloped land—such as the Levee Board's lake suburbs—and these plans view people as citizens whose most pertinent attributes (to the developer) are how much money they have and the kind of house and neighborhood that will attract them. This simplified view allows planners to focus chiefly on the design details of attractive neighborhoods, and is another significant reason city planning has been criticized throughout its American history for caring about buildings and their arrangement on an urban landscape more than the life actually experienced by the people who live in what has been designed for them. The view of citizens as a targeted market is also the reason that Peirce Lewis can call "ornaments" those parts of New Orleans built on a garden-city concept: the plans, and what resulted, didn't take into account other parts of the city and who lived there and what *they* desired from the future.

You could say that a primary flaw of garden-city plans is that they ignore the criticisms of planners' middle-class biases and of planners' single-minded focus on structures. Both criticisms illuminate something about the planning profession's self-regarding and academic preference for well-conceived, elegantly worked out and complexity-averse plans—objects more worthy of aesthetic admiration than actual enactment. Garden-city plans were being conceived in England at the start of the twentieth century, about the same time that Daniel Burnham was working in Chicago. And both conceptions—as well as all subsequent plans that followed either model—view cities as intellectual constructs rather than as places where a plan must address a diverse set of citizens with very different economic, demographic, and cultural characteristics. Burnham's Plan of Chicago found beauty in "grandiloquent panoramas" (Lewis Mumford's dismissive phrase); garden-city plans anticipated each and every detail necessary for a town or a neighborhood that wanted to be a pretty, trouble-free garden.

In either type of plan, grandiloquent or ornamental, citizens come along later. Burnham believed people who were put down into orderly surroundings would act in orderly ways. Garden-city plans came somewhat closer to basing their design on what individuals seemed to appreciate about where they lived—peace and quiet in sylvan surroundings. But these plans concentrated exclusively on providing for those who could afford middle-class sanctuaries. In either case, plans modeled on Burnham's or on garden-city designs ignored the humans outside the plan's purview—and in effect, treated cities like stage sets on which citizens enter like actors once the curtain rises on the designed set.

Yet both plans endure as archetypes. The Orleans Levee District's bourgeois lakefront communities are richly landscaped versions of the garden-city concept. But even low-income suburban tracts that only provide cul-de-sacs, a few street-side saplings, and skimpy front lawns to evoke a "garden development" are themselves variations on the prototype plan Americans first saw at Radburn. The idealized Plan of Chicago likewise inspired many permutations—from the audacious programs devised by Robert Moses to clear New York City's slums and build massive public works, all the way down (and decidedly down) to the callous map the Bring New Orleans Back Commission presented to New Orleanians whose homes had been washed away by Hurricane Katrina.[2]

One reason for the endurance of the Plan of Chicago as an icon is that it still represents what draws many planners to their profession: the possibility that they will be asked, as Daniel Burnham was, to draw up a plan for an entire city. And Burnham's plan, even with its omission of working-class people, is indeed so thorough that it remains a good starting point for modern planners such as those who came to New Orleans to work for the Bring New Orleans Back Commission. However, plans like Burnham's are very expensive to formulate (and even more expensive to execute)—which is one reason so few have been written. His plan was paid for by the Commercial Club. Most cities can't afford such a grand plan, though they still aspire to have one. The Plan of Chicago endures because it continues to represent what many citizens think a plan should provide: an idealized version of their city in the future.[3]

The reasons that garden-city plans remain icons—despite their flaws—are a little different. One powerful reason is that for a long time after Radburn, New Jersey, was built in 1927, Americans had little need to develop new city plans of any type—and therefore better plans weren't imagined. With the stock market crash in 1929, and continuing through the depression and the Second World War, economic growth in America, which usually results in houses being built, offices and shops being constructed, came to a twenty-year standstill. Plans became too-expensive luxuries. City planners in this period concentrated neither on making plans nor on imagining a new form that plans might take, but on regulating how owners could use existing property so they wouldn't harm their neighbors. It was important work, to be sure, but it didn't inspire new planning models. When, in 1939, the Orleans Levee District had finished creating two thousand acres of lakeshore land and needed a plan for development, it hardly seemed worth the expense of devising a plan tailored specifically for the property when the old model of garden cities was available—and was already known to be attractive to home buyers. Holding down the expense of planning in 1939 was proven fiscally prudent because the Levee Board had to struggle each year to repay its loan from the state until the 1950s, when parcels of land in the Levee Board's lakeshore communities were finally purchased and the old loan was retired.

From 1929 through the late 1940s, a few architects and planning scholars imagined new designs for cities. The most famous of these were imagined by the visionary French architect Le Corbusier, who in the late 1920s and early 1930s proposed sweeping away entire cities and erecting in their place high, unornamented residential towers surrounded by parklands; factories would lie beyond the parkland and broad highways would connect the physically segregated functions of living and working. However, American cities took no interest in Le Corbusier's sweep-away-and-start-over theory of urban planning because they did not have the money to execute such a scheme. Therefore, his ideas for city plans remained dormant until after World War II, when America's urban renewal programs began. Until then, the Plan of Chicago as well as the garden-city plans remained unrivaled planning models. You could say that in the period between the stock market crash and the end of World War II, city plans weren't *necessary* to most American cities because there was so little to plan for.

After World War II city plans became necessities rather than luxuries. During the twenty-year period beginning in 1929 when America saw little construction, urban citizens had crowded into whatever housing existed, which in turn resulted in the nation's industrial cities becoming desperately run-down and overpopulated. The federal Housing Act of 1949 was passed to improve deteriorated cities by offering them financial assistance—the federal vernacular was "central area redevelopment funds"—for clearing urban districts of dilapidated buildings (especially slum tenements), following the theory that more lucrative economic activities than housing poor people would commence in these newly "renewed" urban spaces. The same theory had it that new urban economic activities would provide jobs and tax revenues, which would eventually benefit the cleared-out slum dwellers, wherever they went—another version of trickle-down that Burnham's Plan of Chicago relied on.

The Housing Act of 1949 was, as we know now, the beginning of urban renewal programs. The failures of urban renewal—including its reliance on Le Corbusier's planning theories—are so famously known and widely researched that it's possible to summarize them by saying that urban renewal left vast tracts of land in American cities completely desolate. Slum buildings were cleared, to be sure, in cities from Boston to St. Louis to Seattle, replaced most often with crosstown incursions of the 1950's federal highway system. Despite the Housing Act's theory that new economic activities would be attracted to the newly cleared areas, in city after American city, it was roads and vacant lots—often used for surface parking—that were the primary replacements for the crowded, low-income slums in deteriorated downtowns. And the Housing Act took little interest in what happened to the people who'd been living in the slums.[4]

Planners eventually learned many hard lessons from the results of urban renewal plans. However, the original 1949 Housing Act made American city plans *necessary* after a twenty-year hiatus, and amendments to that original act eventuated in an evolution of American city plans.

One stipulation of the 1949 act is supremely noteworthy. It provided that "central area redevelopment funds" would be given only to cities that had adopted a comprehensive plan for community renewal. However, few cities initiated such plans because they were expensive undertakings and because most municipalities thought their money was better spent on something more obviously urgent than developing plans. Still, the important feature of the Housing Act was its precedent that the federal government could require local jurisdictions to adopt plans.

Five years later this precedent was actually invoked and enacted, which resulted in city plans becoming widespread throughout America. The Housing Act of 1954 authorized federal mortgage guarantees for millions of new home buyers, but only if the houses being purchased were in towns that had adopted land-use plans. This stipulation—an amendment to the 1949 act—thus made planning a necessary concomitant to population growth. Importantly, Section 701 of the 1954 Housing Act provided federal funding for half the cost of writing such plans—which made the effort seem more economically rational to cities and towns than had been the case in 1949. Municipalities needed plans that met federal underwriting standards if they were to attract new housing developments.

It is no exaggeration to say that the 1949 and 1954 Housing Acts required land-use planning throughout America and defined its methods. These acts saw the specific utility of planning for the hundreds of thousands of Americans who wanted to buy houses—very few of which had been built since 1929. When the federal government decided to underwrite new home purchasers, it relied on an original justification of city planning: plans would ensure increasing property values and thereby reduce the probability of mortgage defaults. Furthermore, the Housing Acts relied on the fact that local governments, which collect operating revenues by taxing private property, would want more residents because they brought an attendant increase in local property valuations. These were the reasons that Section 701 of the 1954 act was drafted to include a grant program that allowed cities to hire consultants to draw up the required plans.

As the federal government had supposed, local jurisdictions embraced the federal requirement, and thousands of "Section 701 plans" were written by professional consultants in the twenty-five years after 1954—at a cost of over a billion federal dollars.[5] Although the federal government provided some guidelines to describe its preferred notion of a good city plan, most planning consultants after 1954 simply took as their model Section 701 plans that had already been approved. And as it happened, approved plans divided cities into four component land uses (housing, retail centers, offices and business parks, and civic facilities such as libraries and schools) and kept those categorical uses physically apart so as to avoid conflicts among them (annoying hours of operation, problems of traffic and noise, and so on) that might reduce property values. Section 701 plans also provided a system of streets and roads so that people could move among the different land uses as they needed. Providing for four component land uses, each separated from the other, as well as defining a roadway system that connected them, was the conception that underlay the first Section 701 plans approved by the federal government—and therefore became the conceptual model for all subsequent plans.

According to directives made separately from the 1954 Housing Act, however—directives written by the federal mortgage underwriting agency—the federal "good planning" model did not include rental housing, and it did not include home ownership by African-Americans. As a consequence, Section 701 plans didn't provide for rental housing and banks did not approve loans for black families in the planned cities.

Planning consultants who were hired to write so-called 701 plans started by making an estimate of how many people might come to live in the jurisdiction they were planning for. From this, they projected how many houses and schools such a population would need, how much retail space it could support, even how many churches would be needed. These estimates were then given spatial representation by designating different portions of a city's mapped area to be spaces where the four categories of land uses could be built—housing, retail, industry, and civic facilities—each separated from the other, yet connected by streets and roads. Housing wasn't near commercial areas, and neither use was located close to industry. In this way, 701 plans were formulaic, and because so many plans were needed to accommodate the post–World War II demand for housing, many planners

opened shop as consultants and went to work carrying out the federal government's formulas throughout the country. While most of the plans were
written for suburban communities, they were also written—using the same
"good planning" model—for undeveloped sections of already existing cities.

Consultants earned Section 701 grant money by using a simple and
familiar theory: that a well-planned town or city or neighborhood resulted
in domestic harmony among similar people living in single-family homes
that they owned, going about middle-class pursuits of raising children, going to work, attending church. When a consulting firm completed its first
Section 701 plan and saw that plan approved by the federal government, the
firm's success became a selling point for seeking work in other towns. By
this chain of events, consulting planners soon found it efficient—in terms
of the time it took—to use a previously successful plan as a model for subsequent plans in other cities and towns that hired them, rather than trying
to imagine a whole new plan. Adapting a previously successful 701 plan to
different cities reduced the risk of disapproval by the federal government.

Though towns and city neighborhoods built according to the Section
701 model turned out to have a dreary sameness—their street patterns were
predictable, their narrow choice of landscaping materials was "applied"
over and over to residential neighborhoods, and the only difference among
individual houses was their color, which was chosen from a limited palette
of pastels. It was a simple planning template.

There were many criticisms of towns built according to Section 701
plans: critics said they provided only monotonous neighborhoods, and
that the separation of land uses meant only women were in neighborhoods
on weekdays, their husbands off at work and their children at school. Everybody was approximately the same childbearing age—and there weren't
black families, and few minority households of any kind. Critics further
noticed that residents had to drive wherever they wanted to go—even to
get a quart of milk. Diversity in terms of race, income, and age was absent
among residents of these towns, although isolation was in great supply. But
these were criticisms mostly from *outside,* not from people who lived in
Section 701 planned communities.

For local governments, the urban communities that resulted from the
701 plans avoided many of the tedious conflicts that bedevil cities where
different land uses exist side-by-side and elected leaders routinely have to

solve such problems as patrons of fast-food restaurants strewing litter on sidewalks, tavern revelers waking up neighborhoods every Friday night, delivery trucks speeding past playgrounds. On and on. In this regard, both governing and living in towns built according to the federal template were relatively uncomplicated, and complaints about life's dullness there were easy to ignore. Planning consultants, too, had an uncomplicated task—and a lucrative one—of following the federal model for 701 plans, though probably none of the consultants imagined the plans they wrote were capable of stirring anybody's blood the way Daniel Burnham had said they should.

Section 701 of the federal Housing Act determined how three-quarters of the nation's huge population increase after 1950 was planned for and accommodated, and for that reason the 701 plans have come to be seen as archetypes—if dubious ones. But Section 701 was also a powerhouse for the American urban planning profession, putting into play many attributes of what is still usual planning practice. For one thing, it became commonplace for cities to hire consultants to draft their plans. And because the federal government helped pay for the plans, cities got used to how much they cost. Because these plans were written principally to satisfy federal underwriting requirements, no other evaluation of their utility seemed worthwhile, and therefore cities that followed the 701 model got used to *not* evaluating the work of planners.

Furthermore, planning consultants found that they could seize on a single way to write a plan, and like those who wrote Section 701 plans, apply it over and over. Finally, and perhaps most important, consultants found they could write successive plans for many cities, yet their contracts did not make them responsible for executing those plans. Presumably, a city's own planners would perform that duty. As it worked out, neither the planners who were hired specifically to write a plan nor the city planners put in charge of executing it were held accountable for what resulted. To me, this flaw of the Section 701 plans is more fundamental than the monotonous developments they spawned. The ultimate and most insidious effect of Section 701 plans is that planners are not evaluated for what they plan.

All these planning archetypes—the Plan of Chicago, garden-city plans, and Section 701 plans—stand aloof from what we think of as urban problems and urban life, aloof from the messy interactions among people of different economic classes, among people with different cultural values and unequal educational accomplishment, among regular citizens with colliding aspirations for a better life. You might say that these plans stand apart from most of the life that goes on in the confines of a city. Yet it's how a city works out all this potentially chaotic life that determines the daily experience of its citizenry. And good city planning ought to participate in these messy transactions among citizens, which means that a good plan is something more than a beautiful stage set, more than an infinitely replicated template. Furthermore, a *good* city plan would have results that citizens and elected leaders could see and evaluate.

One can analyze city plans to find their rationales, their attractions, their benefits, their liabilities as part of a city's life. But this may be a kind of taxonomic illusion or fallacy—like the exploded view of a motor, which "reveals" all the parts to the motor, while the actual mystery of its real life (that it works) remains intact. Although I've spent years studying cities, whenever I'm exhilarated (as I often am) by finding a city that's unknown to me—or by discovering a new part of a city I already know, or by passing through a section of a city I once knew that's been newly enlivened—I rarely attribute any exhilaration to the *planned* aspect of what I see. How could that be? Is there something in us all—even us planners—that feels diminished by discovering that what we're drawn to is something somebody has *planned* for us? Or that realizes our delight is the predictable result of steadfast adherence to what somebody imagined years ago? Somebody who didn't even know us?

Though it might seem an odd trait in a planner, I rarely think about a city's plan unless my attention has been for some reason specifically drawn to notice, say, the aesthetic beauties of L'Enfant's plan for Washington, D.C., seen as a map; of Burnham's exquisitely drawn plan of Chicago, or Baron Haussmann's imperial plan for rebuilding Paris. Like the underlying structure of a good novel—essential but easily overlooked while reading—a good city plan is not easy to perceive when you walk around a city. In my own case, I usually think about a city in terms of its plan only when one is obviously absent—when traffic congeals at important interchanges, or when I see big-box stores surrounded by acres of unrelentingly hot, mostly empty asphalt parking lots without a single shade tree. Or when I pass a derelict shopping center just a few hundred yards from a new one under construction of the same design. Or when I see a neighborhood where there's no public park, and notice children playing around a boarded-up gas station.

Of course, there is no single way for good plans to come into existence. A degree in city planning requires studying plans drawn up for cities around the world and created in different historic periods. From this study, students judge the success and failure of government policies conceived for a variety of urban conditions. And by their study and appraisal, planners in essence engage in a conversation within the profession past and present about how citizens and their leaders have written plans to positively influence the important factors of an urban environment: how different cities have attracted new industry or responded to population decline; how they've improved conditions of immigrant workers; how they've saved historic buildings from demolition. What planners learn from their study is more than a template for writing plans. Instead, they learn there is never a single means of bringing about a better future, and that a plan has to be formulated for the particular chaos of conflicting views, clamorous opinion, and rivalrous interests that coexist in a particular city.

In New Orleans after the great storm in 2005, the city lost its cohesiveness, its integrity, its implicit internal "plan." The city was devastated and needed a good plan to cope with a vastly changed world that was strange, overly complex, apparently intractable, quickly changing, and seemingly immune to the common sense of ordinary citizens. Yet all cities—devastated or not—face these same issues, and all need good plans to deal with them. A good plan invites invention, invites freedom and even error, but inspires solutions to such an age-old problem as people living in flood-prone neighborhoods. A good plan invites surprise, but also shows how to accommodate it so that what citizens value in their city doesn't disappear. Flux is the single constant in cities: people are born and come of age, have new ideas; new people move to town with different cultural interests; new ways of making a living become profitable. Hurricanes or wildfires or earthquakes are just extremely harmful examples of flux.

Good planning consists of devising a language to unify a city dealing with events both foreseeable and not, with new enthusiasms and even with new citizens. The language of good city planning doesn't suppose it can reconcile contradictory aspirations among its residents, but instead provides for their coexistence. The language of a good plan makes a place cohesive and holds its citizens together, makes them see their destiny as intertwined. The art of a good plan doesn't lie in grand drawings such as Burnham made, not in the pastoral beauties of a garden city, not in the conflict-free templates that Section 701 produced. A good plan is more than an arrangement of buildings and does not have to aim toward a specific physical result. A planner's art is to engage in a conversation about the future that accommodates different personalities and tastes, different economic activities, different cultures, even different components of the way people get along with one another. This quality of planning so simply expressed, though evidently so hard to accomplish, is essential to every city at all times, not just in the wake of disaster.

Though irrespective of the quality individual plans achieve, how they might—or do—take effect continues to mystify so many citizens that it is worth some effort to explain.

SEVEN

How Plans Take Effect

It was on August 31, 2005, two days after Hurricane Katrina left New Orleans devastated, that General Russel Honoré of the U.S. Army arrived to take charge of the military's relief effort in the city. General Honoré, a Louisiana native, was widely welcomed as he took up his duties of overseeing search-and-rescue missions, transporting storm victims from inside the Superdome and outside the Convention Center to more suitable shelter, and organizing the evacuation of citizens who'd remained in the city through the storm. Honoré was also ordered to patrol the "dry"—unflooded—neighborhoods until their residents returned and the city could take over policing its own streets. General Honoré was furthermore commissioned to oversee repairs to breached levees, restoration of the city's broken pumps, and the task of getting floodwater returned to Lake Pontchartrain. Exhaustively, the general was also to coordinate his efforts with those undertaken by the New Orleans mayor, the governor of Louisiana, the U.S. Coast Guard, the National Guard, and the Army Corps of Engineers—all for the purpose of determining when New Orleanians could safely return home.

General Honoré, of course, arrived with a plan for his schedule of duties. When he announced the plan to reporters and saw relief rise on their faces, however, he pleaded: "Don't confuse a plan with execution. A plan is good intentions. You don't win with good intentions."[1]

The general's word—"win"—is in the diction of the military man. But "win" was sadly applicable to New Orleans' predicament on August 31, when every prospect of resuming the city's former life seemed at least embattled, if not completely *un*-winnable. Although General Honoré's plan was spe-cifically designed for the urgent dilemma of New Orleans, a city that lay in ruins, his distinction between plan and execution could extend to any other city with a plan to improve its civic future. You really don't improve a city with good intentions.

The confusion between a plan and its execution finds an illustration in the case of Stamford, Connecticut, a city nearly as old as New Orleans but lacking its fabled intoxicating charms and also its unyielding economic problems. In 2002, Stamford undertook the creation of a new master plan, one purpose of which was to ensure that "affordable" housing would be built for people who worked in Stamford but didn't earn enough to live there. Civic-minded residents met with planning consultants to craft the plan's central goal—that newly built multiple-family developments (apart-ment buildings or townhouse complexes) contain at least some units priced within reach of teachers, civic employees, and other working classes who wanted to live in Stamford. There was little public argument over this well-meaning plan, particularly because it would benefit an identifiable and familiar stratum of individuals who'd kept Stamford safe from crime and fire and taught the town's children how to read. In the glow of community consensus, Stamford adopted the five-hundred-page master plan in the autumn of 2002.

But a year later, one citizen—a woman who'd attended public meetings to help develop the master plan—was heard to lament its apparent effect. "We thought things would happen automatically," she said, then added that several new developments had been constructed in Stamford, "but not according to the master plan. We were naive."[2]

This public-spirited citizen had assumed that Stamford's optimistic master plan would perfectly predict and bring about its own execution and outcome. Any planner, however, would recognize this as a common misunderstanding of how plans work. As clear and appealing as "execute a plan" might seem, this phrase does not at all reflect how a city's plan is literally brought to fruition.

In the first place, with the best possible plan devisable by man, each and every good intention such a plan includes requires a local government to take specific action to bring that intention about. Take the following as a simple example of specific action in behalf of achieving a plan's stated goal:

a city's plan calls for building new community centers to improve the lives of senior citizens. The city council—to make the plan work—will have to finance the construction of the planned facilities. The council might be aware of federal programs that explicitly help pay for community centers, assuming the city "matches" (that is, pays an equal amount) what it is granted. Therefore, to qualify, the city council would have to allocate funds in its annual budget to match the amount it seeks from the federal government. Such necessary fiscal decisions—no matter what the plan says—always have to compete with other demands made on the city council and its budget, such as when the police chief says he needs more money to hire additional patrolmen to prevent crime in new apartment developments.

An alternative way a city could build the new community centers included among its plan's good intentions would be to issue bonds to pay for construction. But because states routinely limit how much bonded indebtedness cities can incur, should the council choose to issue bonds, the city may reach its statutory limit, thereby precluding the sale of additional bonds to make *other* necessary public improvements, such as replacing dilapidated sewer systems or structurally weakened bridges.

The matrix of variables that affect a municipality's budgetary decisions are importantly difficult to forecast and rationalize, inasmuch as local budgets always involve one crucial variable that plans themselves have virtually no control over—namely, the local economy. For a variety of plausible reasons, the municipal budget—and the competing demands made on it—can preemptively prevent a city from taking actions that would "execute" its plan. Yet even with this being true, actions that rely on budgetary decisions make up only a small part of what is required to execute and realize any plan's vision and likewise only a small part of what become obstructions to the plan's fulfillment.

Most city plans seek to envision how land within a municipality's boundaries should be used into the future. Clearly, if the city owned all the land inside its limits, executing a plan to perfection would be a simple matter, if not necessarily easy. Where the plan requires houses should be built, the city would license their construction; where the plan requires industry should operate, the city would allow it.

However, almost all of the land in a city is owned not by the city but by individual citizens who typically have their own ideas for using their property—ideas quite different from what the city plan intends and specifies and that make execution more complicated and difficult. Therefore, plans can be fully executed only by somehow influencing or controlling what citizens can do with their land. In order to act on what a plan stipulates, city councils must adopt legislation that regulates how individuals make use of their property.[3] If the uses of land were not legislatively limited, a plan's vision would likely never be realized because property owners would do whatever they pleased. For all these reasons, regulating the uses of private property is without exception the linchpin for determining whether a city's plan will be precisely executed.

When Stamford adopted its new master plan in 2002, the city council had to pass what planners refer to as a *land-use regulation* to cause the plan's intention of providing "affordable" housing to become a requirement of future development. Stamford executed this intention in a regulation stipulating that 10 percent of the units in new apartment buildings be affordable, which was defined as units offered at a price families who earned less than the town's median income could afford. One can see that the land-use regulation gave an explicit (legislative) directive for how many affordable dwellings had to be offered, and also defined clearly what "affordable" meant. Once the city council passed this land-use regulation, individuals seeking to build apartment buildings could be forced to comply with it. Without the regulation and its effect on individual landowners, the plan's objective to provide relatively inexpensive housing would remain only a good intention, and one that could be freely ignored.

States authorize municipalities to enact a variety of methods for regulating the use of land. These regulations are the principal mechanisms by which a city-as-planned can become the city-as-built. Cities can adopt building codes requiring that houses be constructed to withstand hurricane-force winds; a city can prevent development on protective levees, and it can designate historic districts where every detail of construction (down to the paint color chosen by a homeowner) must be approved by an appointed review board. And cities can even acquire property to ensure that it will be used for, say, libraries or schools.

In passing land-use regulations that execute a plan's good intentions, city councils almost instantly incite and encounter their constituents' complex ambivalence about those good intentions and the plan itself. Plans, no matter their ideal vision, almost always embody a citizenry's implicit desire that nothing fundamentally change in the city's "essential character." This essence usually refers to a city's historic culture, or its rural atmosphere, its mixture of economic classes or its neighborhoods where several generations of the same working-class families live in close proximity, its commitment to green development, and so on. In the example of Stamford, citizens would most likely *not* have wanted the provision of affordable housing to jeopardize the serene town-and-country life that generations had tradition-ally valued. Therefore, before it took action to require such housing, the city council had to first balance its sense of a citizenry's good intentions (the plan) with that same citizenry's desire for unchanged civic life.

A plan's likelihood of being precisely executed can be vitiated as a result of elected officials debating and then deciding the relative importance of their constituents' competing desires, no matter the particular land-use regulation under consideration. Stamford's requirement of a percentage of affordable housing was one such regulation, though among the several ways cities, towns, and suburbs can regulate land use the more long-standing and more widely used are subdivision requirements and zoning ordinances.

Throughout the nation's history—and long before the American planning profession was founded—local governments imposed simple subdivision requirements on private landowners who sought to sell some part of their property. Early municipal procedures required owners to provide local government with a survey of their whole property, including the specific portion of it that they wanted to sell. On such surveys, the surveyor drew lines to show the parcel divided into separate lots—each of which was num-bered for identification. This drawing, which represented how the property would or could be divided and put up for sale, was—and still is—known as a *plat,* an American usage of the ancient English word that was vari-ously used to refer to a place, a spot, a locality or situation, but singularly in the United States refers to a "ground plan" for some particular part of the earth's surface.

American plats are surveys that show land divided—subdivided, that is—into parcels that can be sold, and are permanent municipal records that all towns and cities maintain in perpetuity.[4] The original purpose of plats was to make land conveyance orderly, and early subdivision requirements were little more than record-keeping procedures that allowed landowners to sell their property. Simultaneously, because changes in land ownership were recorded within a municipality's boundaries, cities and towns were able to track who was responsible for paying property tax levies.

Late in the nineteenth century, middle-class Americans realized that suburban housing offered escape from the onerous living conditions common to most industrialized cities. The suburbs that existed at this time were sparsely populated, though land speculators foresaw eventual suburban growth and for that reason bought and subdivided vast tracts of land around all the nation's cities. Such vast acreages were subdivided that much of it was never sold. As a consequence, municipalities became the legal owners of unsaleable land wherever speculators defaulted on property tax payments. But even when speculators were able to sell their land, the purchasers of subdivided lots often confronted serious problems. Often, the plats describing the subdivisions had been erroneously surveyed, or else they created lots on land so steep that nothing could be built on them, or the speculator failed to connect individual lots to public streets. But having sold the subdivided lots, speculators typically went elsewhere and became effectively out of reach. Some purchasers—whose lots were erroneously surveyed, or whose lots could not be built on—simply lost their money. Other purchasers, who by owning property became town residents, had to be provided ordinary public facilities (such as streets) that hadn't been installed in their subdivision, and municipalities had little choice but to pay for them.

These consequences of speculative subdivisions occurred throughout the nation, but New Jersey was the first to put a stop to them. In 1913, the state enacted a statute regarding subdivisions that mandated that municipalities review proposed plats *before* accepting and recording them—thereby ensuring that subdivided lots were buildable, accurately surveyed, and given access to public roads. And though some states adopted their own versions of New Jersey's subdivision regulations, it was the federal government that ultimately made subdivision regulation coherent and effective. In 1928, the U.S. Department of Commerce published a model set of land-use regulations, which were similar to those in New Jersey by providing that before any municipality could approve a proposed subdivision of land, it would review the proposed plat, making sure that lots shown on it were accurately surveyed and buildable. Most American municipalities—new suburbs and old cities—adopted these prudent model regulations for conveyances of property that involved a division of previously existing lots.

States in the American union have always provided criteria that allow new centers of population to incorporate themselves as towns (or cities), following which they can levy their own taxes, manage their budgets, choose a form of local government, and (in the twentieth century) adopt plans and land-use regulations. Before 1900 there were several independent suburbs within commuting distance of old cities, but it was not until after World War II that thousands of newly incorporated suburban towns appeared across America and became the primary location for new housing and population growth.[5] There was little commensurate growth in old cities. The great increase in suburbs was in part the result of the federal government's decision to enhance interstate commercial activity by building a national highway system that connected existing cities. As it happened, this interstate system simultaneously provided access to undeveloped—and easily subdivided—farmland. Another post–World War II initiative authorized the United States government to insure mortgages for single-family houses. The highway system and home mortgages underwritten by the federal government spurred the formation of independent suburban towns on what had once been farmland surrounding American cities. Thus the pattern of suburban growth was set, and has been followed ever since.

The preponderance of new housing built in the sixty years after World War II—units numbering tens of millions—has been on subdivided land in American suburban towns. With such a great volume of subdivision activity, it's unsurprising that new problems have surfaced and that modern subdivision regulations reach far beyond what the Department of Commerce promulgated in 1928.[6] As they did in the eighteenth century, property owners comply with modern requirements because municipalities will accept and record plats only for proposed subdivisions that meet all legislated requirements, and only with a recorded plat can subdivided property be sold.

Whether they refer to land in central cities or in suburban towns, modern plats still show property surveyed and divided into sequentially numbered lots. But in addition, plats now include information detailing what is to be built on the land—details that include construction of common facilities such as streets, drainage systems, and utilities. The rationale for increasing the scope of subdivision regulations has been to protect future buyers (and mortgage lenders) from substandard development, as well as to protect cities from the cost of reconstructing streets or repairing drainage problems in those same substandard subdivisions. It is not unusual for contemporary cities to require that new subdivisions include such amenities as open space—thereby offsetting the public cost of buying additional parkland for new citizens who buy the individual lots.

A great amount of contemporary suburban America has been developed according to these and other subdivision regulations. However, in cities that existed before World War II (as opposed to new postwar suburbs), most development has been governed by the other standard land-use regulation—the municipal zoning ordinance that is normally referred to simply as "zoning."

Zoning refers to a legal instrumentation first made famous in America in 1916, on the occasion of New York City's concerted efforts to preserve Manhattan's midtown Fifth Avenue as a distinctive carriage-trade district of department stores and expensive shops. At the time, the proprietors of B. Altman and other fine clothing establishments had noticed that an increasing number of garment-making factories were turning up near their prestigious Fifth Avenue addresses, and these owners feared that their lady customers' delicate sensibilities might be disturbed by seeing sweatshops where poorly paid and underage immigrant workers sewed lovely dresses for fifteen hours at a stretch under terrible conditions. To prevent these affluent ladies from being given offense—and taking their custom elsewhere—these Manhattan store owners petitioned the City of New York to prevent garment makers from locating in the proprietors' high-priced neighborhoods. The city complied. New York's legislative invention eventually became what we now know as *zoning*, which in its original application prohibited manufacturing activities from operating near the elegant shops along a few specific blocks of Fifth Avenue. The rationale for zoning in 1916 was little different from its contemporary rationale: zoning was and still is employed to prevent land uses from locating where it is deemed by city authorities they would cause detrimental effects to other property owners or other city interests.

In 1926, ten years after the first New York City zoning regulation, the United States Supreme Court rendered a decision that eventuated in zoning becoming the most favored means of regulating what property owners can do with their land. In *Village of Euclid v. Ambler Realty,* the court reviewed zoning regulations enacted by a suburb of Cleveland to create "zones" within which only specified land uses were authorized. The dispute before the court arose when a property owner wished to operate an industry in a zone where only housing was permitted. Through his agent, Ambler Realty, the landowner claimed that the village of Euclid's zoning ordinance had deprived him of the full economic value of his property.

The Supreme Court found in favor of Euclid, concluding that zoning ordinances enacted to achieve a "community purpose" represented constitutionally permitted limitations on owners' use of their property. The justices reasoned that Euclid's ordinance had been enacted to solve problems that develop "with the great increase and concentration of population" in cities.[7] The national implications of this case were unmistakable: the pivotal constitutional issue regarding any city's zoning ordinance was whether or not it identified a community's purpose.

Zoning ordinances are often referred to as "Euclidean" in observance of the importance of this 1926 decision. Yet, despite *Euclid*'s monumental influence, the high court's definition of the term "community interest" has remained a point of contention ever since. For perhaps understandable professional reasons, planners have interpreted the Supreme Court's ruling to mean that cities should find and express their community purpose in a city plan *before* adopting zoning ordinances. However, courts throughout America have only rarely agreed with this "planners' interpretation." Instead, courts have consistently found zoning ordinances constitutional not exclusively if the "community purpose" they serve is defined in a plan, but also—more leniently—if the zoning ordinances themselves include a statement of their purpose. An initial result of this lenience was that many cities in America adopted Euclidean zoning ordinances after 1926, but few adopted city plans. (A related result is that since 1926, American courts have found zoning ordinances constitutional whether or not their purpose matches what is expressed in a city plan.)

Citizens' confusion about the execution of plans originates in the Supreme Court's failure to stipulate that zoning ordinances must be predicated on a plan that expresses a community purpose. After 1926, and because of the *Euclid* decision, zoning (*not* the overarching institution of a plan) became—and still is—the most common regulation for controlling how private property owners put their land to use.

It wasn't long after the *Euclid* decision that complaints about zoning ordinances began, and for reasons that haven't changed in decades. Citizens complain (as the citizen in Stamford did) that zoning does not result in a city's changing according to its plan. Landowners complain that zoning reduces their constitutional rights to use property, and elected leaders complain that zoning inhibits needed economic development. It could truly be said that except for planners, there are few citizens who understand how zoning ordinances can actually carry out a plan.

A small case from New Orleans demonstrates the point. A young man skilled in caring for dogs inherited his aunt's house located in Tremé, a neighborhood fabled for having been where slaves gathered on preemancipation Sunday afternoons, and that was among the nation's oldest African-American communities. The nephew thought to convert his inherited house to a boarding kennel, in anticipation of a thriving clientele from the nearby French Quarter. The conversion required permission from the city, and it was at the point of applying for the necessary building permit that the nephew learned the zoning ordinance prohibited boarding kennels where his aunt's house was located. An official in the permitting office went on to say that if the nephew spoke to city planners, he might learn how the zoning prohibition could be changed.

This is how most citizens learn that a zoning ordinance affects them: when they're told they can't easily use their property as they've imagined. As it transpired, the nephew did speak to city planners, who explained that boarding kennels weren't allowed in Tremé because they might annoy neighbors with the odor from outdoor runs, the sound of barking dogs, and so on. Changing the zoning ordinance to accommodate a kennel was therefore unlikely. Planners, however, advised the nephew that he could make use of his inherited property if he rented it as a dwelling. This choice, planners added, was permitted by the zoning ordinance and wouldn't require his obtaining a building permit. Happily for all, the nephew chose to follow planners' advice and quickly rented his aunt's house. There was no disruption to the peaceful residential atmosphere Tremé had long enjoyed;

the nephew realized a profitable return from his property. These outcomes are boilerplate intentions to be found in any city's plan, and planners would say that the zoning ordinance carried them out in New Orleans.

As means of executing plans, subdivision requirements and zoning ordinances have quite different application. As the tiny example from Tremé showed, zoning mostly takes effect where property has already been developed, and is meant to ensure that proposed uses will not disturb neighboring owners. Subdivision regulations, on the other hand, mostly take effect when owners make use of undeveloped land, and are meant to ensure that adequate streets, buildable lots, and a variety of other community amenities are provided for residents whom the plan projects will move in someday. Because of their different application, zoning ordinances turn out to be most important for executing plans in existing cities, while subdivision requirements take most effect outside cities, where surging demand for housing causes owners of pastures and woodlots to develop their property into suburban housing tracts. Because this book takes greater interest in planning for existing cities, the remainder of this chapter centers on zoning ordinances, though without ignoring instances in which subdivision requirements are pertinent.

Zoning ordinances, well known for exhibiting tangled procedures and for maintaining an opaque relationship to a city's plan, often require expert deciphering. Indeed, planners in city hall spend most of their working day explaining how—and why—the zoning ordinance as an instrument of land-use regulation will affect development of a single piece of property. Citizens ask for explanations, but so do mayors and even members of the very city council that at one time in the past enacted the ordinance. One could only conclude that zoning is complicated.

Zoning ordinances have two essentials. First is a map that shows a city partitioned into geographic areas—what planners refer to as "zoning districts." Second is an accompanying set of regulations that governs how land can be used within each geographic area. Some zoning districts, for example, allow only residences in their boundaries; other zoning districts allow commercial enterprises as well as residences. The zoning map also gives each district a name that identifies the predominant land uses to be found there. A district named "single-family residential" obviously suggests that houses are the primary use of land in the zone. What might be found in a "high-density residential" zoning district is less obvious, though the implication is that single-family houses coexist with duplexes, small apartment buildings, and high-rise condominiums.

Many noncontiguous geographical parts of a city belong to the same zoning classification. A "single-family residential" district, for example, appears on the map wherever this type of land use is predominant—often in different parts of a city. It is possible to visualize what I mean by taking a mental drive through a familiar town, recalling neighborhoods where single-family houses line the streets. One neighborhood might contain grand and obviously expensive houses, whereas a different neighborhood might contain modest bungalows on small lots. Both would be designated as "single-family residential" districts on the city's zoning map because that is how land in each has mostly been used. Within either neighborhood, there might be some nonresidential uses that exist as remnants of the historic uses land was put to, but residential uses predominate.

A map portraying predominant land uses in partitioned districts of a city represents the first practical instrumentation of any zoning ordinance. The counterpart to this map is the second instrumentation of any zoning ordinance: the specific body of rules that authorizes and also governs land uses within each zoning district identified on the map. These stated rules are referred to as "district regulations," a phrase which connotes that land in each zoning district will be used according to how the plan (and the zoning ordinance) have determined the land *should* be used.

District regulations enumerate "authorized" land uses that can operate in particular zoning districts. In "neighborhood shopping districts," for example, coffee shops, dry-cleaning establishments, and convenience stores might be authorized to do business. Correspondingly, any land use not on the list is prohibited. The notion of "authorized uses" is a direct descendant of New York City's early zoning law that prevented the manufacture of dresses near Fifth Avenue.

Having established a list of authorized uses, district regulations next specify the standards each must meet. New homes in a "single-family residential" zoning district, for example, might be required to comply with such standards as minimum lot size, building height limitations, a building's placement on its lot, and how close a building can be to a neighbor's property lines. A house in a "multiple-family" zoning district might be required to fulfill a different set of requirements—to occupy a smaller lot size, for example, or maintain a narrower distance between neighboring structures. Some regulations are based on considerations of safety (the distance between houses prevents the spread of fires), but others find a rationale in axioms of property value: that houses on similarly sized lots, with similar setbacks and a similar scale, provide a coherent appearance that increases the value of each owner's property.

Finally, district regulations prescribe the specific *manner* in which authorized uses can operate. In "high-density residential" zoning districts, for example, apartment buildings might be required to provide parking on the premises for each dwelling unit. In densely developed "downtown residential" districts, however, parking might not be required at all. Or, in "neighborhood commercial" districts, which, as the name implies, are areas of commercial use located near residential neighborhoods, a recording studio might be required to install soundproofing; owners of a fast-food restaurant might be required to remove any litter their patrons drop on surrounding streets. And the regulations might stipulate that neither the recording studio nor the fast-food restaurant can install neon signs to advertise. None of these conditions would be imposed in a regional shopping district where no houses exist nearby. Importantly—and because courts have consistently mandated it—the requirements imposed by district regulations are constitutional only if, within a single zoning district, *all* properties are subject to the same rules.

What has been explained is how the two instrumentations of zoning ordinances—the maps of zoning districts and the associated regulations for each district—limit what property owners can do with their land. Cities enact these limitations primarily to ensure that new land uses cause no harm to what already exists. But cities also enact zoning ordinances to "execute" city plans. By limiting uses of land to such activities as envisioned in a plan, zoning ordinances can bring about a plan's good intentions.

A useful illustration is the new city of Irvine, California, built in the 1960s on what had been a vast lima bean and sheep ranch. Few structures existed on the land, and therefore planners could simultaneously create a plan and provide for its execution in advance. No old neighborhoods, no previously platted land, no existing streets confused the clarity of planners' vision. Public parks and playgrounds, libraries, and community centers were sited within walking distance of any residential neighborhood. A system of roadways was designed—in advance of any development—so that, for example, trucks would not pass through residential areas en route to their destinations, children would not cross major thoroughfares, and the noise and odor of manufacturing enterprise would not affect homes and businesses. Planners could bring about their conflict-free vision by partitioning land into a small number of zoning districts: single-family residential, neighborhood commercial, office buildings and "clean" industries. Irvine was built as planned, and presumably, people who'd found the plan antipathetic went elsewhere.[8]

But in the nation's already existing cities—from Boston to San Francisco, Chicago to New Orleans, and the many large and small cities in between—executing a plan through zoning faces much greater complications. These cities have developed gradually, and neighborhoods present a complex array of new and old land uses. Even where there is a predominant modern use (such as houses—the zoned norm, one could say), other uses almost always exist, sometimes for anomalous reasons civic historians delight in explaining.[9] Another illustration, this from New Orleans, reveals the complications involved in devising zoning regulations for such cities.

Citizens at work on New Orleans' 1999 Land Use Plan expressed a popular vision of industrial operations no longer intruding on residential neighborhoods. Executing this vision seems a standard task, requiring planners to analyze zoning regulations and prepare amendments that would preclude industrial uses from being built among residences. Upon the city council's adoption of such citizen-driven amendments, no further industrial intrusions would occur.

However, having attended the public meetings devoted to creating the 1999 plan, I knew that the "industrial intrusions" citizens referred to were those that already existed, such as a milk-producing plant that operates within a zoning district classified as "one and two-family housing." This district is well named: it encompasses many city blocks of modest bungalows. The area was once a large dairy farm, though much of the farm's acreage was sold more than fifty years ago and the farm's sole remnant is the thriving milk-producing operation. But to residents, the dairy operation now intrudes: large dairy trucks pass along streets in the neighborhood at every hour, creating obvious hazards to children playing in front yards, and also these trucks sometimes leak milk that then creates unpleasant odors on hot New Orleans days. And so forth.

New Orleans is three hundred years old, and most of its oldest residential neighborhoods include similarly intrusive industrial uses that private developers find too expensive to convert into housing. Therefore, until these industries cease operation, they cannot be eliminated unless the city purchases them and closes them down. Like most other cities, New Orleans does not have the public money necessary for this method of eliminating anomalous land uses. Instead, the city relies on a provision contained in most zoning ordinances, which has it that upon "ceasing operation" a no-longer authorized land use cannot start up again. If, for example, the dairy were to burn down or otherwise be destroyed—or if it suspended operation for more than a year—it could not resume business, and could only be replaced by a use authorized within the district. Thus, the zoning ordinance executes the plan's intention of preventing industrial uses from intruding on neighborhoods, albeit through a very slow and unpredictable series of events.

Zoning regulations can execute plans only sporadically because execution depends on actions that individual property owners take. For example, owners might decide to inaugurate new enterprises on their land, at which point—like the nephew in Tremé who wanted to open a kennel—they must follow zoning district regulations. Other owners might decide to cease operation of industries that have intruded on residential neighborhoods, at which point regulations prevent other intrusive industries from taking their place. Each such decision and thousands of others like them appear randomly, not coordinated by the city and without a pattern for where and when they occur. Indeed, neither a city nor its plan can force owners to make decisions about using their land. Nonetheless, the central paradigm of executing a plan's vision relies on steady and predictable regulation: working with planners, city councils adopt zoning ordinances that execute a city's plan, and thereafter property owners literally are *required* to develop their land as the regulations—and the plan—stipulate.

Of course, if this simple paradigm truly reflected the relationship between a plan and how a city ultimately develops, then this chapter—How

Plans Take Effect—would not be necessary. A city would gradually, though sporadically, become what its plan intended because zoning regulations would superintend property owners' use of their land. Instead, and for a great variety of reasons that anybody who observes the continuing civic drama of development well knows, cities allow land uses that are neither authorized by zoning ordinances nor foreseen by plans.

City councils frequently use the statutory authority states give them to change zoning ordinances when they think it makes sense. Such as when, for example, a constituent learns that where he proposes to build a dry-cleaning establishment lies in a zoning district that does not permit such an enterprise. He argues that the tax revenues and jobs to be created outweigh the importance of the zoning ordinance's prohibition; the city council agrees, and votes to remove the "less-important" prohibition from the ordinance. In this way—at least in this one isolated instance—the plan's vision is defeated.

In any city there are many, many of these "isolated" decisions. When changes to the regulations accumulate, the city starts to look far different from how it was planned to look, and the plan itself is then likely to be characterized as "out-of-date"—no longer useful for directing how landowners may use their land. At this point planners often urge the city council to undertake writing a new plan.

The reader has by now been introduced to most of the topics pertinent to a city's plan—who creates plans, how plans are executed, and how the city council is involved in that execution. Needing more explanation, however, is how and why city councils allow development that is different from what's authorized in a plan's vision.

Land-use regulations can be modified, reinterpreted, and even rescinded by a city council for a variety of reasons. In the case of an individual seeking to operate a dry-cleaning establishment, the city council found that the proposed use brought benefits—taxes and jobs—and therefore modified the zoning ordinance. But zoning ordinances are changed for other reasons, too: because conditions that once prompted legislative action have changed, and now require a different response; or because archaic language in an existing law now seems ambiguous; or because experience proves a law did not work as expected, although simple modifications would make it work;

or because a different cohort of legislators takes office and finds a previously enacted law unnecessary and for that reason removes it from the books.

Few citizens would disagree that the power of city councils to change existing law is necessary for government to meet changing needs of a complex society. Of course, some legislators exercise their power well and thoughtfully; others can foresee possible bad results of a legislative act, but vote for it anyway. Still other lawmakers use their right to change law for personal reasons—to enrich a family member, to reward a campaign contributor, to make good on an election-year promise. And only eventually can an electorate hold leaders accountable for how they have changed such laws as zoning ordinances, and vote for or against their continuance in office.

There is in addition a particularly understandable rationale for legislative flexibility regarding land-use regulations. City councils and city planners never suppose that any plan—or any regulation—can foresee every single use to which an owner might imagine putting his land. Indeed, many land uses that were unforeseen when a plan was adopted improve cities. Nor do planners and city officials suppose that artfully drawn zoning districts and well-thought-out regulations can anticipate all possible ways that neighboring uses might conflict with one another. Citizens routinely report new annoyances—beyond traffic and parking and noise—that have been caused by lawful use of land. When city councils hear constituents express such annoyances, they often decide that new zoning regulations need to be written, or old ones modified. In effect, the option of changing zoning ordinances—or any other land-use regulation—is a recognition of human ingenuity.

Any part of a zoning ordinance can be amended. City councils can redraw boundaries of individual zoning districts and adjust the list of uses authorized in each. Specific regulatory requirements that particular uses must meet (how large a building can be, whether it has to install soundproofing) can be modified. Furthermore, requests for change to zoning ordinances can be made by city councils or by individual landowners. Following any such request, planners analyze it and make a recommendation to the planning commission, which holds a meeting so the public can speak on the requested change; the commission then recommends the city council take action to approve, modify, or deny the request, and finally the council holds its own public meeting and votes.[10]

This process—as an example—was followed when a bar was authorized to operate near Tulane University in New Orleans. The landowner successfully argued to the city council that because his property (zoned for residential use) bordered a commercial district, the boundary of that district should be redrawn to include the existing residential zone where his property lay. He would thereby be released from the residential zoning district's standards—though also from the city plan's intention of keeping bars apart from undergraduate dormitories. Though in a similar case of an owner's requesting a zoning change, the city council allowed a cyber-café to operate in a neighborhood shopping center by adding this altogether *unplanned* use to the list of those authorized. It is through such small decisions that zoning ordinances can and do occasionally leave a city's comprehensive plan behind. Although in cases such as the cyber-café, unforeseen by the city's plan, the decision to change zoning to allow its operation was a benefit. And to have *not* permitted it, to have treated the zoning ordinance as unchangeable, would have been an obvious hindrance to entrepreneurial imagination and to the needs of modern citizens.

What's right about city planning is all it pays attention to in a city—its geography, its development history, its citizens old and young, rich and poor, and where they work and live and spend leisure time. City planning is a repository of hopes for the future, and of course of failed hopes from the past. At their best, a city plan and the zoning ordinance that executes it don't hold citizens back from newly imagined uses of land, but superintend new ideas so that benefits aren't accompanied by detrimental effects. It's a tall order, which city planners have some trouble fulfilling.

PART TWO

Locating the Trouble with City Planning

EIGHT

City Planning in Action

Several years before Hurricane Katrina, Albertsons—one of America's national grocery chains—sought to open a large, boxy store in a severely blighted section of uptown New Orleans, only one block away from St. Charles Avenue, the city's historic, carefully maintained, and beautiful street. (Blighted areas close to beautiful streets are a feature of New Orleans' urban physiognomy.) The site Albertsons chose for its store encompassed several blocks of poor and deteriorated lots where many formerly splendid buildings had fallen in or been cleared away over the previous twenty years. What remained in the neighborhood were a few large houses converted into mean apartments standing like sentries guarding an abandoned, weed-filled landscape where people threw old mattresses and household trash. Using realty agents, Albertsons quietly began acquiring contiguous properties. Upon consummating those purchases, the grocery chain publicly announced its design for a new store. However, the sprawling design seemed more appropriate to a suburban location than to the old city of New Orleans.

Albertsons proposed merging separate city blocks by closing infrequently used streets, then constructing a new grocery atop the closed roadbeds—some of which bore historical significance as the original boundaries of plantations subdivided long ago to create the modern city. Another part of Albertsons' design involved a wide thoroughfare between uptown and downtown New Orleans, which was to be rerouted as a dogleg street skirting an asphalt parking lot (no part of which was dedicated to trees or shrubbery). To build its new store, Albertsons also proposed to demolish ten vacant structures on the newly acquired property.

One could look at Albertsons' design and conclude that the chain's architects theorized that investment in the rundown area would be so welcome that *any* design would be acceptable to the city, even this one: an automobile-oriented arrangement Albertsons had replicated in suburbs from Montana to Florida.

For several reasons, every part of Albertsons' proposal had to be reviewed by city planners. For one thing, New Orleans' zoning ordinance required any single enterprise—housing, manufacturing, retailing—to be located on a single lot. Albertsons' desired site comprised several parcels of land, including those occupied by the ten vacant structures and old roadbeds. Although it seems counterintuitive, since the word "subdivision" implies dividing land into more than one parcel, in municipal law "subdivision" actually refers to drawing new lot lines, irrespective of how many lots result. Therefore, to create the required *single* lot on which its new store could be built, Albertsons first had to subdivide into one parcel all the separate lots and former roadways. By statute, city planners review proposed subdivisions to certify that plats meet the city's regulatory criteria.[1]

In addition, Albertsons asked that changes be made to the district regulations of the zone that included the proposed site, and by statute such amendments must also be reviewed by city planners before being adopted by the council. Although it was an authorized use in the zone, the grocery store could not be as large as what Albertsons proposed and neither could there be as many parking spaces as the chain intended. Modern grocery stores want to provide enough parking spaces to accommodate shoppers on the Wednesday before Thanksgiving, their busiest day of the year. But New Orleans meant to prevent overlarge parking lots in this particular zoning district, and therefore limited the number of spaces to what was needed on an ordinary business day.[2] Albertsons saw that the city's zoning ordinance prohibited a store and a parking lot as large as it proposed at the chosen location, and asked that the district regulations be changed in all ways necessary to accommodate the chain's new grocery store. And the list of ways was long.

The grocery-store proposal, then, became a classic example of what happens when an owner proposes a use that is neither authorized by a city's zoning ordinance nor (as it happened) specifically foreseen in its plan. As they had been trained, New Orleans' city planners sought guidance by reading through the plan's adopted goals while they reviewed the proposal. Several goals seemed pertinent: "an improved economy" was one. "Preserving historic culture" and "reducing the economic isolation of the poor" were two others. However, the plan offered no guidelines for choosing among these goals, or for balancing the goals' individual good intentions should they come into conflict.

And the goals of New Orleans' plan *did* conflict, which is usual when unforeseen land uses are "debated." Albertsons claimed that its store would serve two of the plan's good intentions. First, the grocery would improve the economy (create construction jobs, offer new employment at the store, increase sales and property taxes); and second, it would reduce poor citizens' economic isolation by selling food to a diverse clientele. Residents of poor neighborhoods could walk to the store; wealthier citizens could drive, but all would find the same array of groceries—at the same price.[3] Albertsons, however, made no claim of preserving historic culture, and accordingly preservationists opposed the store inasmuch as its construction required demolition of ten vacant but possibly important historic structures.

Preservationists proffered an array of measures to save the ten buildings, suggesting for example that the store be completely redesigned so that demolishing the old structures was no longer necessary. Preservationists filed a lawsuit to stop the development, and they lobbied members of the city council to vote against Albertsons unless the chain paid to relocate the old structures. Albertsons countered by threatening to take its project elsewhere—to the adjoining parish, where it wouldn't have this "hassle"—and also pointed out that without the chain's investment, the ten vacant historic buildings would crumble just as the surrounding premises had.

The issue festered in the city's newspapers, each side enlisting partisans and readying arguments for the planning commission's public hearing. For their part, city planners continued reviewing the proposal prior to the commission's hearing, and suggested that Albertsons change some aspects of its design. In particular, planners urged Albertsons to reduce the size of its store and also redesign it to resemble a row of separate shops such as those that still operate throughout New Orleans' older neighborhoods. Planners also suggested reducing the parking lot's size, surrounding it with a hedge and planting shade trees to "break up" its monotonous asphalt expanse. If the parking lot's size were reduced, historic old streets would not be closed, nor would the major thoroughfare between uptown and downtown New Orleans be expensively rerouted. City planners further argued that with the changes they proposed, Albertsons would still have a huge—i.e., profitable—store, but one that "fit in" better and wouldn't be so disruptive to the city's historic culture.

When Albertsons' proposal was presented at the New Orleans' planning commission's hearing, what transpired was predictable. The developer unfurled detailed and brightly colored drawings of what the handsome new store would look like, along with several charts portraying its positive economic effects. Poor residents who lived in the neighborhood surrounding the site stood up to say that they not only needed a grocery store with a healthy assortment of food at reasonable prices, but that they also needed substantial investment in their blighted environs.

Preservationists cited details proving the site's significance in the city's history, noting for example that Felicity Street (which was proposed to be closed) was once New Orleans' uptown boundary, and concluded by describing important architectural features of the ten buildings that they argued the developer should save. Corroborating comments for each side went on for several hours. The last comment of the afternoon was made by a frustrated citizen, and put to preservationists: "Where have you been while we endured the devastation of our neighborhood? If these buildings are so important, why haven't you worked to save them before now?"

Preservationists had answers to these questions. They had been saving *other* buildings, they said. And what better time than *this* time, when the buildings were being threatened? And, is it the job of preservationists to save neighborhoods? The terms of this public argument were both ad hoc and spontaneous, largely because neither the plan nor the zoning ordinance explained which of the city's competing goals—its good intentions for an improved economy, for reduced isolation of the poor, for the preservation of historic culture—was most important.

Finally, the planning commission agreed to recommend that the city council approve a modified design that Albertsons would offer after meeting with city planners. But the commission also recommended that the council ask Albertsons to delay demolition of the ten historic buildings for six months, thereby allowing preservationists to find a way to save them. This seemed such a reasonable recommendation that when the city council voted in favor of Albertsons' requested zoning changes, it also voted to impose a six-month moratorium on demolishing the ten buildings.

As it transpired, during those six months the council itself dedicated a portion of its "emergency" budget to help pay for the historic buildings' removal.[4] And this vote encouraged Albertsons to pay the larger share of the move. Subsequently, preservationists found locations for the ten historic structures, and city planners advised the grocery chain that when it redesigned the new store, it should fit into its urban surroundings. A planner would say that preservation, good urban design, and good public policy decisions had all prevailed—albeit after several months of highly charged public discussion.

For their part, preservationists saw this entire incident differently, and were frustrated by listening to inconclusive testimony from citizens who attended public hearings. The preservationists expressed their frustration as a question every city planner has heard: Why hadn't the plan foreseen this proposal and solved it ahead of time? This question, of course, articulates the odd, though common assumption that plans can foretell the future.

And with that question, this chapter returns to a press conference after Hurricane Katrina, when the man charged to oversee recovery efforts in ruined New Orleans, General Honoré, saw relief rise on reporters' faces when he assured them that he had a plan. He quickly added, "Don't confuse a plan with execution." On retelling the Albertsons' saga, I would add: "Don't confuse a plan with foreseeing the future." Both the general and I would agree: a plan is only good intentions.

The public process of planning can be an authentic effort to discover the sense of harmonious life that struggles to exist among any citizenry. In New Orleans, the pressure of Albertsons' proposed development changed how some people viewed a run-down neighborhood they'd frequently passed and most probably written off. The controversy also made elected officials realize that just *any* investment, or just *any* design, might not be desirable— even in the most desperate, "slumlike" parts of the city. And finally, the dispute over Albertsons caused preservationists to think of new strategies for salvaging buildings, something beyond simply insisting that somebody, somehow must save them.

Could all of this have been imagined and planned before Albertsons proposed to build a new store at this location? Would leaders in New Orleans have chosen to devote some of the city's meager "emergency" money to moving buildings *just because it was prudent?* Probably not. In other words, this public drama—a drama ostensibly over zoning—brought about complex civic actions that could not have been foreseen—or planned. A planner, of course, would find the outcome encouraging because so many people tried to imagine how to solve a problem of city planning.

Planners are trained to put up with the messy, unpredictable clamor of public discourse. Planners are successful to the extent that they have an appetite for the clamor and also know how to orchestrate public discourse. In the Albertsons case, a good conclusion came by stages: the suggestion by the planning commission to delay demolition of the vacant historic buildings; the agreement of city council members to find special money to relocate them; the willingness of the developer to redesign the store and its parking lot. Planners ultimately oversaw every stage. But not one of these actions was foreseen by New Orleans' plan—or by its zoning ordinance—yet the result was widely thought to exemplify successful city planning.

There is a coda to the story: the Albertsons store had been approved and the historic structures moved to new locations when Wal-Mart unexpectedly proposed building a new "superstore"—the corporation's term for a mercantile establishment that includes groceries—only a few blocks from Albertsons' proposed site. With its economic prospects changed, Albertsons decided not to build. And as it happened, Wal-Mart endured an even longer and more fractious public process regarding its proposed store than Albertsons, though Wal-Mart ultimately succeeded. This outcome reinforces a point made earlier: development occurs only when property owners decide to make use of their land—and Albertsons decided not to, based on what another property owner decided.

The case of Albertsons dramatizes the major elements of city plans in action—how plans are used—but rehearsing this incident goes beyond showing how planning operates in practice. The relationship among plans, the land-use regulations that would execute them, and the ultimate land-use decisions a city makes are potentially mysterious to everyone *not* able to see all sides. For this reason, the Albertsons incident stands as a useful introduction to discussing the consequences of how city planning is practiced. A fundamental question underlies the chapters that follow: do plans and land-use regulations serve the purpose planners think they do?

NINE

Plans that Only Planners Use

As Hurricane Katrina flooded New Orleanians from their homes, some survivors found safety atop elevated sections of the interstate highway that runs through the city. Soon after, Coast Guard helicopters lowered other refugees down to the highway alongside them, and for several days every viaduct and exit ramp became an island, places where victims awaited rescue in relative safety. Even the sheriff of Orleans Parish transported prisoners from his flooded jail onto one such elevated interstate crossing. There they could be safe.

Although these isolated viaduct-islands stand out in photographs taken of New Orleans after the storm, visitors to the city before the tragedy of Hurricane Katrina would likely not have noticed them. They are nothing more than ordinary parts of modern urban settings—all but invisible conduits leading travelers to their destinations.

There was one viaduct, though, that visitors might have singled out, since it took them close to an unusual art deco sign featuring an outsized, uniformed neon chef (complete with a big white chef's toque), smiling while he stirred a huge pot of something good. The sign wasn't placed like most billboards that dot American highways—easy to see and far enough away that an entire "message" can be absorbed. Instead, this smiling chef suddenly loomed up from the side of the viaduct, and just as suddenly was hidden from view behind a looping exit ramp. Any New Orleanian knew that the smiling-chef sign designated the site of Baumer Foods, manufacturer of Crystal Hot Sauce—a Louisiana institution. But why would Baumer

Foods, a visitor might wonder, not have put its wondrous sign in a more visible place?

The answer is no mystery. The sign had been erected long before Interstate 10 was bulldozed through New Orleans in the name of economic progress, bringing about what all urban interstates seem to ordain: many buildings cleared away, many others left orphaned with a new highway as their next-door neighbor; plus, existing roadways rerouted and traffic suddenly appearing where it's never appeared before. This is what had befallen the Baumer Foods building, leaving its sign to loom mostly unobserved behind a tangle of roadways. The Baumer factory itself was built nearly a century before Hurricane Katrina, at a time when its site was on the outskirts of the city and alongside a busy road. It had been a *good* location, offering ready highway access for trucks. In addition, because Baumer's rear boundary in those early years of the twentieth century was a local street too narrow to carry truck traffic, across that street was a relatively quiet residential area of modest homes where many Baumer employees lived.

Once this section of Interstate 10 was completed in 1972, however, driving trucks to Baumer's entailed a complicated navigation through ramps and local streets, stop signs and pedestrian crossings. The chef cooking up Crystal Hot Sauce enshrines one of many places where New Orleans' major interstate disrupted the city's economic and residential life.

In the case of the hot sauce manufacturer, operations started becoming obsolete soon after the highway's completion. Not only was access difficult (and consequently more costly), but Baumer's was hemmed in because the interstate had consumed land where the plant might've expanded were business to boom. As for the residential area located behind the factory and previously undisturbed by Baumer's operations, this neighborhood began to decline once I-10 was completed, a result of trucks hauling heavy products over local streets, and the noise and exhaust fumes of the interstate. As time passed the neighborhood became a ragtag assortment of occupied and vacant houses, its streets full of potholes, its original character lost.

Baumer Foods stayed in business at its original location for thirty-three years after Interstate 10 was completed, and many residents continued living in the increasingly run-down neighborhood nearby. But then Hurricane Katrina occurred, and the plant's machinery stood in five feet of floodwater for several days. A few months later—long after the water was gone—Baumer's owner announced he was selling the site and salvaging his ruined sign. He'd needed a new location for years, he said, but it had taken the storm to extinguish his desire to keep the Crystal plant in New Orleans. He'd found a buyer who would tear the plant down and replace it with affordable housing in a complex to be named the Preserve Apartments. Most people who read about this project in the newspaper thought it a worthy substitute for the old factory, especially because the run-down adjacent residential neighborhood had been devastated just as Baumer Foods had. And of course at the time of this incident—early 2006—there was fierce demand for new houses and apartments where returning New Orleanians could live.

"Affordable" housing became an anthem among many developers in New Orleans in the months after Hurricane Katrina. So many houses had been destroyed and so little money had yet been made available for repairs that housing was scarce and also expensive. After the storm, calling apartments "affordable" made their construction seem beneficial, just as the same phrase and concept had seemed in Stamford, Connecticut, four years earlier. In Stamford, a change to the city's zoning ordinance had been necessary to execute the city plan's goal of providing more affordable housing. Stamford, as you will remember, amended its ordinance to stipulate that 10 percent of the units in newly constructed apartment buildings had to be "affordable," a word the ordinance defined.[1] Once this zoning amendment was made, landowners had to comply with it. Without the amendment, the plan's objective of providing affordable housing would have remained nothing more than a good intention.

In New Orleans, building the "affordable" Preserve Apartments also required changing the city's zoning ordinance, though not in order to execute a plan's good intention. At the time of this incident, New Orleans' Land Use Plan of 1999 was still in effect, and it did not envision apartment buildings at the Baumer Foods site. Nonetheless, the city amended its zoning ordinance to allow housing where residential structures had never before been authorized. Cities throughout the country make similar changes to their zoning ordinances: not to execute plans, but to allow particular one-of-a-kind developments that actually violate plans. The dynamics described might seem unique to New Orleans because the Baumer Foods incident occurred in a city that lay devastated, but the same dynamics are repeated in every American city. Therefore, the case of Baumer Foods/Preserve Apartments demonstrates what leads a city council to disregard a city's plan. Some aspects of the Preserve case will be familiar from the earlier account of the Albertsons grocery proposal, though that familiarity might result in a more robust understanding of the interplay between city plans and development decisions.

One preliminary point should be emphasized. Most of what is built in any city does *not* require a zoning change, nor does it require city officials to consult the city's plan. Instead, property owners initiate land uses that are authorized by the zoning ordinance—and the plan it executes. These owners are like the man in Tremé who used his inherited house as rental property rather than seeking the zoning change necessary for operating boarding kennels. And when development proceeds as authorized by the zoning ordinance, planners conclude that a city's land-use regulations are reliable indicators that the city will develop as the plan envisioned.

The converse of this basic planning axiom is true for the small number of owners who want to put their land to uses that are different from how the city's plan—as enacted in the city's zoning ordinance—envisions. Because so few developments require zoning changes, citizens can live in a city without knowing much about how such zoning requests are decided. Neither do citizens typically know much about the relationship between a plan and the zoning ordinance itself. Like most of us, city residents are not bothered by what they don't know—or even are aware that they don't know it—until someone proposes or builds a project they object to.

When city councils deliberate about changing zoning ordinances, they weigh the relative strength of three competing points of view. The first is that taken by city planners, who according to most municipal statutes must review any development proposal for which approval necessitates changing a zoning district map or its accompanying regulations. Planners assess how such changes might affect the long-term future envisioned by a city's plan, and also estimate any likely effects on neighboring property. By analyzing these aspects of a development proposal, planners see both the big and the small picture.

Individuals seeking zoning changes advocate a competing and a narrower point of view to that taken by planners. Landowners and developers focus on the profit their proposed uses of property will bring, and support their applications for zoning changes by painting a "big picture" of their own, which portrays new jobs being created and municipalities enjoying increased tax revenues.

A third view is taken by citizens who live near a proposed project and who concentrate on the local effects of its being authorized: whether traffic will increase, whether historic buildings will be demolished, whether the proposed development will bring about such desired public improvements as additional landscaping along local streets.

While taking into account the advocacies of planners, developers and property owners, and the local citizenry, city councils are necessarily influenced by their own responsibilities regarding land and how it is used—responsibilities having to do with the city's budget, employment opportunities for local citizens, and future tax revenues.

To explain how these different viewpoints and responsibilities figure into decisions about changing a zoning ordinance, I will recount how it happened that the New Orleans city council authorized affordable housing—the Preserve Apartments—where Baumer Foods once manufactured hot sauce. The explanation will take up each viewpoint in the order in which it became pertinent to the council's ultimate vote. Because that council vote went against what the city's plan advised and also required changing the zoning ordinance, this incident typifies decisions that ultimately result in cities' developing differently from what their plans propose.[2]

The Baumer Foods episode commenced as most land-use matters do. A developer requested a zoning change that would allow him to build the Preserve Apartments. All such requests are submitted first to city planners, who analyze the developer's request. In this case, the Baumer factory was located in a "light industrial" zoning district, which authorized neither apartments nor any other residential use. However, the zoning district that lay across the street from the old factory was designated "residential," as its neighborhood character would suggest. Houses and apartment buildings were authorized there, but industrial uses were not.

The point of these details is that it was nominally possible to authorize the Preserve Apartments by using one of two easily understandable changes to the zoning ordinance. First, the boundary of the existing residential zoning district could be redrawn to include the Baumer Foods' light industrial site. This change would mean that the Preserve project could be built because the regulations for that particular residential zoning district listed apartment buildings as authorized uses. Alternatively, the "light industrial" district regulations could be amended to include "multiple-family housing." Thereafter, apartment buildings would be allowed.

There were problems with either strategy. To change the boundaries of the residential district would then allow all forms of housing—single-family homes, duplexes, apartment buildings—to be as close to the nearby interstate highway as the chef on the Baumer's sign had been. This was not a good location for people to live, for fairly obvious reasons: exhaust fumes, noise, and so on. Conversely, the other way of changing the zoning ordinance—by adding apartment buildings to the list of uses authorized in a light industrial zoning district—would mean that apartments were thereafter authorized in *every* light industrial district in the city, many of which were even more inappropriate for human habitation than the one alongside Interstate 10. Some of New Orleans' light industrial districts had previously been the site of landfills, and in others underground gasoline tanks remained in use. People probably shouldn't live there, a planner would reason, and allowing apartment buildings in all light industrial zoning districts was a bad idea.

However, there was yet a third way to allow an apartment building on the Crystal Hot Sauce site. And that was to declare apartment buildings a "conditional" use in light industrial zones. Such a declaration is a common and popular method that cities use to shoehorn new uses into zoning districts where they are not authorized. A "conditional use" takes effect by amending the zoning ordinance to add a single new category of uses to those already authorized in a specific district. This conditional-use category allows a particular new land use to exist on a chosen site, but only if it can meet conditions specifically tailored to overcome any conflicts it might cause there. A bar in the middle of a residential district might be authorized conditionally if it closed at ten o'clock on weeknights and at midnight on Friday and Saturday. This restriction would presumably lessen the likelihood that the bar's patrons would make noise—talking, shouting, starting cars, and so forth—at a time when neighbors would ordinarily be asleep. Or, a restaurant on a site without space allocated for parking could be allowed conditionally if the owner instituted a valet-parking program—

which would lessen the likelihood that diners would block nearby drive-ways. Presumably, a proposed use that could not meet these conditions would be denied.

Designating a particular land use "conditional" in a zoning ordinance is very appealing to city councils that want to approve some proposed proj-ect and are allowed to do so by figuring out "wise" conditions that make it possible. One could term conditional uses the Solomon's wisdom aspect of a zoning ordinance. In any case, once a conditional use is approved, city planners redraw the map of zoning districts so that a single "conditional use" becomes, in effect, its own separate district. The zoning map of New Orleans has many, many such separate districts, and each one has specific and unique conditions associated with it. However, in the case of the Pre-serve Apartments, wise individuals—including city planners—might have a hard time imagining conditions that would overcome its proposed location beside the interstate.

To bolster a position against authorizing the Preserve Apartments, New Orleans' city planners looked to the city's land-use plan adopted in 1999. There, specific mention of the Baumer site was made in a historical summary of the industries that once operated in this part of town—the Blue Plate Mayonnaise Plant, the Falstaff Brewery, . . . and Baumer Foods. When the 1999 Land Use Plan was written, of course, the hot sauce fac-tory was still in business, and on the plan's map of where future land uses should be located, the Baumer Foods site was designated as it always had been designated—as part of a light industrial zoning district. To a planner, this is prima facie evidence to keep the zoning "light industrial."

There is yet another, potentially overpowering reason to maintain the light industrial designation: a planner would know that the nature of "light industry" has changed since the hot sauce factory opened nearly a century ago, and now includes research facilities and telecommunications centers. These modern light industries cause little truck traffic, and if one of them replaced the hot sauce factory, trucks would no longer pass through streets in the neighborhood behind old Baumer Foods. That is, a modern light industrial use could actually restore some of the residential tranquility that had been ruined by the construction of I-10. In any event, planners found nothing in the 1999 Land Use Plan to support siting an apartment build-ing in the light industrial zone where the hot sauce factory once operated.

In addition, a close look at the future land use map included in the 1999 plan would show that a narrow strip of green had been drawn along the boundaries of this particular light industrial district, indicating that a vegetative buffer (such as a hedge) was envisioned to separate it from the adjacent residential district. Vegetative buffers serve to ameliorate the effects of one zoning district on another by, for example, blocking the glare of headlights that might shine from parking lots into residences, or by reducing the volume of noise that might travel between commercial and residential districts. In addition, buffers provide a visual border that differentiates one part of town from another. A reader of the 1999 Land Use Plan might characterize this green strip as a reflexive gesture planners employ whenever incompatible land uses abut. But a planner who saw such a buffer proposed as a border between the residential district behind Baumer Foods and the light industrial district would understand that the plan *intended* that the boundaries of the two districts should not be changed.

Upon analyzing the proposed Preserve Apartments, making use of the 1999 Land Use Plan and their knowledge of zoning ordinances, city planners concluded that residential uses should not be allowed in a light industrial zone, and light industrial uses should not be allowed in residential zones. In other words, planners believed New Orleans' zoning ordinance should not be changed to authorize the apartments.

Planners communicate to a city's planning commission their analysis of the zoning changes a proposed development might require in a report that concludes by recommending how the commission should advise the city council to vote. City planners complete all such reports several days before the planning commission meets, and send these documents to the commissioners for their review, as well as to the applicants themselves. The reports are also made available to any interested citizen.

Once the planners' report regarding the Preserve Apartments was complete, the next step in the legally defined process for considering such proposals required the planning commission to take the application up at a public meeting. Such meetings start with an applicant—in this case the developer seeking approval of the Preserve Apartments—describing the project under consideration. City planners next summarize their analysis of the proposed project. Then the planning commission invites the public to comment. In New Orleans, the commission's practice is to allow those in favor of a proposal to speak first, followed by those opposed. When the public comments come to an end, the commission typically asks the applicant to respond to what's been said. Finally, the commission votes on the action it considers appropriate for the city council to take on each application: to approve it, approve it with modification, or deny it.[3]

With this as an outline of how land-use decisions are advanced, the case of the application to authorize the Preserve Apartments describes what can—and often does—transpire at each step of advancement.

When planners recommend denial of a proposed development, the applicant marshals responses to present at the commission's public meeting. At the meeting regarding the Preserve Apartments, the developer-applicant pointed out that in post-Katrina New Orleans, "affordable" housing was so evidently needed that planners' objections should be dismissed. This same argument, it's worth noting, is universally used by developers, and not just because housing shortages have been created by a hurricane or a flood or a tornado—but also because, as in Stamford, Connecticut, there is an inadequate supply of housing priced within reach of the local working class.

In addition to appearing at the planning commission's public meeting, the prospective developer of the Preserve Apartments had also been busy complaining privately—to planning commissioners and to city council members—that the city planning office was a hidebound stickler for plans and regulations, that planners were unsympathetic to the devastated circumstances of the city and were unappreciative of how unusual and how beneficent was the developer's willingness to invest in this problematic site. City planners in every city have heard this before, and know that such contentions lie at the root of the common complaint that city planning has an anti-business bias. Nonetheless, an applicant's claims of bias can cast doubt on what city planners recommend.

At its meeting, and after the developer presented his proposal, the planning commission next invited the public to comment on the Preserve Apartments. Before I describe what transpired in this part of the meeting, it must first be acknowledged how few citizens attend any planning commission meeting at all. Based on their experience, planners know some reasons for poor attendance: interested citizens have to work when scheduled meetings take place, or because citizens evaluate land-use proposals mostly in terms of how they might be affected personally, they only appear at public meetings when they have strong feelings *against* a development.

When the Preserve Apartments application was considered by the planning commission, *no* citizens appeared to speak at the public meeting. Knowing that it is chiefly citizens' opposition to a proposal that incites attendance at meetings about development applications, planning commissions tend to interpret a lack of public comment to mean that a proposal has few opponents—which might have been true regarding the proposed Preserve Apartments, inasmuch as affordable housing was in very short supply after the great storm. (Although there is also an obvious possibility that residents who lived near the site and would've been affected by the decision had been displaced by Hurricane Katrina and couldn't attend.) In this case, the planning commission went against planners' initial analysis, recommending that the city council approve a zoning change that would designate apartment buildings as conditional uses in light industrial zoning districts, thereby authorizing the proposed residential development of the Baumer Foods site.

Following every application that comes before the planning commission, planners write a summary of the commission's public meeting—including the planners' original analytic report—and forward that summary to the city council prior to the council's public meeting that takes up applications for which the planning commission has rendered an opinion. City councils usually conduct their meetings as the planning commission does: first, the applicant presents his proposal; next, city planners speak about their analysis of the application and about the deliberations of the planning commission; and last, the public is invited to comment. Finally, the council discusses all that it has heard about the application, and then votes for or against it. In the case of the Preserve Apartments, only city planners opposed the application—and no citizens voiced opinion at all.

The council *did* approve construction of the "affordable" Preserve Apartments, relying on a familiar logic that planners' objections—based as they were on the city's land-use plan, on the zoning ordinance, and on their professional judgment—were less important than getting this project built. The proposed development, the council reasoned, would provide desperately needed "affordable" housing, and would also create construction jobs; the developer would pay annual property taxes that exceeded those levied on the abandoned Baumer Foods factory. In addition, elected leaders in New Orleans might well have thought, new construction would herald New Orleans "coming back" from its devastated state, meaning that tourists and investors would also return. And a final justification for authorizing the Preserve Apartments was that no citizens had expressed opposition.

City planners work on a daily basis with all these discrete views, which one might call the internal logic of developers, citizens, and their elected leaders. Planners' work is to widen and inform each view by directing attention to the city's plan and by interjecting their professionally trained analysis of development proposals. Indeed, widening the perspective of each party—the developer, the planning commission, the city council, and the public—is one purpose of the reports planners prepare regarding every application made to them.

However, as the incident with the Preserve Apartments shows, land-use decisions are typically argued by employing other, more ready-made logic that ignores planners' advice and ignores city plans. In this case, a logic of "affordable housing" proved impermeable to what the plan advised, and impermeable also to planners' wider concern about allowing people to live so near an interstate highway. The citizenry expressed no opinion. It is predictable, I suppose, that my sympathy lies with planners' efforts, and that I chose to narrate the hot sauce episode because it identifies an important misunderstanding about the basis of planners' arguments. Where developers see planners as rigid "sticklers for the plan" and where citizens typically turn to plans only when they oppose a specific development proposal, I see plans and planning through different eyes, and see that both are misunderstood.

Planners are rarely rigid sticklers for a plan, as the developer of the Preserve Apartments complained. Truthfully, plans almost never offer directives so specific that they are susceptible to rigid interpretation—directives such as "*this* is what should replace Baumer Foods if it closes down." Planners look to a plan for its more general—and therefore malleable—guidance. In the case of the Baumer Foods site, planners found that the plan's map for location of future land uses at this site showed the property unchanged from its existing light industrial designation. This designation offered mild support for planners' conclusion that the Preserve Apartments should not be authorized as the developer requested because the proposed site was so close to an interstate highway.

Said another way, planners are often the only party to discussions about a proposed development who understand clearly how the contents of a city's plan are related to land-use regulations such as zoning ordinances. The consequence is that only planners know how to use a plan's seemingly nonspecific advice with regard to such proposed developments as the Preserve Apartments. Ultimately, the fact that only planners know how to use city plans becomes the underlying reason that city councils so easily dismiss advice based upon plans. Thus, in New Orleans and in most other cities, the contents of plans are overruled or ignored by elected leaders. Why would this be the case? The answer can be found in the document itself, and it's therefore valuable to spend some time describing the contents of city plans.

Planners, like any other citizen, cannot hold in mind all parts of a city at once. Cities are too big and too complicated, and they aren't static. Therefore, planners divide a city into a conceptually manageable set of geographic areas—known as planning districts—each of which comprises several contiguous neighborhoods. In the early 1970s, New Orleans' planners grouped the city's seventy-two neighborhoods into thirteen planning districts. As in every city, citizens know neighborhoods by names history has given them—the French Quarter (also known as the Vieux Carré), Hollygrove, and Gentilly in New Orleans—and planners generally retain these old designations rather than assigning newly devised names that would only confuse. In the case of New Orleans, planners specified the city's planning districts by simply numbering them from one to thirteen. Planning District One includes the oldest parts of town: the French Quarter, the downtown business district, and the oldest working wharves uptown of the Vieux Carré, which citizens now refer to as the warehouse district. Planning District Five is quite different, consisting of such neighborhoods as Lakeview, Lake Vista, and Lake Shore, all built on land drained by the Wood pump before 1926 or created by the Levee Board. Planning District Eight is the Lower Ninth Ward, and includes neighborhoods settled on the natural levees along the river and those that were created much more recently on low-lying ground that abuts the Mississippi River–Gulf Outlet. Planning Districts Nine, Ten, and Eleven as a group contain the neighborhoods referred to as New Orleans East—the large section of New Orleans that was built after 1970.

The contiguous neighborhoods of a single planning district share similar histories and their residents are generally of a similar age and economic circumstance. Therefore, planners are able to identify common problems with how land is used in each district and can also discover common aspirations of residents. Planners in other American cities use a different term from New Orleans' "planning districts," such as "community quadrants" or "planning sectors." Whatever these geographic divisions are called, planners organize city plans in terms of them. The New Orleans land-use plan is a good example of the resulting organization: the first chapter of the plan is devoted to the whole city; a second chapter has thirteen sections—each of which takes up one of the thirteen planning districts (and the neighborhoods therein) in turn.

Irrespective of how they are organized, however, all city plans include the same sort of information that the 1999 New Orleans Land Use Plan contains: maps that show how land is used in each planning district, followed by a history of how individual neighborhoods in a single district were founded and how they developed over time—what was built, and when and by whom. The history of Planning District Two is about the neighborhoods in uptown New Orleans, first settled in the form of long, narrow plantations that at one end gave river access to their owners. Later, these original owners subdivided their land but kept the highest ground for their families and domestic slaves. Reserving the high ground of subdivided plantations was how the wealthiest neighborhoods of the old city of New Orleans were founded—although after emancipation in the nineteenth century, whites and newly freed slaves continued living close to one another in these areas, a pattern that survives to this day.

All histories found in city plans culminate in statistics that planners employ to describe a contemporary city in land-use terms: how many acres are taken up by residential uses in a given district, or how many acres are used for industry or parkland. Different city plans of course emphasize different land-use facts depending on what is of most interest in a particular city. In Denver, the plan emphasizes the suburban development that has sprawled across the land lying east of the Rocky Mountain front; in Detroit, the plan emphasizes the great number of idle factories and vacant corporate headquarters once busy with the automotive industry. And in New Orleans, its 1999 Land Use Plan reported the number of houses rendered vacant in each planning district due to the city's population decline after 1960. Most plans present factual statistics alongside comparable information from the past so that planners can discern trends. The 1999 plan included data showing that between 1980 and 1990, the number of vacant houses in the Lower Ninth Ward increased nearly 86 percent.

In addition to information about land use, all plans offer a second array of facts, these having to do with residents of each planning district—their median age, income, race, education, and so on. And just as land-use statistics are presented so that trends can be detected, information about residents includes comparable data from the past ten or twenty years. Based on a statistical analysis of such trends, planners can project how population characteristics are likely to change in the future. In the Lower Ninth Ward, for instance, population fell nearly 20 percent between 1980 and 1990, then declined only 5 percent between 1990 and 1997. Based on these figures, the 1999 plan projected that the district's population would decline by about 4 percent in the next five years. Such projections are found in nearly all city plans.

When writing a plan, planners conclude their documentation of statistical data by explaining what it means. New Orleans' 1999 plan explained that the Lower Ninth Ward's declining population and increasing number of vacant properties "reflect the isolated nature of the district, resulting in further population loss and increasing vacant houses." Most plans also point out problems the data portend, although problems are typically phrased in palliative terms. Here, for example, is how the 1999 plan—which I had a hand in writing—described the circumstances of the Lower Ninth Ward (Planning District Eight):

> The last quarter of the 20th Century has brought a decline in
> the neighborhood with large industrial users leaving the area
> and a depression in the city's economy in the 1980s. Many of
> the homes built in the 1930s & 40s now stand empty and ne-
> glected. . . . However, a recent renaissance of restoration and
> rehabilitation of older homes is beginning to revitalize District
> Eight and deliver residents hope for a brighter future.

Anyone who attended the land-use meeting held in the Lower Ninth Ward might well wonder how "hope for a brighter future" could summarize what citizens said that night—and might conclude it's a planner's bias to find the optimistic phrase.

The contents of plans described above are primarily useful for planners: maps of how land is used in a city; a history of how the city was established and subsequently developed; a description of how a city's population has evolved with regard to age, racial characteristics, and income. Planners make use of this information—which, it must be said, is a substantial portion of a plan's text—because of what it implies about the future. However, few citizens ever read their city's plan, and therefore they are typically unaware that it contains such descriptive statistics.

What follows the descriptive information, however, are the contents that citizens typically assume they would find in a plan: a stated vision of how the city should change in the next twenty or so years, based on what a citizenry declares are its expectations during that period. The explanation of a plan's vision makes up a substantial amount of text, typically organized into three discussions. The first discussion has to do with problems citizens say they encounter because of the different land uses that exist near them; the second discussion takes up the set of goals a citizenry thinks new development should achieve; and the third discussion pertains to a map that shows *where* a citizenry agrees new development should be directed. All three discussions constitute what is known as a plan's "vision," and to articulate this vision planners must obviously have learned what citizens think about their present circumstances and how they might be improved as new development occurs.

To write a plan and to articulate its vision, planners set about learning the views of citizens in an orderly way lest some views be inadvertently left out. Planners' usual method for developing a plan's vision is to conduct well-advertised public meetings in individual planning districts, at which planners ask the citizens who attend to speak about their vision of the future. Thus, citizens are asked about land-use conflicts they have perceived in their neighborhoods and throughout the city, about what types of future land-use development would be improvements, and about where they think new development would best be located.

It is at these meetings with citizens—so obviously crucial to developing a creditable vision for a city's future and thus its plan—that the information planners have gathered becomes useful. A small example serves to explain. At the previously described meeting held in the Lower Ninth Ward, a meeting meant to include citizens in the preparation of the 1999 Land Use Plan, one man rose to declare that in his view there were too many churches in his neighborhood. No more of them should be allowed, he added. Information planners had compiled in advance of the meeting verified that several new churches had recently located in this district, and that the congregations of these churches were people who mostly lived in other parts of New Orleans. Planners hypothesized that it might be the behavior of some of these parishioners that caused the problems that prompted the citizen's complaint about too many churches. Drivers late for services often drove too fast down the Lower Nine's narrow streets where children were playing; once a church's parking lot was full, churchgoers routinely blocked residents' driveways. And there was more. All these problems were, to a planner's conceptualization, "land-use conflicts" that a new land-use plan would resolve.

When planners explained to the assembled group that they supposed the man's remark referred to these problems, the man agreed. He'd suggested no more churches should be allowed, but planners countered with a different solution: that the new land-use plan could stipulate that in the future, churches would be required to provide enough parking to accommodate their parishioners, and could be located only where it was not necessary for people attending services to traverse the streets in nearby neighborhoods. The man said that this would solve the problem.

To my mind, this meeting shows planners engaging citizens in an exchange that was useful to the plan's vision and could be included in it. Yet no matter how useful planners find such incidents, they rarely lead to citizens' taking an interest in reading the plan that is finally adopted, except perhaps to determine if what was said at a meeting they attended was faithfully included. Therefore this very small incident—no more than a short conversation, really—reveals something more important than showing how planners make good use of information they include in a plan.

Only twelve citizens came to this particular public meeting, which occurred in the Lower Ninth Ward, in a planning district where more than twenty thousand people lived (before Hurricane Katrina). What planners heard at this meeting, some of which I've described earlier, were the typical congeries of complaints that planners hear whenever a citizenry speaks: reports about potholes, vacant properties, and weed lots. "Too many churches" is surely unusual, but no more so than what planners in any city commonly hear. From this mélange of usual and unusual public comments planners must derive a citizenry's vision.

As it happened, the man's remarks proved useful to the plan's recommendations about future development—which constitute part of the plan's vision. However, at the same meeting planners asked citizens to locate where a future grocery store should be built, whereupon the assembled participants dutifully did so, and the location they identified was shown in the 1999 Land Use Plan. But as we saw earlier (for this was the same meeting described in Chapter 5), one woman said that answering the question (and, by extension, putting the group's answer into the plan) was a waste of time, since no grocery store was likely to open in the Lower Nine, and the observer from the Bureau of Governmental Research also said the whole evening was a waste of time because so few citizens were there. Nonetheless, despite the few citizens who came to our meeting—and their doubts about what they were asked—we planners, like planners in all other cities, were able to use what we heard that evening as we wrote the 1999 plan.

New Orleans planners that night in the Lower Ninth Ward *did* learn about churches and the preferred location of a grocery store; we *did* hear many comments about land-use conflicts in the neighborhood. Therefore no one could fairly think the meeting was a waste of time, although it was unfortunate that more residents were not there—residents who might have made comments of use to formulating the plan. Obviously, missing such useful comments can render a plan's vision incomplete. In addition, there is a less obvious though more important effect of so few citizens attending meetings about a city's plan. An essential feature of a plan is its success at gaining the intelligence to accurately represent what a citizenry wants from the future. When most of that citizenry is absent—or makes no useful comment—planners are left to deduce (or imagine) a citizenry's aspirations. It is at this point of deduction that a city planner's *own* vision often comes into play, which may or may not accurately express the desires of the larger citizenry.

I will return to the crucial issue of expressing a citizenry's point of view later, but conclude this discussion of city plans by summarizing their usual contents. No matter how they are organized, plans provide background information about how a city has developed up to the time of the new plan and about who lives in the city. Though plans have a knowable internal logic and content, they are typically so long that it is difficult to imagine a citizen or a developer or even a city council member actually reading an entire plan. New Orleans' 1999 Land Use Plan was more than three hundred pages long; Stamford's master plan was five hundred pages; and the Unified Plan for New Orleans' recovery was promised to consist of two thousand pages. In anyone's judgment, that's a lot of pages given the news a plan brings—a list of problems to be corrected, a short list of commonly held aspirations for future development, and a map showing where that future development should go. The length of most plans almost ensures that only planners will read and try to use them. When citizens try to use the plan, they typically do so amid a land-use controversy, seeking guidance specific only to a contested site, which most plans do not provide anyway. Instead, plans offer a vision of general expectations from future development: that churches, say, must provide adequate parking for their congregations.

All the information included in a city plan is important. But that information—which is set out in many pages of text and even more devoted to statistical tables—is useful primarily as background for city planners, whose job is to translate a plan's good intentions into land-use regulations, or to evaluate individual land-use proposals and to determine how they will affect the vision a plan describes. The volume of information—all those pages—effectively hides a plan's utility from anyone but planners who've been trained to use it. And of course, what is hidden from citizens or their elected leaders won't be used, or worse, will be misused. It makes one wonder why my profession continues to write plans we know will have this result.

Much of the answer to this wonderment lies in the reason many people are attracted to the planning profession in the first place: they have an urge to improve what others have built, and believe they can see what would make a better city. Something like this inspires most planners—enthusiasts for "self-sustaining" cities or "green" suburbs or "smart" growth—who arrive to the profession thinking their ideas are sound and that an opportunity to remake the world in their model will be given to them just as Daniel Burnham was handed his chance.[4] There's nothing wrong with this. It's just how planners start.

Modern professional training tries to educate these young enthusiasts, to teach them to learn what citizens want before they start planning. Planners are trained to help formulate the vision of people who live in a city, rather than impose their certainties about what is desirable. Yet in most states the legislation that provides for city planning still requires master plans to be adopted for cities, and this requirement can inadvertently encourage mastermind visionaries. As post-Katrina New Orleans demonstrates, planners still relish the opportunity to devise a plan for a whole city based on *their* own vision. In other words, professional training has not tempered and informed what first attracted students to become planners.

And one can detect the reason: it's a professional delight—a sort of intoxication—to draw a plan. In this way, planners are like John Ruskin, who once described drawing an aspen: "Languidly, but not idly, I began to draw it; and as I drew, the languor passed away. The beautiful lines insisted on being traced—without weariness. More and more beautiful they became, as each rose out of the rest, and took its place in the air. With wonder increasing every instant, I saw that they 'composed' themselves, by finer laws than any known of men. At last the tree was there, and everything I had thought before about trees, nowhere."[5] Many plans I've read contain the swoony delight of Ruskin, but none demonstrate it as regrettably as plans for rebuilding New Orleans after Hurricane Katrina. In one such plan, the future would be achieved by first clearing away ruined public housing projects, then making better use of the cleared property—building new commercial districts and new upscale housing where neither had thrived before. Another plan contained drawings of new city playgrounds and open spaces, and spoke of "opening up" the riverfront for development of expensive condominiums that "world-class" architects would design. No provision was made for the people who had lived in the public housing until the day of the storm; nor were their voices heard or their opinions used to identify a vision.

All such plans are written by a planner who can, and often does, feel that he or she has *revealed* a city where everything bothersome about urban life has been magically set aside—much as if, like the Irvine ranch, nothing was there before. But planners must write plans to serve citizens already living among the decidedly unmagical facts of any city—the quotidian matters of where they can afford to live and where they can find a job, or what has been built before and is unlikely to change. The delight for planners envisioning a future from unmagical circumstances is not really akin to the pleasures of Ruskin. Rather, delight arises from a simple satisfaction of improving the life ordinary citizens experience in a city.

The distinction between planning for a citizenry rather than to bring about a planner's own professional vision is important. City plans often reflect the vision of professional city planners rather than the vision of a citizenry, and the two visions can be quite different. Because discovering what a citizenry desires is a fundamentally important subject in the practice of city planning, citizen participation merits special discussion.

TEN

Plans that Don't Include
What Citizens Know

It was August 1996, and unsurprisingly nasty humid weather in New Orleans—although the land-use issue before the planning commission that day was about refreshment. A young man whose smile displayed a gold-capped front tooth addressed the commission to say that he wanted to open a little store that would sell snowballs—the southern staple: a paper cone heaped with sweetly flavored crushed ice. Snowball stands are common in commercial areas of every southern city and are easy to recognize for being tiny, bright-colored huts decorated with paintings of what look like, well . . . snow cones.

Inside each snowball stand one or two employees concoct snowballs and sell them to customers through a large window facing the sidewalk. A citizen can walk toward home from the bus, buy a snowball, and continue on his way. The proposal before the commission asked for permission to build such a stand in one of the oldest black neighborhoods in New Orleans, on what was currently a vacant, overgrown lot surrounded by modest bungalows. One might suppose that neighboring residents could be pleased to see this lot put to good use, as it was undoubtedly a nuisance in the same ways neglected lots were a nuisance everywhere else in the city: uncut weeds, lurking feral dogs, urban drug trolls.

But because the vacant lot in question sat in a residential area, the zoning ordinance would have to be changed to authorize small neighborhood stores—including snowball stands—to operate among the houses. The young entrepreneur argued in behalf of this zoning change, saying he was "putting a vacant parcel back into commerce," the code phrase that implies increased tax revenues, more jobs, and general improvement. Virtually all developers seize this argument, no matter how small their project. The snowball entrepreneur also said that because older parts of New Orleans contained small stores located amid residential areas, his proposal was consistent with the city's development history. He further noted that allowing small shops would serve the modern purpose of encouraging people to shop on foot, thereby reducing gasoline consumption and air pollution.

The commission's chairman asked if any opponents to the snowball stand wanted to speak. A gray-haired gentleman approached the podium with his wife, and identified himself as a retired police officer who lived near the proposed snowball stand. He declared that he'd learned from years on the NOPD that such enterprises mostly sold products other than flavored ices. His observation was loudly applauded by the audience. Someone standing in the rear of the room shouted that drugs were the "other products." The ex-cop presented a petition of opposition signed by one hundred residents, then stood back to allow his wife to speak. She had brought a hand-drawn map of their neighborhood, on which she'd circled the area where she thought the stand's customers would originate—its market area, so to speak. She had then sketched a red line to show the route teenagers from a housing project located inside the circled area would follow back and forth to the snowball stand. If these teenagers were buying drugs, she said, violence would follow the same route. She ended her presentation in a soft voice, saying, "We know where we live and we're willing to put up with our fair share of murders—but we don't want to put up with more than our fair share."

Her words and her map were powerful arguments. City planners had already written a staff report that argued against the requested zoning change, but their report used more neutral reasons than that the proposed snowball stand would redistribute the location of homicides in New Orleans. The planning commission ultimately voted to recommend that the city council deny the request.

Another commission or another staff in another city might have seen the matter differently. But each would seek—as was done in New Orleans—to balance a city's needs for commerce against the legitimate concerns of individuals. This small drama succinctly explains city planning's importance to municipal government in New Orleans and elsewhere: that planners guide new development, and sometimes prohibit it, according to a citizenry's expressed vision of an agreeable future. Even with regard to such seemingly minuscule matters as snowball stands, important ethical decisions about ordinary lives are made whenever a city council votes on a proposed use of land. Planners are trained to help councils make such decisions well, although planners rarely have such winningly articulated assistance from citizens. And more noteworthy than the woman's unusual explanation of her hand-drawn map—and her ex-cop husband's validation of her conclusion—is the fact that she demonstrated citizens' savvy about urban dynamics, and how much knowledge citizens can bring to city planners.

Ultimately, the snowball incident influenced us to change our method of conducting planning meetings in New Orleans. In particular, when planners commenced work on a new land-use plan two years after that hot August day, we brought a large-scale map of the Lower Ninth Ward to a planning meeting we'd convened there. Our thinking was that citizens could focus on future land uses if they could make reference to—and draw on—a *map,* just as the policeman's wife had. Our new idea for involving citizens, however, was not fairly tested at that meeting. Only twelve citizens attended, despite the event's being well publicized. We eventually held twenty-six such meetings in pursuit of the 1999 Land Use Plan—two in each of New Orleans' thirteen planning districts. At several of these meetings, participants praised our big maps for helping them focus on how land had been developed in the city, and how it should be used in the future. As it happened, the maps—along with our many efforts to publicize the meetings where the maps would be used—were among the specific reasons Louisiana's planning association gave an award for excellence to the 1999 Land Use Plan. That award was a satisfying outcome of our efforts to create this plan, of course, though the award did not extinguish my uneasiness as planning director about how few citizens had taken part in formulating the plan. Although nearly five hundred thousand people lived in New Orleans in 1999, fewer than a thousand had come to our twenty-six meetings.

It should be said that involving citizens is a relatively recent add-on to the planning profession's traditional way of creating plans. Planning did not start by involving citizens, but—at best—by planning *for* them. Burnham's revered Plan of Chicago ignored that city's residents. Garden city plans and

Section 701 plans provided for residents *yet to come,* who would choose to live in a place because of its sylvan beauty, or because of federal mortgage guarantees granted to home buyers in towns developed according to the 1954 Housing Act's notion of good city planning. All these plans were based on what planners presumed citizens wanted or what planners thought made a good city. But planners did not consult the citizenry.

Urban renewal plans written in the 1950s were similarly drawn up without conferring with citizens. These plans concerned the future development of large tracts within cities made vacant when local governments—using money from the federal government—cleared run-down buildings away, along with most of the people who had lived in them. Urban renewal relied on the theory that once dilapidated structures were removed from central cities, new enterprise would invest where the buildings had stood. But instead of the lucrative new enterprise these plans foresaw "renewing" cities, urban renewal had quite different consequences: interstate highways gouged their paths through downtown neighborhoods, leaving vast expanses of land idle for years.

The results of urban renewal can be seen vividly in New Orleans, where great numbers of buildings were demolished, although much of this cleared land has never found a better use than for highways and paved parking lots. After Hurricane Katrina those asphalt parking lots seemed an especially cruel reminder of failed urban renewal programs of the past, since what had been cleared away to "renew" New Orleans were buildings that had occupied high ground where people could have lived (and had once lived) safely through devastating floods. However, in New Orleans—as in every other city that endured urban renewal—virtually no provisions were made for the people who'd once lived in the cleared-away areas. They were simply gone, left to find their future homes unassisted by a plan of any kind.

In every American city, urban renewal was a disastrous program in most every way. And every aspect of the program drew fierce criticism from scholars, journalists, and community activists. The critics explicitly or implicitly blamed government's reliance on misguided experts who presumed to know what was best for cities and their citizenry. It is no exaggeration to say that because of the disastrous failure of urban renewal, every agency of American government engaged in planning eventually started involving citizens. Even when qualified experts were hired to draw up specific plans, citizen participation became virtually mandatory. As a consequence, in the 1960s, increasing numbers of citizens demanded to be involved in planning decisions. The result is all around us: federal highways are no longer built without citizen comment; neither are state-regulated landfills, or jails meant to serve several counties. Over the past forty years, every level of government has come to require some form of citizen involvement when planning public facilities.

Contemporary methods cities use to formulate their plans for the future also require citizen involvement—what city planners refer to as "citizen participation." All contemporary city plans, such as the 1999 Land Use Plan for New Orleans, describe how planners have involved citizens. Despite nearly fifty years of effort to cultivate citizens' interest in planning, however, the small number of people who show up at planning meetings and the even smaller number who ever make reference to their city's plan prove that the profession has yet to secure the citizenry's interest. In fact, it is typical that planners hear from citizens only when they are aroused against a proposed development and arrive at a public hearing to say so. In that frame of mind, citizens' interest in a plan is generally limited to learning whether the plan corroborates what the citizens already think. Furthermore, no matter how hotly a citizenry has publicly argued over a specific development, only rarely does that specific intensity lead individuals to participate in writing a new plan later on. Evidently, most people do not find participation in planners' meetings to be productive except to oppose some such proposal as a snowball stand.

For this reason, under the rubric of "what works," planning journals offer helpful articles describing innovative strategies to quicken a citizenry's interest. One such article pictured a billboard that graphically posed the question "Where Would You Draw the Line" to advertise public meetings about relocating the boundaries of that city's zoning districts. It's arguable whether this appeal would be effective: it made sense only to people who already understood what zoning ordinances contain and what effect drawing district boundaries would have. Furthermore, those very citizens who ordinarily keep track of the activities city planners undertake would attend the meetings without the billboard's provocation.

In any case, most articles about how planners can increase a citizenry's participation rely on particular circumstances that other cities cannot replicate. This was the case when one city's mayor was himself trained as a planner, and emphasized the value of the city's plan so convincingly that large numbers of citizens turned out when he said the plan needed revision. In another instance, the U.S. Navy announced its intention to close a base that had been a significant part of a city's economy for decades. Hearing this, citizens took an unusual interest in planning because they could imagine that without military personnel and their families, the housing market would change, as would the prosperity of local stores and restaurants. In addition, citizens could see that their future depended on the nature of any new activity that might replace the naval base. A new industry, for example, might offer only low-paying jobs. Families who'd foreseen their children growing up and working at the naval base might worry that their offspring would only find work in a distant town. Or, more complicatedly, citizens might have worried that a new enterprise would employ only highly skilled, highly paid workers, whose incomes and housing demands would increase everyone's property values—but might also increase taxes because newcomers could demand new public facilities such as libraries and public parks. In the event of a base closure, citizens can suddenly perceive their civic future requires taking an interest in planning. This, instead of taking the usual course of letting city planners and a few public-spirited citizens write the plan. The point, however, is that particular success stories about citizen participation rarely offer wisdom transferable to other cities.

After nearly fifty years of planners' seeking participation by the public, the fact that relatively few people ever take part in creating a plan might indicate that citizens have not found their participation worthwhile.

What goes on at public meetings devoted to developing a city's plan, where planners seek citizens' comments, is typified by the experience of devising New Orleans' 1999 Land Use Plan. At the time, we city planners convened several meetings at which we explained to the assembled citizens the importance of land-use plans: that they are crafted to improve a neighborhood as new uses of land are introduced.[1] We said the 1999 plan would take into account all types of future uses of property, and would suggest, in general terms, where new schools, fire stations, shops, houses, and public parks should be located (and newly situated) over the next twenty years. We also explained how our phrase "in general terms" meant that the plan would not say specifically where every occurrence of future development should go, but rather would suggest the *types of locations* where a few broad categories of land uses would bring the most benefit. Shops where small household items are sold, for example—a quart of milk, razor blades, newspapers— are ideally situated close to where customers live. And we explained that planners call this broad category of land use "neighborhood commercial."

Each of these preliminary explanations required considerable talk and many examples, and citizens—even those most intent on participating— often lost interest. As quickly as possible, therefore, we planners turned to the second portion of the public meetings, in which we asked citizens to talk about how they wanted the city, as well as their particular neighbor- hoods, to change.

This second part of the meeting, of course, is what most citizens come for. In advance of such meetings, planners figured out methods to allow every citizen in attendance an opportunity to participate. As they set about working on the 1999 plan, New Orleans planners prepared large maps of each planning district to help participants visualize city geography and locate different land uses—those now existing and those that might occur in the future. Planners also prepared the questions they are most interested in having citizens answer: How do you want your neighborhood and your city to look in twenty years? What features of the city would you like to see developed, enhanced, or diminished? What new uses of land would improve your individual neighborhood? All these questions—and many more like them—are standard planners' queries. In response, New Orlea- nians declared that they'd like to see more open space, more houses . . . and fewer churches, then sketched on the large maps planners had provided the best locations for new land uses. At the end of each public meeting, planners summarized citizens' ideas and the sketches they'd drawn on the large maps, and declared a "consensus" had been reached. This consensus about how the city should look two decades hence constituted the specific contribution citizens made in developing the new plan.

In New Orleans, planners used large-scale maps to summon forth citi- zens' perceptions and vision of the future, but the questions we asked are standard among city planners. The questions are premised on planners' professional training—and on the continual reminders all planners receive throughout their practice. For example, the State Planning Office in Maine recently advised municipal planners that local plans (which towns and cities in Maine are required to have) can be "meaningful" only if citizens have agreed on "a mental picture" of what they hope their community will "look like, feel like, and be like" in twenty years.[2] Hence endure the standardized questions that planners throughout America—including myself—have proposed to citizens.

In response to questions about their envisioned city, some citizens can provide very good answers: they can identify where new roadways, new buildings, new commercial development, and new uses of land could be situated, and they can explain how this vision of the future would improve the contemporary urban circumstance. However, such useful answers are rare in my experience, and most citizens offer what could best be termed inadequate replies.

Many citizens respond to planners' questions with their own recollections of the city's past. Seemingly, these citizens' preferred vision of a future city would find it largely reverted to an earlier time, which they remember liking better. In the case of New Orleans, citizens who attended meetings to develop the 1999 plan wanted the future city to replicate a city where "nice" department stores were downtown; where children walked to school unescorted, and where mail got delivered twice daily. However, such responses involve memories that often gloss old problems and exaggerate old virtues. The gritty buzz and implication of ordinary life in the good old days becomes, in memory, indistinct and charming—but often quite unreliable. Those "nice" department stores in downtown New Orleans would not allow black women to try dresses on; those unescorted children in the old days walked to segregated schools; those residents who got mail twice a day lived in neighborhoods that flooded after every heavy rainstorm. All such answers—and citizens in every city have their own version—compose a past-laden vision of the future that no planner (or anyone else) can replicate.

Other citizens respond to the question "What do you want your city to look like, feel like, and be like in twenty years?" by declaring that they want the civic amenities that other, more-favored neighborhoods already have. These civic jealousies are often quite specific, as in the case of a meeting held in New Orleans East at which citizens agreed that the 1999 Land Use Plan should encourage New Orleans' famous restaurants to open branches in their part of town. Other civic jealousies are more general, as when citizens tell planners they want community centers, playgrounds, and elementary schools "nearby," or that they want safe places to walk—all of which they believe (whether or not it's true) other neighborhoods enjoy.

Citizens also respond to planners' questions with overly broad ideas, such as (in most cities) that "the economy should be improved," or (in New Orleans) that the "isolation of the poor should be reduced." Such visions of an improved civic future are indisputably desirable, but impractically vague. Writing a city plan requires the establishment of a specified relationship between the present and an envisioned future, and requires a clear and stated understanding of the ways by which guiding the use of land could bring that future to fruition. Overly broad responses to planners' questions are inadequate because they express no more than a generalized civic *hope* that's of little practical use to guiding development.

Still other citizens envision their city twenty years hence as if the municipal budget were not a constraining factor. They may describe a future in which neighborhoods are joined by a series of bike paths, or are provided a daily cycle of garbage collection, or enjoy well-maintained landscaping on all thoroughfares. These responses ignore budgetary practicalities, including the hope of the same respondents that their taxes never be raised.

Of course, there are many varieties of inadequate answers to planners' questions but one seems universal. Though urban residents realize that such facilities as landfills, sewage treatment facilities, public housing, welfare offices, and power stations are necessary components of modern cities, when asked where those facilities would best be located in the future, most citizens are quick to answer that they do not want these uses located nearby—nor, in many cases, do they want nearby the people who might use them. Such responses reveal what might be termed "issues citizens don't want to think about."

These several responses to planners are inadequate because they do not specifically contribute to the formulation of a city plan—which cannot return a city to a fond (and often inaccurate) memory of itself, which must be constrained by the municipal budget, which must be specifically connected to guiding the future uses of land, and which must provide for unwelcome (though necessary) civic facilities.

Faced, then, with inadequate comments from citizens, planners are often left reliant on their own vision or on instinct, and frequently feel no choice but to write plans that consist of what *they* think a citizenry desires and needs, or what *they* think are the specific land-use policies that will achieve a vision that citizens have specified only insufficiently.

Of course, any plan that ultimately results from planners' meetings with citizens has to be presented for additional public comment before a city's planning commission would adopt it. As seen, however, plans are long and dense, and most citizens are not entirely clear about what purpose a plan serves. Nor are citizens fluent with how professional planners go about discovering common themes among the multiple aspirations citizens have voiced. Therefore, citizens rarely feel competent to disagree with how planners have articulated a vision for the future ostensibly based on what the citizens themselves have said at the smaller public meetings convened to work on the plan. This lack of vocal disagreement might seem to indicate citizens support a newly written plan, but it might also indicate that planners have written a plan that only they know how to use.

The observation that "only planners know how to use plans" is worth emphasizing, since absent valuable comment by citizens, planners can be said to write plans *for* citizens, not *with* them. In addition, the interpretation planners give to citizens' comments can actually impose a vision of the future based on professional considerations and values that citizens themselves might not share.

Unlike New Orleans, summertime in Maine is *not* hot and humid, though a planner in Kennebunk (near where I live) sent a fiery letter to the local newspaper about new houses and convenience stores springing up in the fields and forests surrounding the town. This was ugly rural sprawl, he said, and a threat to Kennebunk's economy, which depended on tourists flocking to the pristine seaside village. He exhorted readers to tell their legislators how they wanted the town to look in fifty years. His strategy is common among planners, who often exaggerate the typical twenty- or twenty-five-year time frame of plans so as to emphasize the dire importance of the future itself.

Using a similar strategy, city planners in New York City recently criticized the Bloomberg administration for "not asking what the city should be like 50 or 100 years from now."[3] There's little to fault in planners' preoccupation with such long-term views, since they know firsthand the length of time it takes for cities to be improved. Large components of social and physical change—racial integration, for example, but also construction, deterioration, and reconstruction of buildings, highways, and parks—take years to have an effect or even be completed. And small changes—opening a snowball stand, siting a grocery store, or building an affordable apartment building—though each can be quickly realized, occur one-by-one and only over time make up a perceivable pattern of change.

Yet when planners employ these exaggerated exhortative time spans they are trying to convince their audience (citizens) to think about the future in planners' terms and to do something about that future, also in planners' terms. New York City's planners would have the Bloomberg administration consider what the city should be like in fifty to one hundred years. The planner in Kennebunk would have citizens tell leaders what they wanted the town to look like in fifty years. In both cases, planners' words bespeak a faith not only that a city's or a town's future so many years hence can be described, but also that it can be guaranteed by a plan.

For most citizens, however, the future is a far different concept. Their future involves shorter periods of time and is less concerned with the notion of what "should be" than with improving what presently "is." Most citizens think of what affects their day-to-day lives—their present—however cities have been or will be built. But planners frame questions from a professional concern with the physical form a city could take in the long run. From the answers citizens give, planners are able to find corroboration of their professional views. The unfortunate result is that plans written *with* citizen participation are not much different from plans written *without* citizen involvement.

Planners, of course, employ many methods to engage citizens beyond asking them what they hope their city will look like someday. Most of these methods, however, achieve the same result: plans that are written according to planners' beliefs about what constitutes the most promising civic future, yet are adopted on the failed premise that the plans represent what citizens aspire to. One final example will illustrate the various unsuccessful methods planners use to engage citizens, and illustrate as well the results of failing to enlist the best of what citizens can offer.

This story took place in post-Katrina Louisiana, after the state had hired several professional consultants to help local communities plan for recovery and future development. The consultants set about their work by conducting a survey of Louisianians—some of whom had returned home after the storm, some of whom were still displaced and living in Houston, Atlanta . . . and even Oklahoma. All respondents were asked what was most important about the future, once storm-ravaged Louisiana had been rebuilt. "How should we grow?" consultants asked, directing respondents to choose among three answers, each of which was accompanied by a brief explanation:

1. We should keep building and developing as we have—single-family homes, located mainly at the edge of metropolitan areas, connected by roadways.
2. We should modify development patterns—building more in-town condos, apartments and townhouses, as well as single-family homes. Balance new public transit with road improvements.
3. We should focus development on Existing Cities and Towns—build mostly in-town condos, apartments and townhouses, connected by public transit such as modern buses or commuter trains.

In their subsequent report describing the results of this survey (which had been hopefully entitled "Louisiana Speaks"), the consultants remarked that only 18 percent of the respondents preferred development to continue as it always had. The consultants interpreted this low percentage to mean that the vast majority of "citizens want to change development patterns towards more compact cities and towns, with more transit options and alternatives to single family houses."[4]

Maybe this interpretation of how citizens responded in the "Louisiana Speaks" survey is accurate. However, asking citizens "How should we grow?" and then restricting their responses to a choice of three answers demonstrates something not immediately obvious about how planners seek out—and then put to use—public opinion. The American Planning Association (a professional organization that most practicing planners belong to) offers some insight. In 1993, the association reported the results of a survey of its membership titled "What Planners Value." The survey—which of course might have had biases of its own—found that most planners preferred two patterns of growth: "compact development" and "convenient public transit co-ordinated with land use and development."

These preferences are the subtext for the question asked in the Louisiana Speaks survey: "How should we grow?" Citizens were presented with three choices, two of which express what *planners* prefer—development that is compact and coordinated with public transit. Over 80 percent of the respondents chose options 2 and 3—which would result in compact development organized around public transit. Perhaps in the wake of the hurricane, citizens realized how foolishly Louisiana had been developed up to then, though the planning consultants did not ask citizens why they had chosen one option over another. Nonetheless, from the results of their survey, the consultants concluded that a vast majority of Louisiana's citizens believed that development should be compact and coordinated with public transit. And from this conclusion, the consultants recommended that all plans for Louisiana's municipalities should concentrate development around public-transit stops. However, the consultants had not investigated how citizens would respond to a wider array of potential development options.

Most planners, myself included, would have no quarrel with the consultants' proposal for guiding future growth because it is consistent with what our training suggests is most desirable. However, as in this case, when planners write plans that do not elicit a full array of citizens' responses, a city loses touch with the intelligence of such citizens as, for example, the woman who anticipated that a new snowball stand would result in her neighborhood's enduring more than its "fair share" of homicides. Or, when planners insist citizens identify the best site for a grocery store—as we did in the Lower Ninth Ward—the plan might overlook residents' better ideas about developments that were much more likely to occur in their neighborhoods.

The questions that planners ask citizens during public meetings or through widely distributed surveys—or through the many other methods planners have devised for seeking out a citizenry's opinion—those planners' questions do not typically or systematically draw on the potent knowledge of citizens. Instead, planners discover citizens' useful perceptions only unpredictably and often accidentally, such as happened when a snowball stand was proposed in New Orleans.

* * *

Planners ask citizens the wrong questions, questions that are premised on how the planning profession looks at the world. The philosopher Simone Weil said, "The only important question to ask another human being is, what are you going through?" Yet we planners ask questions that make sense only to people who think the way we do: who imagine how the built environment might appear in a distant future, for example. We have not wondered whether different questions might result in better answers and might also cause citizens to take a greater interest in planning. Clearly, formulating better questions requires a concentrated effort to reimagine citizen participation.

Earlier this chapter described the exuberance of a planner in Maine who exhorted citizens to tell their legislators what they wanted their town to look like in fifty years. Asking questions that do not lead to citizens' expressing what they're going through in their current circumstances is just another self-referring exuberance among planners. This exuberance can take the form of overbearing certainty, such as can lamentably be recognized whenever planners write a plan that represents what *they* think is best, based on their professional training and on their experience in a particular city—and not a plan that represents what citizens think.

Most planners have written such plans, certain of the good intentions and aspirations that our profession would have us fulfill. Surely, such certainty explains how planners wrote the sequence of plans for rebuilding New Orleans after Hurricane Katrina—all of which proved unsatisfactory to the citizens of that devastated city. Absent satisfactory plans, city planning is unable to demonstrate its necessity to a citizenry. The worse result is that without an evident constituency for planning, elected public leaders can, and do, make land-use decisions that effectively dismiss city plans.

ELEVEN

Plans that Elected Leaders Ignore

It was December 1992, scarcely two weeks after I'd become New Orleans' planning director, when a land developer stopped by to congratulate me on my new job. He unrolled several architectural drawings on my desktop and said, "I've got five votes on the city council, but I thought I'd show you the four-star hotel we're about to build. We'll need a map change."

"Need a map change" meant that the zoning district where his hotel site was located did not allow hotels (although, as shown on the zoning map, an adjacent district did). If that district's boundaries could be redrawn to include his site, then he could put up his hotel. "I've got five votes" meant that he'd already persuaded five members of the city council to vote in favor of his proposal even before he brought it to city planning for review. The New Orleans' city council has seven members, and a simple majority (four votes) is necessary for the council to decide as the planning commission recommends. A larger majority (five votes) is required to overrule the commission. "Five votes," therefore, meant that the city council could approve what the planning commission thought should be denied; or the council could deny what the commission said should be approved. Win-win, in his view. His "map change" was assured, and with it, his hotel.

The law in Louisiana—as in most states—requires planning commissions to review all proposed changes to zoning ordinances (including map changes). This developer, like many before him, had simply found a way to transform that legal requirement into an inert procedural formality. Planners would analyze his request; the planning commission would recommend how the city council should vote; public hearings would be held—all as the law required. The law *intended* that these proceedings and their outcome be taken into account when the city council voted. But in this instance the developer had prearranged a vote in his favor. No law was being illegally skirted, as he saw it, and his visit to my office was a courteous way of telling a newcomer how things worked.

Like most city planners, however, I was already wise to this practice of securing votes in advance on land-use matters. In addition, I had read the informational handout that New Orleans city planners gave to anyone whose proposal required review by the planning commission, plus a subsequent vote by the city council. "Step One," the handout read, "Go See Your District Councilman." The handout went on to describe the succeeding steps: the planning staff's analysis of what was proposed; the planning commission's hearing on the matter; the city council's own public hearing and decision. Only after all this rigamarole, the handout said, could the developer secure a building permit and start construction. And if the council voted against the project, there were avenues of appeal.

The handout also included factual information about legal procedures that city councils must follow when presented with a development proposal, although a wily citizen reading Step One might theorize that the ultimate decision could be influenced in a district councilman's office well before any of the subsequent steps involving city planning. Go to your councilman first, New Orleans' city planners officially recommended, *then* proceed through the city-planning review. The handout was effectively telling its readers how things really work in New Orleans. And to me, a new director, it implied that something—whether it was planners' discouragement, or planners feeling unpersuasive before the city council, or that planners suffered from failed leadership, or that they had no advocates for their work—*something* had caused New Orleans' planners to all but abandon their professional skills and ethics to the politics practiced by developers and elected officials.

It was certainly a situation to correct. And I started to correct it by revising the handout so that it no longer included old Step One.

Revising the handout, however, was unlikely to put an end to developers securing votes in advance, because this practice was both traditional and entrenched in New Orleans. I also knew the entrenched practice had to be *overcome* rather than expecting it to be reformed by state legislators strengthening the procedures cities must follow when making land-use decisions. Typically, after granting (the legal word is "enabling") cities the authority to conduct a loosely defined set of planning activities, most states take little further interest in local land-use decisions and their protocols. Louisiana's lawmakers would undoubtedly take even less interest in what an ingenue planning director had found deficient in the state's existing planning statutes and practices. A more productive strategy would be to find informal ways of giving city planners a stronger hand in the face of council members making unofficial land-use decisions.

As it happened, I was often present when such unofficial decisions were reached. Several city council members invited me, as planning director, to attend meetings with prospective developers. Perhaps this invitation was extended so the council member could gauge opposition to a particular proposal; or perhaps a council member herself wanted to change some aspects of a proposed development and sought corroboration from a professional planner's perspective; or perhaps the council member wanted to signal the director what decision was going to be reached.

Nonetheless, from such meetings held in advance of official decisions I learned that New Orleans' elected leaders were inclined to support development proposals because they believed increased municipal tax revenues were the preordained result. Seated beside a developer in a council member's office, I sometimes pointed out that approving his proposed subdivision meant the city would have to provide additional public services there—services that cost more than the city could collect from property taxes it levied. When making this case in New Orleans, I had documented proof for my argument. Statistics showed that subdivisions built in the eastern sections of New Orleans over the previous twenty-five years had cost the city multiples of the property tax revenues collected there. The developer answered my argument simply by ignoring it and advancing his own, describing the jobs his new subdivision would create—construction jobs first, followed by permanent jobs for lawn-maintenance firms, boarding kennel custodians, and many, many others. Residential development, he concluded, is always accompanied by new enterprises to serve it. Of course I had an answer to his conclusion ready, though the council member cut the discussion short. He'd heard enough. One informal strategy bites the dust.

Meetings like this are political deliberations, and therefore are not conducted like formal debates in which arguments must be answered—rather than ignored—and a decision is given to the side that makes the best case. Rather, decision makers weigh arguments in part by considering who is making them. A developer may have a personal relationship with the district councilman—sometimes based on campaign contributions, other times on family connections or longstanding friendship. Or a council member may simply philosophically agree with a developer's assertion that all planners share an anti-business bias. Or, like many of his peers, a councilman may suspect planners have greater loyalty to the aims of their profession than to elected leaders. Each of these extra-professional considerations can give a developer the advantage over a planner's logic. City plans, of course, might seem able to bolster that logic, but few people other than planners know how to apply the general advice of a plan to a particular development proposal. This fact, too, gives an advantage to developers when they meet with council members. The plan inevitably seems arcane.

In addition, there is also the crucial matter of any planner's ability to persevere. No matter how many times I met with a particular council member to explain the professional logic regarding particular land-use issues, it seemed that I started anew with each proposal. I was almost never able to predict whether my logic—welcomed in the same council member's office on a previous issue—would succeed or be disregarded on a new visit. In obvious ways, this experience can so discourage planners that they capitulate to "how things work."

It might be supposed that the relationship among city planners and city councils would be less mercurial than I've described in view of the fact that city councils hear the arguments of city planners so frequently. In most cities the council's agenda is predominately taken up with land-use matters. However, a planner's credibility and value provided by cumulative experience with city councils tend to evaporate when a council member already knows he wants to approve a development.

For example, the boutique-hotel developer mentioned earlier chose his site without seeking guidance from the city's plan or from the zoning ordinance (documents that indicate where New Orleans' citizenry prefers new land uses to be located). His ignoring these documents confounds planners' rational paradigm in which a developer *first* reviews municipal rules to discover locations where hotels are authorized, and *then* sets about finding a property in one of those approved locations and building his hotel there. By following this rational paradigm, the developer would find a location for his hotel that required neither a review by city planning nor a vote by the city council because it was consistent with the city's planning documents. But the more true-to-life paradigm has a developer first finding a property at an attractive price located where he thinks a boutique hotel ought to succeed, and buying the property.[1] Typically, it's only after a developer has settled on a location that he takes into account what the plan or the zoning ordinance might say about his chosen site. And if the developer discovers that hotels are not allowed in the zoning district he has chosen, he has the choice of either putting the property to some other use, selling it, or asking for a change in the zoning ordinance.

Another version of this real-life decision sequence recalls the citizen who wanted to convert the house he'd inherited to boarding kennels. Still another version is the developer who bought the devastated Crystal Hot Sauce factory after Hurricane Katrina, and set about getting the city's zoning ordinance changed so he could construct the Preserve Apartments. In all these cases, and in hundreds similar, a city's zoning ordinance (and, implicitly, the city's plan) only come into play late in the process of making land-use decisions.

It is worth repeating that most construction in any city occurs without the involvement of city planners or city councils. In most instances, individuals simply seek and receive building permits for planned activities that are consistent with what the zoning ordinance authorizes (and, by implication, what the city's plan forecasts). Planners might claim such "consistency" indicates a city's land-use regulations are successful in guiding development consistent with the city's plan. Usually, however, this "consistency" occurs not because individuals have previously looked through a city's land-use regulations or its plan, but because they have noticed the parts of town where their own plans match what is already thriving there.

Some critics of city planning would say that "consistent" development proves city planning is unnecessary. And many citizens would agree. For example, if a grocery store were to open in the Lower Ninth Ward location approved by the 1999 Land Use Plan, I doubt many citizens would think this welcome event occurred *because* of the plan. To the extent citizens take favorable notice of any new construction, it is unlikely they connect it with zoning and planning at all, but instead would typically credit the developer's efforts. And that credit would not be misplaced, since the developer has taken the financial risk of operating a new business or building a new subdivision.

Citizens, it seems, most often take notice of city planning in its day-to-day business of working with people who, for any number of reasons, have bumped up against land-use regulations. Such individuals might have misread what was allowed in some part of town, or they might want to open a business that is not allowed, or want to erect a bigger sign, or a taller building, or operate longer hours than the zoning ordinance authorizes. In each of these instances, citizens discover city planning and city plans and local land-use regulations *abruptly*—when in full expectation of receiving a building permit to operate, say, a kennel, they learn it won't be that simple. Most of these citizens arrive at city planning only once in their lives. They are not entrepreneurs, and might for that very reason be more open to a planner's advice than skilled developers are. Planners told the prospective kennel operator that his idea would require a vote by the city council—which was unlikely to be favorable for reasons planners could explain. But planners also told him that he could realize income from his inherited house simply by making it a rental property. No vote by the city council was required, nor would he have to pay the fee that cities assess when applications are made for city-planning review. This man found planners' advice useful, and took it. Elected leaders took no part—and took no notice of—his decision.

Skilled developers such as those who proposed the Preserve Apartments and the boutique hotel know from experience that their projects require a land-use decision by the city council, and they also know they must submit an application to city planners. Most developers do not prearrange a favorable vote from the city council, nor do most of them seek an audience with council members. Instead, these developers simply follow the legally prescribed process for seeking a land-use decision from the council, and submit their applications to city planning. However, these same developers do not ordinarily seek (nor have I much found them open to) advice about alternative uses of their property—uses that require no decision by the city council because both the city's plan and zoning ordinance endorse them.

Unlike the citizen in Tremé, most applicants who meet with city planners do not change their original proposals along lines planners might advise. Their most common reason for not changing proposed developments can be found in the example of the application to authorize "affordable" housing in the light industrial district where Crystal Hot Sauce had been made. By the time the developer completed his application for the Preserve Apartments, he had already paid architects and engineers for the project's design, and probably had also purchased an option to buy the old manufacturing plant. Choosing an alternative use for the property—as planners might advise him to do—would mean he'd wasted the money spent to devise his project.

When individual citizens actually find the advice of city planners useful and persuasive, that does not mean they represent a constituency for city planning. These citizens' interest is randomly occurring and typically does not extend beyond a single concern. Furthermore, and as is perhaps obvious, many other individuals in similar one-time encounters with city planners do not take planners' advice, choosing instead to seek city council approval of their developments. Whether that political strategy is successful or not, in my experience these latter individuals tend to sympathize with detractors of city planning who claim its procedures waste their time and accomplish nothing worthwhile. In any event, city councils do not feel political pressure from their constituents to take more notice of planners' advice when making land-use decisions.

However—and irrespective of their failures to make planning concerns persuasive to elected leaders—planners are required by state statute to advise elected leaders on land-use matters. Certainly, elected leaders sometimes heed planners' advice—though the reasons they do can seem neither predictable nor susceptible to rational explanation. I'll demonstrate what I mean with an incident that involved the most important *other* elected leader city planners work with: the mayor.

City councils vote on numerous land-use decisions at every meeting, and city planning offers advice on them all. Most of these matters involve small parcels of land on which an individual wants to operate a beauty salon or an apartment building or a restaurant. Only over time do decisions on these small matters combine to make a perceptible change to the city.

In New Orleans, for example, a run-down part of town near the Mississippi River was transformed from dereliction to vibrant urban activity as a result of several individual land-use decisions made by the city council over a ten-year period. The first such decision granted a speculator the zoning change necessary for his converting into apartments an abandoned warehouse once used by the Port of New Orleans. When the conversion was completed, young professionals who worked nearby soon rented all the newly created units. The success of this conversion encouraged developers to seek—and to obtain—zoning changes to rehabilitate other vacant industrial buildings as apartments or condominiums. As more people moved into the new apartment complexes, still more developers saw additional opportunities for profit in the same neighborhood, and secured zoning changes to authorize celebrity-chef restaurants and art galleries. One by one, the city council's decisions to grant individual zoning changes—unforeseen and not approved by the city's plan—gradually resulted in what became known as "the Warehouse District," a lively residential area where restaurants and nightclubs and shops attracted great numbers of tourists.

Most big-city mayors leave decisions about the development of small pieces of land to the city council, preferring to concentrate on projects that quickly transform cities according to the mayor's own vision of good change and good politics. Yet despite the different scale of land-use matters that distinguishes the work of city councils and mayors, the manner by which city leaders discuss prospective developments with city planners does not differ. The nature of such conversations can be exemplified in the story of how New Orleans came to approve the construction of a casino on its primary thoroughfare in the downtown—Canal Street.

The story begins in what New Orleanians refer to as the oil bust of the mid-1980s, when the price of oil tanked and several multinational oil-and-gas corporations shut their doors and left town, closing down a blue-chip industry that for decades had prospered and afforded generations of New Orleanians promising career paths. In the aftermath of the shutdown, the city refocused its economic hopes and dependencies onto a tourism-based economy whose fortunes follow national business cycles and whose jobs are mostly low wage and immobile. Unemployment rates in New Orleans became morbid, as did the city's crime statistics.

For several years thereafter, New Orleans' leaders courted other businesses to replace oil and gas, but saw so little success that the mayor and city council agreed to Governor Edwin Edwards' high-stakes economic solution of legalizing gambling in New Orleans. Mississippi's well-established casinos suggested to city leaders that there was an endless demand for gambling, and an endless source of revenue. Governor Edwards' solution intended for the state to take the first share of profits, followed by the casino operators. New Orleans was to get what was left. The mayor and city council agreed to this split, believing that Mississippi's experience proved New Orleans would turn a fortune no matter how the take was divided.

The city also agreed with the governor's logic for demolishing the old downtown convention center and building the new casino edifice at its former site near the river, on Canal Street—the city's grandest commercial boulevard. The city owned this site, which meant that a prospective casino operator wouldn't have to buy it, which in turn meant increased profit margins for everybody involved. The site was close to both the French Quarter and to a *new* convention center, allowing plenty of tourists access to the casino. New hotels would be necessary, as would new restaurants and shops. All would create new jobs. A revived economy for New Orleans was in the offing.

By the time I became director of city planning, the governor, the mayor, and a majority of the city council had shaken hands on the casino deal. Construction would start the instant the council amended the zoning ordinance to authorize the casino as a "conditional use" in the downtown commercial zoning district. Louisiana law prohibited the city council from taking a vote on the conditional-use decision until after city planning had reviewed the application that would authorize a casino. But the council's vote had been determined months earlier.

City planners had taken no part in the negotiations among the governor, the mayor, and the city council. And our after-the-fact review of the foregone decision was limited to fitting a politically favored land use into a politically chosen location. At city planning, however, we set about tailoring specific conditions that would prevent the casino from disturbing New Orleanians' use and enjoyment of their city. We noted the site's proximity to already existing luxury hotels on Canal Street, whose revenues—and the city's economy—would suffer if guests were shocked awake by the noise of demolition and jackhammers. We proposed limiting the hours during which any high-decibel construction activities could occur. We turned our attention to the casino's proposed parking structure—a tower of ugly concrete sure to blemish a district of historic two-story brick buildings—and we proposed conditions to reduce the structure's size, and also obligated the casino to provide remote parking for its employees as well as a shuttle to transport them to and from work.

In addition, we required the parking structure to be redesigned so its facade would be compatible with the architectural details of adjacent buildings. We stipulated that a security plan be devised to protect the winning blackjack players who'd parked in spaces the casino had built. Beyond all this, we proposed that awnings be installed over public sidewalks adjacent to the parking structure to protect pedestrians from sun and rain. We demanded that landscaping be planted along city street frontages. All these proposals represented commonsense, commonplace planning considerations that would help accommodate an anomalous use to a historic downtown commercial district.

Planners were also aware that most casino jobs offered no path to promotion, and therefore we included a condition that all employees be offered schooling where they could learn management skills. And because in 1992 downtown casinos existed only in faraway Nevada—where new cities had been founded specifically to serve the gambling industry—the New Orleans city planning staff had little to guide us as we tried to foresee all that might result from forcing this new, high-profile leisure activity onto our old, low-profile city. Gambling losses could increase eviction rates in low-income neighborhoods; math teachers in public schools might leave for better-paid, more glamorous jobs as blackjack dealers. New Orleans' famed restaurants might fail if tourists preferred the free-food-cum-entertainment offered at the casino.

So, in recognition of all that we could *not* predict about the effects of the casino—effects that citizens worried about—city planners suggested that a consortium of New Orleans universities conduct empirical studies of what the casino brought to the city: good effects and bad. This unbiased research by scholars, planners believed, would offer the city an informed factual basis for (if nothing else) annual renegotiations with the casino— which we also made a condition for this use.

The conditions proposed by city planners responded to what had been brushed aside by the mayor and the governor and the city council, who'd concentrated on touting the jobs and tax revenues the casino would bring. After a lengthy public hearing, the New Orleans planning commission advised the city council that the casino should be authorized as a conditional use, but only if its plans were modified as the city's planners suggested. On hearing this decision, the casino developer complained that the conditions were ruinously expensive. And less than an hour later, the mayor of New Orleans was on the phone: "What do you think you're doing, Kristina, getting the planning commission to require all these changes to the casino's proposal?" I had at this moment been on the job one month.

I began to explain, but the mayor interrupted, observing that planners were always anti-business, always unconcerned about jobs and tax revenues, always oblivious to the real needs of the city. Following which he hung up.

I knew the mayor would immediately set about convincing the city council to vote in favor of authorizing the casino as a conditional use—and to ignore the conditions proposed by city planners. He had only to find four of the seven council members who agreed with him.[2] I deemed patience and tenacity to be my best allies, although they seemed weak in the face of all that the casino—and the governor and the mayor—promised for the economy of New Orleans.

Eventually, I met with every member of the city council, and they eventually voted in favor of the conditions we city planners had suggested. In those seven discussions conducted with city council members, I found that some favored the management training program planners recommended, while others favored conditions meant to keep the tourism industry vital, and still others said they would vote against city planning because it was more important to get the casino open and people to work than that management training classes be devised.

The short version of the outcome—that the city council approved the casino, but also required it to fulfill planners' conditions—had nothing to do with my ability to persuade the council. Instead, the casino developer was so certain of huge profits that he suddenly agreed to comply with planners' conditions. Furthermore, he also asked the mayor not to incite bad feelings in the community by sweeping the planning commission's recommendation aside. Because of the casino developer's unexpected compliance, the city council's decision to approve the casino was easy to make. Though it was also humbling that planners' conditions of approval had been voted up *not* because they were sensible, but because the developer unexpectedly agreed with them in order to get his casino under way.

Following the city council's vote to approve the casino, the mayor said he was pleased and invited me to attend a small celebration of the event. Somewhat later, and relying on the mayor's satisfaction with the outcome, I met with him, intent on championing the work of the city planners who worked in my office. I explained that the conditions we'd imposed meant problems would be avoided and the city would be improved. I offered several examples—that the casino's parking garage would *not* be an ugly, out-of-scale building. Instead, the garage would fit in among the Warehouse District. There would be attractive, camouflage landscaping on streets near the casino, and pedestrians would be protected from rain and the hot sun as they walked beneath awnings the casino had been required to install. All of these improvements, I told him, would enhance the city's continuing ability to attract tourists, which was a goal included in the city's policy plan, *New Century, New Orleans.* That plan had deemed tourism the principal foundation of New Orleans' economy in the early 1990s, and had stressed the importance of attending to its well-being. I also told the mayor that our management-training requirement at the casino would help the city realize another of *New Century*'s goals, which was to improve long-term job prospects for the city's residents.

The mayor—who was a polite man, first of all—listened politely, though he was visibly bored. As a token memento of our conversation, I placed a copy of *New Century, New Orleans* on his desk, where it remained, un-opened, until he left office and it was removed.

As it eventually transpired, much that had been feared about the casino's operations did not come to pass: math teachers did not leave their classrooms to run blackjack tables, world-class restaurants did not close, the numbers of evicted renters did not increase. But neither did much of what had been promised: the casino made only a fraction of its projected revenues; the state of Louisiana scaled back its share of profits; and the city never got more than a nominal rent from the casino for operating on the city-owned site. Overall, unemployment remained high, crime statistics remained notorious. In short, the casino took its place as another under-performing enterprise in a southern city with a foundering economy.

An instructive part of this story lies in a postscript. When the Louisiana legislature legalized the Canal Street casino in New Orleans, it also legalized riverboat casinos like those that had made Mississippi rich. And even before construction on the Canal Street site was completed, a new casino entrepreneur proposed to dock a riverboat at the Toulouse Street Wharf alongside the French Quarter. This wharf was the most central part of the French Quarter's riverbank, and a prime destination for tourists. The mayor, however, saw that a riverboat casino docked at this premier location could siphon profits from the yet-unfinished casino a few blocks away on Canal. And perhaps remembering that city planners had appraised the Canal Street casino through what he'd characterized as an anti-business attitude, he called me again—this time to ask me to help develop a strategy that would put a stop to the riverboat casino at the Toulouse Street Wharf.

As it happened, his was a welcome invitation because I also thought the proposed Toulouse Street site was unsuitable, albeit for different reasons. The new traffic would cause congestion, as well as despoiling wear-and-tear on the historic buildings and streets in the French Quarter. Residential neighborhoods would be disrupted. But I saw that the mayor and I could work together. I would use my objections to argue against the proposed riverboat during the planning commission hearings, and he would voice his objections in private conversations with at least five members of the council.

Our arguments prevailed, and the riverboat chose to dock elsewhere—well before the council had even taken a vote. Once again I recognized that patient tenacity constituted the suit of armor the council president had advised me to wear. But I also recognized that it was the unexpected ally I'd found in the mayor that determined the outcome of this land-use argument. Though there is more to this story than these obvious conclusions.

The tale of New Orleans' casino contains important, though imbedded and possibly even invisible, points of interest. Foremost is contingency, by which I mean that the success of planners' advice depended to a great extent on chance—the chance that the casino developer would unexpectedly agree to planners' conditions, and later on, the chance that the mayor himself would become an ally of planners. I would argue that such contingency plays a larger part in city planners' success than does their professional logic. A related point of interest is that while an elected leader might dismiss a planner's logic for being putatively anti-business—that is, ignorant of the real economic needs of a city—in another circumstance the same politician can and will fortuitously find favor with the very logic he previously dismissed. Planners can succeed, often unpredictably, by being persistent and principled, *but also* by being supple enough to let other people's slippery principles give them a windfall.

Another imbedded point of interest in the foregoing saga is planners' inventive use of professional expertise when unforeseeable uses—such as a casino in downtown New Orleans—muscle their way to approval. In this particular case, planners knew the zoning ordinance's mechanism of conditional-use designations gave them a means to interject useful ideas into a land-use decision after it had, in effect, already been made. But the casino saga was only one instance of planners making inventive use of what they know. All planners—in whatever city they work—are fully capable of similar invention.

Critics frequently accuse city planning of being a "reactive" function of government (meaning that planners, despite their title, do not look to the future, but only come along late in the story), particularly when a plan or a zoning ordinance has not foreseen what a developer proposes. But I think city planners use their best—and most creative—professional abilities precisely in those reactive instances. Rather than supposing that a plan can foresee and therefore control what people might imagine as beneficial in their city over the next twenty years, planners make better use of their skills in assessing how to fit an unforeseen land use into an existing city so as to improve it. Planners are trained to know that all important circumstances of a city will change: its demographics, its economic underpinnings, its preferred forms of housing. And this means that planners *expect* citizens to propose land uses that a city has never seen and for which its plan makes no provision. Reaction is inevitable.

Finally, the casino story sheds clear, corrective light on the goals contained in city plans, which are frequently criticized for offering contradictory advice. In New Orleans, the mayor seized on the casino as the way to achieve what he saw as the city's most important objective: to improve the economy. He objected to planners' suggestions that the casino should also be required to achieve other objectives listed in the city's plan—such as ensuring New Orleanians could find promising career paths, or enhancing the vitality of the city's larger tourism industry. His objection was that requiring the casino developer to respond to these *other* goals might impede—and in that way, contradict—the casino's ability to serve the goal of bringing economic benefits to New Orleans. However, during my conversations with several council members, it became clear that several of these elected leaders saw the other goals as complementary, rather than contradictory to the city's improved economy. Some council members said they would have opposed the casino, *except* that it might help the city realize these other municipal objectives.

Different, seemingly contradictory goals prove reconcilable because all public policy decisions, including those about how to use land, portend many different effects and rarely, if ever, are approved because all legislators agree on which effect is most important. In fact, the reasons different political leaders vote for a single public policy are themselves often at odds. Thus it is the planner's art to imagine how to advance different goals simultaneously. While acknowledging that the city council believed the casino would improve New Orleans' economy, planners also argued for instituting promising career paths for the casino's employees and for enhancing tourism activities beyond gambling.

And yet. Citizens lose confidence in a plan when they hear—in the course of a debate over a particular proposed land use—that the plan's goals are contradictory. Most people instinctively expect plans will provide an unambiguous, unchanging set of instructions for achieving an agreed-upon future. And citizens may therefore think that a city plan said to have conflicting goals is a plan that's been poorly conceived. This faulty conclusion ignores the ordinary circumstance of individuals themselves having contradictory desires. A woman may want the variety of low-priced commodities that a Wal-Mart offers, but also want to preserve the "rural" character of the town in Maine where such a store might be built. A father knows his children need counseling at a drug rehabilitation center, but opposes such a facility being built near his house because it might decrease his property's value. A city plan always mirrors the citizenry—or should—and therefore will include its contradictory goals.

Indeed, it is in the process of choosing among conflicting goals that elected leaders—the mayor, the city council members—have the greatest effect on a city's future. Some leaders focus on historic preservation, while others try to give all economic classes access to job opportunities. In a planner's eyes, the fact that a plan contains competing goals is one of its important virtues. In the long run—always a planner's professional perspective—all goals might be realized. Multiple and conflicting goals thus provide a useful articulation of a citizenry's complex aspirations, which elected leaders can use to choose policy directions during their term in office.

The word "conflicting" brings up a last point about the casino incident. Land-use decisions always designate who will or won't be allowed to build a building, and where; whose aspirations for the future will be served, and whose will not. Such competition among citizen-actors is the defining characteristic of political decisions, and is the reason that land-use proposals often involve political argument and contumely. Many citizens think the very reason that cities adopt plans is to avoid the fractious debate that accompanies political decisions. However, chaotic public discourse, unpleasant as it can be, is the most efficient way of discovering what citizens, planners, planning commissions, and even elected leaders actually think about land-use matters.

The Education of Henry Adams, that great nineteenth-century keyhole into the world to come, offers a useful perspective on the value of uncertainty and wrangling. "Chaos," Adams wrote, "was the law of nature; order was the dream of man. Since monkeys first began to chatter in trees, neither man nor beast had ever denied or doubted multiplicity, diversity, complexity, anarchy, chaos. . . . Always and everywhere the complex had been true and the contradiction had been certain. Thought started by it." This postulate actually describes public discussion at its best: from chaos comes thought (though rarely order).

The casino example demonstrates that the old and wonderful and troubled city of New Orleans is like every other existing city in that planning has had only sporadic success. But the example also demonstrates that planning often can work well *not* by devising some grand and orderly plan for the city's future development, but by dealing with unforeseen, perhaps conflicting, development proposals that are inevitably thrust upon all that already exists—inherited land-use decisions, prior planning enthusiasms, historical culture, and economic activities. City planning in such instances could be termed supple, though suppleness might be a lost virtue to political leaders—and citizens—who continue to believe (and sometimes even hope) that city plans articulate a strict view of what will be allowed in the future.

* * *

My intention thus far has been to impart a sound understanding of what city planning tries to accomplish and how planners go about their work, using New Orleans as the primary case in point. To do this, I've described the three signature and defining features of city planning: the plan and the land-use regulations that result from it; the way planners engage citizens; and how planners interact with elected leaders who actually decide how a city develops and changes.

I've chosen not to describe the many complicated issues and procedures that accompany any part of what city planners do. By this I am referring to such things as variances to land-use regulations, rules about expanding nonconforming uses, the use of eminent domain to guide development, statutory time limits on how long planners may review development proposals, and even parliamentary procedures city councils use to ignore what planning commissions advise. All these issues, of course, are familiar to any citizen with a passing interest in city planning. But my wish has been to save readers from being distracted by the multitude of accompanying issues, and instead to focus on what I see—regrettably—as the primary causes of disappointment with my profession.

The people whom city planning disappoints constitute a diverse and large group: all citizens throughout America who've been let down, thwarted, or otherwise dissatisfied by city planning wherever it's practiced. As described early in this book, the group includes developers who can't build a subdivision because planners require an expensive common sewerage system. It includes environmentalists who learn that a subdivision development—unchecked by city planners—has wrecked natural bird habitats. The group might include minimum-wage workers living in dingy downtown hotels that city planners have approved for expensive modernization by developers trying to attract an upscale clientele. Or the group might include preservationists who oppose modernizing those same dingy hotels because the buildings played a significant role in local history.

My thesis is that the trouble with city planning lies principally in its signature features. First, that a city plan effectively hides much of its useful information and its wise guidance from anyone but a city planner. Second, that citizens take insufficient interest in city planning, which results both from how plans hide their virtues and also from how poorly planners elicit important information from citizens. We do not ask important questions, and we only randomly gain access to the experience and creativity many citizens can offer. And third, that planners work at arms' length from elected leaders, which cloisters planners' professional abilities from the people whose decisions determine how a city is developed. In the remainder of this book I will develop suggestions for how to fix the trouble with city planning. Using these suggestions will improve both city plans and the practice of city planning, with the important result of improving cities themselves.

PART THREE

Good City Plans

Fixing the Trouble with

City Planning

TWELVE

City Plans for Citizens

President George W. Bush came to New Orleans three weeks after Hurricane Katrina to promise that his administration would pay to rebuild the ruined city. This was in mid-September 2005, when few lights were shining in New Orleans other than the floodlights trained on the president's portable podium, and the people walking the streets were mostly National Guardsmen. Many elected leaders had not yet returned from places of refuge. But after the president's speech these leaders confidently answered phone calls from inquiring reporters, and declared New Orleans would "come back stronger and better than ever." A plan, they said, would see to it.

The story of plans devised to rebuild New Orleans after Hurricane Katrina is a sad tale that no planner could take pride in telling. A first recovery plan was developed, then quickly shelved and replaced by a second plan. The replacement plan itself quickly proved inadequate and was soon replaced by a third plan. This plan, too, was found deficient and replaced. Five different efforts to draft a rebuilding plan for New Orleans were undertaken in three years, during which time few parts of the city were rebuilt and only a fraction of the pre-storm population returned, despite early promises by elected leaders that a plan would bring citizens back. Evidently, creating a plan that provided for the city's recovery was a more elusive goal than anyone had thought in the first weeks after the storm.

The failures in those five efforts are common to most city plans, though the disaster New Orleans suffered made the failures easier to identify. My purpose here is not so much to describe what a recovery plan for New

Orleans should have been but rather to describe how all city plans might be made better.

In the summer of 2007, nearly two years after Hurricane Katrina, a plan to recover the city of New Orleans was at last adopted. This Unified New Orleans Plan met the federal government's requirement that all seventy-two city neighborhoods be included in a recovery scheme.[1] Few citizens bothered to read the hundreds of pages that made up the Unified Plan. Frustrated by a surfeit of plans over the space of two years, New Orleanians merely supported the latest plan carte blanche. The citizenry knew that this fourth plan was necessary for the city to receive the long-promised federal funds that would achieve a nominal full recovery ($14 billion, the plan estimated)—and that only by receiving these funds could New Orleans finally be rebuilt (a ten-year effort, the plan also estimated).

In addition, New Orleanians supported this most recent plan because, according to the consultants hired to write it, the plan envisioned restoring *all* damaged neighborhoods. Citizens of New Orleans—a designation that included displaced residents who were waiting in Georgia and Texas and Oklahoma to return home—supported the Unified Plan because they believed its result would be that they would someday live in neighborhoods unchanged from the days before the storm had changed so much. The plan's supporters (whether or not they read the plan) urged the city council to adopt it.

However, there were critics among the few citizens who did read the lengthy Unified Plan. One voice complained that it did not designate which neighborhoods faced a high risk of future flooding and a low likelihood of quick repopulation—and therefore, the plan was flawed for not helping displaced New Orleanians decide whether their return was worth the effort. Another critic noted that the plan suggested ninety-five different capital projects—such as building new flood protection devices and modernizing the pumps to remove floodwaters from the city. According to the plan, these projects would "repair or correct the effects" of Hurricane Katrina, and also "ensure that a similar disaster" would not occur. However, the critic noted that the Unified Plan provided no maps to show where these recommended projects should be undertaken, and therefore the plan actually offered no vision for how to redevelop New Orleans. A few other criticisms were made—the most blistering by planners who worked for the city planning commission, who faulted the consultants' plan for being "more indicative of the authors' personal and/or political views [about the best vision for a rebuilt New Orleans] than representative of public input."[2]

As a consequence of the criticisms, the consultants modified their plan—added a few maps and inserted a few direct quotations from citizens to prove that the authors' views actually represented public input. And another draft was quickly released for review. But again, most citizens did not read the newly revised document, and the general sentiment among New Orleanians and their elected leaders was impatience, since most felt that further criticism would delay the release of federal funds conditioned on the Unified Plan's adoption. In response to this sigh of public sentiment, the city planning commission voted to adopt the plan in June 2007, and the city council voted to put the mayor's recovery director in charge of investing the federal money as it arrived.[3]

Little more than a year after the Unified Plan was adopted, however, there were many indications that this fourth plan was not bringing about the vision of a rebuilt New Orleans that citizens believed it had promised. Federal recovery funds had not arrived as quickly as expected, and restoration was consequently slowed, particularly in the fifty most severely damaged neighborhoods where it was typical to find only one or two houses whose owners could afford to rebuild. There, surrounding houses were either demolished or unrepaired, with muddy watermarks on their exterior walls to remind passersby of how high Hurricane Katrina's floodwaters had risen three years earlier. Partial restoration of a neighborhood was not the result citizens had expected.

Furthermore, despite the fact that most New Orleanians were renters—not owners—of their homes, the federal government had not awarded reconstruction funds to owners of rental property. Throughout the city there were many still-uninhabitable apartment buildings awaiting restoration—including many in the high-ground neighborhoods where actual homeowners (non-renters) had rebuilt their houses soon after the hurricane. Here and there, a few apartment owners secured private financing to rebuild their properties, believing that the federal government would eventually repay them. But because so few undamaged rental units were available, most New Orleanians could not return. For them, there was little evidence that the Unified Plan was fulfilling its promise of restoring their city.

Plus, and improbably, the federal government decided to demolish several public housing developments in the city, projects that had contained more than five thousand dwelling units and that were undamaged by Hurricane Katrina. All public housing complexes had been boarded up immediately after the storm, with the federal government (the landlord there) explaining that its action would prevent looting after New Orleans was evacuated. However, the buildings remained boarded over and unoccupied after two years—despite inspections that proved they were entirely inhabitable. And again, little provision had been made by the Unified Plan for displaced residents of public housing. They, too, could not return home—as the plan's vision seemed to imply.[4]

In addition, there were so few health-care facilities operating in the city two years after the hurricane that many homeowners put off their return until they felt assured that medical services would be available. Yet when the city approved the Veterans Administration's proposal to build a hospital in a different location from where the storm-ruined VA had previously stood, residents near the new location complained that the Unified Plan was supposed to rebuild the city as it had been before the storm—not in some new way. Before Hurricane Katrina the VA hadn't been in their neighborhood, which meant to these residents that constructing a new VA was contrary to the plan's promises.[5] Using a similar logic, citizens living in restored neighborhoods complained when the city council authorized restaurants in residential areas and apartment buildings adjacent to single-family houses. Restaurants and apartments had not been located in these neighborhoods before the storm, and therefore citizens concluded that these uses were contrary to the plan's vision of restoring all neighborhoods.

The problem that the Unified Plan encountered—and that caused consternation about its vision among New Orleanians—was that planners and citizens often do not understand the same words the same way. Planners' seemingly simple phrase in the plan that said "restore all neighborhoods" lay at or near the heart of the citizenry's various dissatisfactions. Apparently, citizens thought (or hoped) that the plan forecast New Orleans being rebuilt as a replica of itself before the hurricane. Planners, however, would not—and in the case of the Unified Plan, did not—intend such a replication because their professional aspirations always seek *improvement,* rather than copying what had been before. For planners, replicating New Orleans would mean extending the results of bad land-use decisions made in the past—such as allowing residential areas near landfills or on land predictably vulnerable to floods, or authorizing bars near elementary schools, or approving subdivisions beyond the reach of city services.

The Unified Plan forecast an improved city—a city where the plan's recommendation to build ninety-five large capital projects would solve some of New Orleans' most nagging problems. For example, the plan proposed renovating the city's failure-prone pumping system that became crucial whenever hurricanes, or even heavy thunderstorms, flooded neighborhoods. In all its particulars, the estimable plan took on the fierce challenge of rebuilding New Orleans: to restore the city so as to give its citizens what the old city gave them, even though the new city would look different. With the phrase "restore all neighborhoods," planners had meant no more than that rebuilding could occur in any part of the city—that no neighborhood was deemed unrecoverable.

Citizens' misunderstanding of the Unified Plan's language could have been resolved through public discussion. No such public discussion was inaugurated. It should be said that the evident mood among New Orleanians was fatigue with more planning meetings, even if such meetings might have resolved faulty understandings of the plan and given citizens more confidence about the future it intended.

But because the needless misunderstanding of "restore all neighborhoods" was not resolved, the most troubling part of this sad tale from New Orleans was still to come. Only a year after the Unified Plan was adopted in 2007, the city planning commission announced that it was seeking consultants to write still another plan—a Master Plan. The city council agreed to budget funds for this additional plan because so many constituents complained that the Unified Plan was not bringing about the future they believed it had portrayed. This time, the planning commission chose another team of outside consultants, who likewise invited citizens to participate in yet another series of public meetings. The resulting plan, consultants said, would express a "Vision of New Orleans' Future Together."

The announcement of this new plan was of course worrisome to the New Orleanians who had no complaint with the Unified Plan and were busy rebuilding their houses *as they thought that plan*—the fourth—had encouraged them to. What might this Master Plan be, citizens wondered, alarmed that it might imperil the investments they'd made to restore their homes.

As well, displaced renters—including former residents of public housing complexes—were not mentioned in the planning commission's announcement of the Master Plan, and they worried this plan would take no more interest in their plight than previous plans had. Citizens who lived in the single-family neighborhood where the city council had authorized building a hospital, despite what the Unified Plan said, now worried that land-use decisions based on the Master Plan would be no more predictable. Still other citizens wrote letters to the *Times-Picayune* that questioned why it was necessary to start over again. Could the Unified Plan have been so flawed that nothing could be salvaged from it?

Each of these unaddressed worries originates in a misunderstanding between citizens and planners: about the purpose of plans, about what services plans provide to citizens, about how plans are used when city councils make land-use decisions, and about why a new plan would be formulated as if no previous plan existed. Such fundamental misunderstandings about city plans exist in all cities, though they were garishly highlighted in New Orleans by a quick succession of several plans written in three years for the single purpose of restoring the one ruined city. In most cities, plans remain in effect for about twenty years, during which time various dissatisfactions among a citizenry—or their leaders or their planners—about the course of their city's development cause them to think a new plan is necessary. However, the local dissatisfactions might or might not have been a result of the old plan—but instead a result of a variety of other civic events that affect development: new enthusiasms among a citizenry, vicissitudes of the local economy, decisions by the federal government to open or close military bases, and so forth. Furthermore, local governments and newly elected leaders are impatient to enact new policies, and it therefore seems more expedient to write a new plan than to figure out what, if anything, was wrong with the old one during the twenty years it was in effect.

An oddly positive aspect of the efforts to plan New Orleans' restoration after Hurricane Katrina is that the quick sequence of plans offers a unique opportunity to pinpoint what was so unsatisfying about each plan that it was so quickly replaced.

* * *

"Significant and useful" was a phrase the young Woodrow Wilson, a professor of politics, used to characterize activities he believed municipal governments should undertake to inspire a "distinctive city spirit." Wilson was writing decades before city planning became a profession. Still, his words command our attention today in thinking about improvements for city plans. A plan could become *significant* if citizens could just be made to understand its purpose and benefits, if citizens knew how to use a plan and if they did use it. Wilson's optimistic spirit is contained in the notion of a Good City Plan—a term this book will explain. And again New Orleans, with its sad tale of planning in the ruins, will be relied on to dramatize the necessity for such a plan.

Finding a better way to formulate plans is always the planning profession's fundamental task. In just the past few years, various planners at annual conventions of the American Association of Planners have proposed a great variety of "new" plans, including strategic plans for short-term problems, neighborhood plans for individual parts of a city, and sustainability plans to preserve the environment.[6] All these "new" plans offer innovations to an audience of American planners, and in my professional life I have tried to make use of them all. Yet the debilitating flaw all these "new" plans share is that they do not seem to be formulated for the purpose of making a plan useful to the public.

Even the most innovative plans have one or more crucial shortcomings that prevent their becoming significant and useful documents to citizens' lives—prevent them from becoming Good City Plans. Most plans are so voluminous that citizens resist reading them. Few plans explain their purpose in terms citizens can understand, and typically avoid discussing problems that have existed so long they've been deemed unresolvable. Finally, plans ordinarily do not provide continuous records of how—and how successfully—cities have tried to influence the course of their development. Paying attention to the reasons behind each shortcoming might allow them to be overcome.

As an example of excessive length, one consultant who worked on the Unified Plan in New Orleans forecast that it would contain two thousand pages of text. His promise implied, one can only suppose, that the plan would be extremely thorough, perhaps encyclopedic, regarding everything necessary to restore and plan New Orleans. And by being so thorough it would be better than previous plans for the city's recovery. Although the final version of the plan shrank to several hundred pages, this too was a length only a planner (and not a citizen) could tolerate.

To demonstrate how poorly most plans explain their purpose, I'll quote the sentences I myself wrote in the introduction to New Orleans' 1999 Land Use Plan:

> As a part of the vision included here, the Plan foresees preserving the best of what has happened in New Orleans—sometimes by chance, such as the mixture of uses that developed historically—while it recognizes the need for planning to address existing land use conflicts and to prevent incompatible development in the future.
>
> In recognition of the hopeful fact that *good* ideas may occur, a land use plan accommodates flexibility while emphasizing the importance of a reliable mechanism for evaluating unanticipated proposals.
>
> The goal of this [plan] is to present agreement about ways to steer change in our city, based on modes of development which sustain and support the community in a sensible and responsible manner.

Apart from the lamentable writing, each sentence in the paragraphs above relies doggedly on planners' terminology or professional jargon: *address existing land-use conflicts; reliable mechanism for evaluating unanticipated proposals; support the community in a sensible and responsible manner.* Planners understand the latent meaning of these words, and also the particular public policy that each phrase is advocating. Planners continue writing such sentences into plans as if all other readers understood them too.

Citizens who are not planners, however, are likely to be hard-pressed to read and decipher language like this. Much more usefully, plans could translate jargon into explanations ordinary citizens can understand. As an example, I've rewritten the statement of purpose from the 1999 Land Use Plan.

New Orleans is a three-hundred-year-old city whose gradual development certainly began with a plan—a plan drawn up by the French government for how to build a new port on the Mississippi River. The port thrived and the city grew—but without a subsequent set of revised plans.

Until the twentieth century New Orleans was developed according only to how individuals put their land to use: as industrial plants, as housing, or as commercial enterprises. City government's role during this period of expansion was not to plan, but to construct roads as they became necessary, and to provide essential public services such as water and sewerage systems to accommodate random development.

Only in the past seventy-five years has New Orleans adopted plans for guiding growth. However, over time—that is, over three hundred years—New Orleans has become a city with a distinctive character that is prized by its citizens.

The primary purpose of the 1999 Land Use Plan is to preserve New Orleans' distinctive character even as future growth and development occurs.

However, this plan has been written because the same development that gave New Orleans its distinctive character has often been accompanied by land-use conflicts. These conflicts involve new traffic congestion, new noise, and environmental pollution that new uses of land have caused. Another purpose of this plan, then, is to solve these conflicts, which are a part of the city's past and present life.

Looking to the future, this plan anticipates that new land-use proposals will be made, but that they should not be incompatible with what already exists in New Orleans—its distinctive character. This means that proposals for making new uses of land must neither disturb neighbors nor harm what citizens value about the city.

Deciphering and making more felicitous the planners' infelicitous jargon contained in the three earlier sentences has resulted in a substantially longer text. Though if citizens could understand the translated purpose, they would perhaps not quarrel with its length and would read it. The above translation is not necessarily how, exactly, a plan's purpose should be explained. Each city is distinct—and certainly has a different history of development from that of New Orleans, as well as different problems that its own plan might resolve. Therefore, each city's plan will have a purpose distinct from plans in all other cities. Translating the jargon planners used in New Orleans is meant only to demonstrate that the purpose of any plan must be rendered in language that most citizens understand.

In addition to being too long and also having poorly explained purposes, a third shortcoming of most city plans is that they fail to take up intractable problems. I saw this failure vividly when, after Hurricane Katrina, a reporter asked me if the city could have done something differently in the past to prevent the calamitous floods of 2005. I took her question as a broad inquiry into New Orleans' city government—and answered that the levees should have been stronger, poor citizens should have been evacuated earlier, generators in hospitals should not have been located on ground floors, all policemen should have been on duty, and so on. Government, in sum, should have exercised foresight. The reporter's question remained on my mind, however—although I have rephrased the question to ask whether *city planning* should have done something differently when we made the 1999 Land Use Plan.

"Yes," I can only answer, "we should have done more than what the purpose of the plan describes. That plan should have included a frank discussion of the severe problems that led to the tragedy of Hurricane Katrina: that people lived in areas predictably vulnerable to floods, or lived in houses built on slab foundations rather than on raised piers that would allow floodwaters to flow under them harmlessly, or lived where land was subsiding beneath them, increasing the likelihood of their being flooded. The plan should have emphasized the importance of solving those problems before a tragedy occurred."

But New Orleans' severe and long-standing problems were not acknowledged in the plan. Instead, the city was described as being afflicted with nothing more severe than generic "land-use conflicts": small bars encroaching into residential areas, auto-repair shops operating among "nice" commercial areas, fraternity houses disturbing the peaceful atmosphere of a single-family residential neighborhood.[7] When this plan was adopted, however, New Orleans citizens and New Orleans city planners well knew that low-lying areas of the city would be overwhelmed by hurricanes and floodwaters, despite the protection that levees supposedly provided. In addition, New Orleans planners (myself included) were certainly aware that the city had overextended its budget to provide services in outlying New Orleans East. But the plan made no mention of the connection between authorizing new development in the future (which the plan presumed would happen) and the city's over-stressed budget. Planners also knew that people living in the Lower Ninth Ward were isolated from the rest of the city. Yet in the 1999 plan there was no discussion of how the city could draw them closer.

Most city plans do not discuss such seemingly unresolvable problems, and for a variety of reasons. Citizens—particularly those not affected—typically do not want to think about them. Elected leaders believe that solving such problems would be either politically unpopular (if, for example, their resolution required relocating all vulnerable residents to safe neighborhoods); or solutions would be prohibitively costly (if, for example, resolution required installing expensive new technology throughout a city). And because both citizens and their leaders tend to be in virtual denial about such difficult matters, planners themselves—perhaps sensitive about their typical failure to persuade using professional logic—don't seem to like to think about hurricanes and earthquakes and wildfires either.

Failure to discuss intractable problems lends a difficult moral dimension to plans and planning, even as the failure renders plans insignificant. Because no matter how unpleasant it is to think about and to discuss such problems, paying attention to them at least implies the problems are worth thinking about and *can* be thought about. No one knows where creative solutions might arise, or what might provoke innovations, but if a plan does not acknowledge difficult problems, it fails to even suggest that creativity and innovation are welcome.

A plan for restoring New Orleans after Hurricane Katrina could certainly have included a frank discussion of the city's many persistent problems laid bare once again by the tragic flood. A recovery plan could also have at least acknowledged that thousands of displaced New Orleanians couldn't come home until there was a plan specifically for them. By frankly discussing these apparently unthinkable problems, planners and citizens and elected leaders could perhaps have been provoked to seek new ways to solve them. Devastated New Orleans could have been rebuilt differently, but still have provided its citizens much of what the old city had. Instead, a plan for rebuilding New Orleans still remains a most elusive goal.

The final shortcoming of most city plans is how they are revised. As explained earlier, all cities make land-use decisions inconsistent with what their plans suggest, and they do so for reasons any interested citizen could recite and even appreciate: more jobs are created, more tax revenue is collected, an increasing number of tourists are attracted if unforeseeable opportunities are seized. Irrespective of the reasons that explain these natural inconsistencies, the cumulative result is that a plan becomes less and less accurate in its portrayal of the city and of how future development should be guided. At some point, usually several years after a plan is adopted, city planners declare it to be "out of date," after which they convince elected leaders to hire outside consultants who will write a new plan. In almost every such case, the resulting "new" plan replaces the "old" plan in its entirety. In most "new" plans, planning consultants routinely describe the sequence of plans that a city has previously adopted. But it is rare that these consultants also analyze those earlier plans to discern contents that might actually remain pertinent and useful. In effect, new plans generally start with a blank slate, as if the planners writing them believe that analyzing previous plans would not yield useful information. Apparently, it is easier to start over—as each succeeding team of consultants did when writing the succession of plans for restoring New Orleans.

Much is lost in this history-blind method of revision, including the good ideas that all plans—no matter how out-of-date—inevitably include. Though the most important loss incurred by starting over each time is that a city maintains in its civic memory no continuous record of how the city has grown, how it has solved (or not solved) its problems, and how it has (or has not) provided what its citizenry desires. Nor is there an ongoing record of the new problems citizens routinely discover, nor of their new desires for civic improvement. Great cities are themselves continuous entities, even those cities that have undergone such destruction as New Orleans saw. And if a city's plan were also continuous, rather than episodically replaced with an entirely new document, the city might make use of past experience to guide future development.

A Good City Plan overcomes the shortcomings common to most plans.

It is of a length that citizens would and can read. Its purpose is explained clearly, using language that means the same thing to citizens and to planners. It discusses problems that seem unresolvable and it acts as an evolving document that is never entirely replaced. These qualities might appear difficult to achieve, although city planners already have the resources necessary to craft Good City Plans.

THIRTEEN

The Trouble with Most City Plans

All city plans are documents that reflect efforts by citizens, planners, and city executives to identify, rationalize, and manage future changes in how land is used. These are changes to what might be called a city's physical environment (where buildings are built, streets constructed, parks provided, and so on). Planners understand city plans because they've been trained to write, read, and use them.

On the other hand, city executives—mayors, council members, and heads of municipal agencies—understand plans because their duties *require* them to. For example, and at least ideally, to authorize new uses of land city councils must take into account whether their action would help achieve the goals of a city's plan. In another example, to qualify for federal financial assistance to rebuild New Orleans after Hurricane Katrina, the city's mayor and his recovery director were required to have a *plan* for reconstruction.

However, the great majority of citizens have no specific necessity to understand plans, nor do citizens share planners' training, their vocabulary, or even their particular interest in how a city's land is used. And partly for these reasons, citizens—planners' core constituents—frequently become confounded when they seek to make sense of city plans and try to put them to use.

What confounds most citizens is that a plan's good intentions are often imprecisely worded *in the plan itself.* As described earlier, this was the case at meetings of the New Orleans' planning commission, where citizens argued—reliant on the 1999 Land Use Plan—both for and against the proposed construction of an Albertsons supermarket. Citizens found, among the plan's many stated purposes, that it sought to "reduce the isolation of the poor." Albertsons assured the commission that its proposed store would specifically advance this purpose. Sited in a poor neighborhood only two blocks distant from the wealthy Garden District, the new grocery, Albertsons argued, was meant to serve both affluent and less-than-affluent customers, who would choose among the same array of food and pay the same price for it. Some citizens agreed with Albertsons' justification. But others found it trivial compared with their own understanding of what constituted reducing poor citizens' isolation. These people believed, for example, that reducing isolation meant that residents of the Lower Ninth Ward should have better access to the rest of the city than two bridges over the Industrial Canal. Indeed, the imprecision of such phrases as "reduce the isolation of the poor" can cause citizens who've been reasonably brought into the planning process not to find plans pertinent. Confusion can reign.

At first glance, it may seem odd that this chapter would take up the process of *writing* plans, since that complex undertaking might seem more appropriate to a technical discussion in a textbook for planners. But a confounding aspect of many plans is that they don't facilitate their own use by citizens, and this is at least partly because of the way plans are written. What, indeed, distinguishes Good City Plans is that their contents *are* accessible and understandable by any reader interested in using them. Therefore, this chapter will describe how to write a Good City Plan by relying on resourceful involvement of those very citizen-users.

In the actual process of writing a typical city plan, planners invite citizens to participate in public working meetings at which planners pose to those citizens a series of questions meant to establish consensus views of the city's hoped-for future. Those questions might be: "How would you like to see your city look in twenty years?" or "How do you want your neighborhood to change in the future?" or "Where should new apartment complexes be located in the next twenty years?" or "What new land uses would make your neighborhood a better place to live in the future?" In the conversations these questions inspire, planners typically expect citizens to respond by standing and verbally providing information that planners can then combine with their own professional knowledge into statements that express what planners believe the citizenry envisions their city could become. Such statements, written by planners after public meetings are concluded, constitute what they call the "goals" of a plan. Taken together these goals are what planners mean when they speak of a plan's vision.

In these dialogues that take place at working public meetings, some citizens of course provide very good answers to planners' questions. Citizens identify where new parks could be situated, where public libraries would be more convenient within neighborhoods, where big-box stores could be located so as *not* to cause traffic congestion. Citizens might suggest that new skyscrapers not be allowed to cast shadows over residential neighborhoods, or that public restrooms be constructed in areas frequented by tourists, or that the city provide landscaping along all major thoroughfares.

But in these public meetings, many citizens also offer what are essentially inadequate answers—inadequate to the needs of guiding a city's future development. As discussed earlier, some answers are constrained by the past, essentially describing a desirable future as a return to some halcyon version of years gone by. Other citizens respond with a vision founded on what they believe—often wrongly—residents of other neighborhoods already enjoy. Still other citizens frequently offer vague responses to planners' questions by, for example, advocating that the "character of a city, or of a neighborhood, *be maintained*," but without first defining the attributes of that "character."[1] And other citizens often respond by foreseeing a future city in which, apparently, the budget for civic improvement is unlimited. Many citizens, as it happens, offer little response whatsoever when asked where necessary public facilities such as garbage collection centers should be sited in the future. In my professional practice—in Maine, Montana, New York, and New Orleans—inadequate or nonexistent answers outnumbered good answers by a wide margin.

Few of these inadequate answers turn out to be purely wrong, inasmuch as all our sense of the future is tempered by the past. And to an extent, we all desire civic improvements in part because of what we see in other neighborhoods. Indeed, we all wish for a bountiful municipal budget and prefer not to be reminded of the "ugly" necessities of urban life. But for planners' purposes such responses are inadequate because plans can never return a city to a fond (often inaccurately recollected) reincarnation of itself, or create money for a municipal budget, or correct a misapprehension about life in another neighborhood. And because citizens' answers about the future are often inadequate in these ways, citizen participation is itself rendered inadequate. Planners are left to rely on their own vision of a city's future when they sit down to write a plan—an unlikeable fact, since citizens later come to find that their expressed (but inadequately articulated) wishes have apparently not been included in the plan and are not likely to take effect. Citizens are confounded.

Yet these same citizens are often in fact acute observers of their own city and come to meetings with valuable experience to share. Think of the woman who was alerted and alarmed by the prospect of a "snowball" stand opening in her neighborhood. Admittedly, her vivid testimony about drug dealing at such enterprises was offered in a discussion of a specific land-use decision, rather than in a question-and-answer session about a new city plan. But in this same manner, citizens are often intimately attuned to important urban dynamics and are themselves living repositories of vital information. City planners and the plans they create lose legitimacy and public support when they fail to discover such knowledge.

The small case of a snowball stand suggests to me that if planners, relying on traditional modes of inquiry, fail to elicit the best intelligence from citizens, then at the very least better questions are necessary. Why, one wonders, would professional planners resort to such unproductive techniques for gaining potential vital intelligence? Conceivably, to put the best interpretation on the matter, planners have been trained to conceptualize a city's future as holding unlimited possibilities and therefore do not want to close off possibilities by asking questions that might be too directed. However, the open-ended questions are themselves uninformed and for that reason only haphazardly elicit informed responses from citizens.[2]

An equally important result of failing to provoke citizens' intelligence is that citizens themselves lose interest in planning . . . and in plans. New Orleanians desperately needed a plan for recovering their city after Hurricane Katrina, so they returned time and again to planning meetings where they answered the same questions posed by succeeding teams of planners. Their complaint of "planning fatigue" was shorthand for their unrewarding experience: inadequate questions had produced inadequate responses; the plan crafted by each of several succeeding teams of planners was subsequently found inadequate; and the cycle of attending planning meetings began anew. In other cities, facing less desperate conditions, citizens' experience is often the same: they answer planners' questions, then realize, on reading the resulting plan, that their answers were ignored when planners articulated the "consensus" vision. Just as in New Orleans, these citizens are eventually less likely to attend public meetings convened to develop subsequent plans, and at the end of the day are unlikely to read and use them.

Nothing that I have just described about failing to engage citizens is unknown to planners. But our profession has not spent sufficient effort to remedy these long-standing deficiencies by, for instance, imagining better questions to unearth what citizens know. And again, the regrettable outcome is that many plans do not accurately portray what a citizenry hopes will be improved in its urban circumstances. Planning fails.

Despite having the simply expressed purpose of making a city better as new development occurs, city plans are of course always complicated documents. The first complication arises because plans must guide development of land—development that results both from public investment (as in the construction of new city streets or parks, paid for by government) and from private investments (such as apartment buildings or grocery stores, paid for by property owners or speculators). A plan should be written so as to tell its reader-users about guiding both types of development. Most complications that are inherent in plans—and in planning, itself—pertain to writing a plan that can address the competing conceptions a citizenry holds about just how these two broad categories of development should go forth.

With regard to public development and investment, city plans must, for example, be written to accommodate the view of citizens who think a city itself should finance new public works to solve existing problems. Old streets should be rerouted away from residential areas; public parks should be opened in poorer neighborhoods that have none. Plans must be made also to take into account citizens' demands that a city should attract new economic activity, or encourage construction of low-income housing by reducing property taxes on such dwellings.[3] Every city and every citizenry has a similar slate of good ideas for publicly financed civic betterment. Any one of these ideas is expensive and must compete with all other good ideas when elected leaders compose annual budgets. Still, over the course of several years and several annual budgets, a city can in fact successfully invest in many of the improvements citizens advocate in their city's plan.

As for guiding private development and investment, plans must designate the best locations for a variety of land uses that a city will predictably require and that will be met by individuals developing land they own. A citizen-owner of a vacant field might contend that his property is an ideal location for a subdivision of single-family homes—which will provide more housing, more tax revenue, more jobs—and for this reason his proposal should be approved because it would fulfill these mandates common to all city plans. Other citizens with competing interests, however, might argue that the best location for a new subdivision should be limited to property where adequate public infrastructure already exists or where schools have classroom space for additional children, thereby conserving municipal expenditures. Thus do conflicts over future development arise.

In public meetings pursuant to writing most plans, planners encourage conversation among participating citizens about the ideas they hold for improving the city—for instance, where future subdivisions should be located. In this conversation, some ideas will prove unworkable and be dropped; others will be easily agreed to by a majority, while still others will represent strongly held minority views—many of which conflict. All the ideas that survive the conversation are deemed to have merit because they reflect the variety of shared, conflicting, and competing views that naturally exist among a citizenry. A planner's task is to elicit and express a citizenry's ideas. Again, these ideas are the goals that compose the plan's vision.

All plans encompass such conflicting goals for how to improve a city, and actually most plans contain the information necessary to help citizens who're using the plan decide whether to support or oppose a specific development proposal. But the material is often not accessible to individuals who have no training as planners. Many plans indeed are flawed not by a lack of useful content but by their being organized according to a logic that only planners can navigate. And as a result of not being useful to citizens, conventional plans remain ineffectual civic documents when land-use decisions are made.

In essence, what you've just read is a description of the problems found in most conventional city plans: that they confuse citizen users; that they represent planners' vision rather than a vision that could be discovered from citizens' acute observations and experience. And because of these common problems, citizens lose interest in city plans and city planning, ultimately becoming resigned to their city's poor land-use decisions.

Good City Plans are imagined to overcome these problems. Such plans state their nature and purpose clearly: that the plan is an expression of how the citizenry, working with city planners, believes a city could be made better. The plan is specifically designed to provide necessary information for citizens to use so as to influence land-use decisions. Because a Good City Plan is useful to citizens when they want to support or oppose land-use decisions, they are likely to maintain their interest in city plans and city planning. To encourage these results, the plans are organized into three sections whose titles respect what a citizen-user will find in each and which will help citizens be effective when land-use decisions are made.

The first section of a Good City Plan is called the State of the City because when using it, a citizen will find descriptions of a city's current situation in terms of how land was used there at the time the plan was written: what had already been built and the problems prior development had caused, as well as who lived in a city then, what those people valued from life there and what improvements they desired. The State of the City also provides an accurate catalog of a citizenry's agreed-upon ideas for how a city should itself invest in new development, and simultaneously keeps these ideas in the forefront of civic attention.

The second section of a Good City Plan is called Projections for the Future, and in this section a user will find inventories of land uses that were deemed likely to be proposed in the years following the plan's adoption. The third section is the Citizen's Guide to Future Land-Use Decisions. This guide informs citizens about the questions they should ask themselves, as well as ask planners and elected officials, regarding current land-use proposals the plan did not foresee. These questions will determine whether the proposed new uses advance the goals of the plan, thereby improving the state of the city.

The next three chapters of this book discuss how each section of a Good City Plan is formulated, and a fourth chapter will describe how the good ideas contained in such a plan are activated.

FOURTEEN

Formulating Good City Plans

The State of the City

The first two parts of a Good City Plan—the State of the City and Projections for the Future—are distinguishable from conventional city plans primarily for the improved ways by which they elicit and incorporate citizen participation in describing the city's current situation and anticipated changes. This chapter and the one that follows describe briefly what these sections should contain, concentrating on how citizens can participate in formulating the sections themselves.

In describing how land is used, the State of the City section of a Good City Plan provides a portrait of who lived there when the plan was written and of how citizens experienced life in the city—what they found precious, what difficulties they met, what improvements they desired as new development went forth.

The information in this section is principally distinguishable from what is found in most conventional city plans primarily for the improved ways that Good City Plans elicit and incorporate citizen participation in formulating the overall plan itself. Indeed, most city plans routinely include an initial assemblage of factual information, which planners refer to as "baseline" data for the fact that it establishes basic characteristics of a city at a single moment in time—the moment the plan is written—thus enabling subsequent change to be measurable. In most plans, planners first set about describing a city's physical environment by establishing and stating how land is currently used there—where streets and highways and public transit lines exist, where people live and the kind of housing they live in, and also where commercial and industrial enterprises operate, where land is used for schools, public parks, and such civic buildings as libraries, post offices, and police stations. Beyond a description of a city's physical environment, most plans also offer the user a city map on which different colors depict where land has been put to various uses: residential, commercial, public, and so on. In addition, most plans generally summarize data about the physical environment in statistical tables that set forth the percentage of a city's land devoted to each use.[1]

Near the beginning of the plan, planners normally include narratives that explain certain facts about a city's physical environment. They write about noteworthy land-use changes that have occurred since a previous plan was adopted—such as large new subdivisions that were built, or manufacturing plants that ceased operation. Another typical example of narrated factual information regards land whose use is governed not by the city but by agencies of the state or federal government. In New Orleans, Louisiana law gives the State Dock Board authority over maritime uses of land lying along the Mississippi River. But the law does not require the board to comply with the city's plan. By describing and including in the city plan areas where the plan has no jurisdiction, planners alert citizen-users that entities other than the city have authorized plans that might affect their property. Plans written for different cities obviously include different factual information, but whatever set of facts is employed to describe a city's *physical environment*—how land is used there—gathering those facts and installing them at the commencement of the plan is a task for planners. Citizens need not be involved.

Most city plans also provide facts about a city's *human environment*—who lived there at the time the plan was written and under what circumstances. Planners summarize these data in charts that describe the citizens in such terms as their median income, age, years of schooling completed, and race. Plans usually summarize facts about where people lived by employing statistical tables that show, for example, the dollar value of homes, the percentage of residents who lived in rental dwellings, and how much they paid, plus the quality of the housing stock and the number of units that were vacant. In addition to these charts and tables, planners include narratives regarding recent and noteworthy changes among a local citizenry. After Hurricane Katrina, the total number of New Orleanians who returned home from places of refuge did not include many of the poor, nor did the total returnees include many of those who had lived in rental housing before the storm. These missing sectors of the population, as it turned out, were mostly African-American. Any city plan written for New Orleans could be expected to specify this change in the city's racial composition: before August 29, 2005, the citizenry had been predominantly black, but soon after it became predominantly white. Again, the factual data and the narratives that contribute to conventional as well as to Good City Plans are material planners would gather and write without involving citizens.

But conventional plans and Good City Plans diverge significantly on this point—where both set about describing for their users those important aspects of a city's human environment that are not purely factual, but that could be said to be anecdotal and experiential. Here I'm referring to how the conventional plan and the State of the City section gather information by different means from citizens during the public meetings planners convene as part of the process of writing a new city plan itself. This is information about the experience of living in neighborhoods: what citizens cherish, worry about, or fear, what they believe could be improved on their streets, what long-standing problems need to be solved—in other words, much that contributes to the plan's goals and its vision. Although the drafting of most plans elicits and includes citizens' perceptions, Good City Plans are unique in the ways they delve, discriminate, and organize these particular experiential and consequential responses to city life.

In their attempt to construct the State of the City section—so that users will maximize the plan's value—planners, prior to meeting with citizens, frame questions that seek to elicit useful experiential information from them. Planners inform their questions by undertaking background research from several sources. They will study, for example, previous city plans to discover what former citizens experienced in their city—what they found valuable, and so on. Planners would also read accounts of prior land-use decisions to determine the reasons citizens have given for objecting to various development proposals. And planners would meet with people who work in other city agencies that routinely meet with citizens—the library board, the city recreation department, to name only two obvious entities—to enhance a sense of what a citizenry values and hopes for.

An example of the type of background information planners gather in the process of formulating questions for citizens can be found in the 1999 Land Use Plan for New Orleans. Among the enumerated qualities of life reported for that year, citizens felt especially strongly about three broad areas, and the particulars they listed under these groups would serve a planner well as source material for drafting questions. First, citizens placed high value on

- a strong sense of community in their neighborhoods
- large parks
- a "fifteen-minute city," where they have easy access to all they want and need to do.[2]

Second, citizens were especially concerned about a number of land-use *problems* needing to be solved:

- they did not like adult entertainment adjacent to residential neighborhoods, which was not compatible with a family living environment, and decreased the level of safety;
- they felt that a particular intersection was overcommercialized to the detriment of residential neighbors;
- they did not like residential streets being used as a detour for commercial vehicles.[3]

Finally, among *improvements* citizens desired:

- they wanted parks, schools, and other city properties to be upgraded and maintained;
- they wanted roads to be resurfaced throughout the city;
- they wanted streetcar lines and bike lanes to be designed and built.

These excerpted samples demonstrate the kind of basic and specific information planners can glean from previously adopted plans, information that can then be brought forward to inspire more informed questions and to provoke citizen intelligence.

At public meetings planners would put on display the results of their research from earlier plans and other sources, and then ask citizens attending the meeting whether adult entertainment was still a problem in residential neighborhoods; or whether New Orleans was still a "fifteen-minute city" and whether this remained a valued attribute. Planners would likewise ask if bike lanes had been designed and built, and if so, whether they had proved to be the improvement citizens in 1999 had forecast they'd be. The answers to such directed questions reveal to planners—and to citizens themselves—how the human situation has specifically changed, and what has perhaps become more or less important since a previous plan was adopted.

In addition to what they find in previous plans, planners will also frame questions for citizens by drawing on their own experience and training. For example, planners in any city know that there are long-standing and unresolved problems that previous plans have avoided: neighborhoods threatened by recurrent flooding or lying in the predictable path of forest fires. By including in their preparation for public dialogue this intelligence gained from specific problems they've encountered and by framing questions that draw on a citizenry's own experience, planners can find—and include in the plan—fresh ideas for how these problems might be solved.

To their preliminary researches, planners would add the issue of land uses that most citizens prefer *not* to think about. I'm referring to landfills, sewage treatment plants, detention centers, welfare offices, and any other necessary but unwelcome uses of land that all cities must provide but few citizens want to live near. To structure a useful discussion about where each such facility should be built (as it becomes necessary), planners would prepare a map of the city on which, for example, several alternate sites for a jail would be shown, as well as a listing of historical factors that led to the choice of the sites shown on the map—proximity to a police station or a criminal court, or proximity to residences and schools, and so on. Planners would then ask citizens to choose among the sites . . . or to suggest other, more suitable locations . . . or to interject other, more appropriate factors to be considered.

A final piece of work planners would complete before public discussion and writing the State of the City involves conceiving questions about budgetary matters. Planners might ask, for example, if citizens would be willing to forgo any of the city services they currently receive in order to receive others. Or, they could focus citizens' attention on the fiscal effects

of development by preparing a pro forma budget that calculates the anticipated tax revenue new subdivisions bring—and conversely shows the cost
of providing municipal services to those same subdivisions. The question
to be posed to citizens would ask whether they supported requiring new
subdivisions to show a net fiscal benefit to the city. Again, asking informed
questions allows planners more useful access to a citizenry's useful perceptions about the future state of their city.

In this short discussion, I have done no more than sketch how planners
prepare material and devise questions whose common purpose is to discover citizens' knowledge of their human experience—knowledge that will
help formulate the State of the City section and the goals and vision of a
Good City Plan. As is surely implicit, such questions must be tailored to
any particular city's circumstances. But once the research is done and the
questions are framed, planners can set about accurately gathering citizen
responses. The process of posing the questions in public forums convened
to help write a plan might require several meetings, since igniting citizens' intelligence can be a lengthy, probing process and lead to tumultuous discussions. In any case, at the end of these more (or less) tumultuous
meetings and questionings, citizens will have thoroughly discussed and,
it's hoped, found greater agreement about what they value in their human
environment, what problems that environment presents, and what public
improvements citizens desire.

At the conclusion of these public meetings, and with crucial agreements
achieved, planners will have the information necessary to write the State
of the City section. As described earlier, this section begins with baseline
information displayed in statistical tables, explanatory narrative, and color-
coded maps that planners create to represent a city's physical environment
and its human environment. Depending on the resources a city wishes
to devote to describing factual information, the State of the City section
might also include maps depicting the elevation of land throughout the city,
thereby highlighting—in cities such as New Orleans—the neighborhoods
most susceptible to flooding. Other maps could use color codes to illustrate
features of a citizenry's income, indicating where the wealthiest and the
poorest citizens live. Again, the number and character of such maps would
vary according to what is of most interest in a particular city.

In the State of the City section, planners narrate the results of what has been deemed, by consensus, as important for the plan to portray about the situation of the city at the moment the plan is written. Again, planners will have created three categories of concerns citizens agree are important: what they value in their city, what problems they want solved, and what improvements they desire. As they write the text explaining these concerns, planners will define items whose meaning is not immediately obvious—such as what "reducing the isolation of the poor" means in a plan for New Orleans, or what calling New Orleans a "fifteen-minute city" refers to.

When planners complete the State of the City section of a Good City Plan, they will have satisfied the expectations of citizens who open a plan and attempt to understand its purpose, as well as better appreciate the city around them. In its particulars, this section describes those planning issues a citizenry wishes their elected leaders to pay heed to as future development proposals come to be made.

FIFTEEN

Formulating Good City Plans
Projections for the Future

The second section of the model Good City Plan is dedicated to inventories of new land-use proposals most likely to occur in the city, as well as expressions of where the local citizenry prefers such new development would be located. As before, most city plans contain such projections. What distinguishes projections found in Good City Plans is how they are developed in close concert with citizens.

New development proposals in a city arise in ways and for reasons that are almost always responsive to the local economy. In a thriving economy, a city's population typically increases as more people come and find work, new commercial enterprises open, new subdivisions develop, and apartment buildings are constructed. As an example, the owner of the proposed casino on Canal Street in New Orleans stated that its operations would require five thousand employees, after which local economists projected twenty thousand *other* jobs would be created to meet the economic consequences of the new gambling enterprise. All of the projected jobs—those at the casino, and those that served and resulted from the casino—would customarily eventuate in new land uses becoming necessary in the city. In New Orleans, these uses were predicted to include additional hotels to house a new stream of casino customers, additional restaurants and catering firms, additional livery businesses to chauffeur gamblers to and from the games, even additional schools for training blackjack dealers; and of course, additional workers would need housing.

On the other hand, a stagnant economy brings with it an entirely different set of prospects. When the 1999 Land Use Plan was written, Harrah's casino had become a stable part of the local economy, and was neither inspiring new development nor attracting new employees. And with few other prospects for economic growth (most oil companies had long since fled), the city's chronic population loss was expected to continue at a rate established in the 1980s. People would simply continue to depart the city, economists observed, seeking work elsewhere. As a result, planners forecast few proposals being made for new subdivisions, new hotels, and new commercial enterprises.

These examples from New Orleans characterize the forces that bring about—or fail to bring about—development and development proposals in any city. And they attest that before a useful and reliable city plan can be written, planners must establish projections for how a local economy is likely to change during the period the plan foresees, how the population—its numbers and demographic composition—is likely to change over the same period, and what land-use changes are likely to result from whatever the plan helps bring into existence.[1] Most conventional plans offer projections. But a Good City Plan again relies on unique and better methods of involving citizens to arrive at these projections, making the plan more useful.

Even in a stagnant economy, of course, entrepreneurs will always detect demand for new uses of land. Because so-called big-box stores such as Lowe's or Target or Home Depot can offer a wide variety of goods at low prices, developers can envision a potential profit from building these stores even when other new enterprises might be expected to fail. Or, among the wealthier citizens of a city (more immune to the general economy), developers may perceive an unanswered demand for new shopping malls organized around posh department stores, or for subdivisions organized around golf courses. In other words, every year finds developers devising new ways to use land.

In anticipation of meeting with citizens to determine what a new plan might include regarding future land uses, planners using the Good City Plan model would seek out descriptions of alternate schemes other cities have used to arrange development as it occurs.[2] Based on their research, planners would subsequently create three or four city maps, each depicting an alternate pattern for arranging projected new development throughout the city. One such map might cluster future housing around public transportation facilities; a second map might arrange new land uses in a pattern that preserves open space. Still another map might focus all future development onto ground that is safe from floods or forest fires. Planners would then be prepared to superimpose these maps of alternate development patterns onto a copy of the existing land-use map found in the State of the City section. By these means, each map of future development possibilities would encourage a participating group of citizens—joined in an effort to write the plan—to visually grasp the differences among alternatives and to notice how new development might fit what already exists, as well as how each alternative reflects citizens' different desires for the future.

As a part of their background research in preparing the Projections for the Future, planners would scout recent national development trends and popular new forms of commercial enterprise occurring in other cities or other countries, and be prepared to discuss in public meetings the planning issues each might bring to the fore. For example, "cohousing" is the ugly name widely used to describe the Danish design for a "living community" in which small clusters of houses are arranged around jointly owned grounds. In some permutations, the jointly owned property includes a house where communal meals are cooked and where guests can stay. Advocates of cohousing believe homeowners will enjoy an increased sense of community by interacting with one another in the common areas. The issues planners would raise about cohousing and introduce in a meeting dedicated to writing a Good City Plan might involve how to adapt the model to fit already existing neighborhoods, or communities where residents live in rental houses.

After gathering background information and preparing alternate maps of future land-use patterns, planners would be ready to convene public meetings to discuss with citizens how this second prospective part of the Good City Plan should be written. At these meetings, planners would explain their background research. They would describe projected changes to the local economy and resident population, and then detail the land-use proposals each change has the potential to cause. Planners would also narrate new trends in development, such as land uses that other cities have seen and that might become popular locally.

Planners would then pose to the attending citizens questions specifically formulated to elicit their most considered responses. Planners would ask citizens to look through the background information—presented in an accessible way—and identify omissions, discuss future trends in development, or add any other land-use proposals that citizens might know of. Following this discussion, in which those in attendance would focus on projected land uses, the audience would be shown the maps planners had prepared to portray three or four alternate patterns that future growth might follow. The rationale of each growth pattern would be fully explained and discussed—again, one map showing housing clustered around public transit stops, another exhibiting preserved open space, and so on.

Having explained the maps, planners would ask citizens for their reactions to the development that each map projects. A lively conversation would no doubt ensue, since citizens typically express very different and very firmly held ideas regarding where they believe new automobile dealerships, big-box stores, low-income housing, parks, and so forth should be located. Furthermore, once they look closely at planners' alternately mapped patterns of growth, citizens might perceive a different—and better—pattern from what planners propose. Throughout the meeting, as citizens suggest modifications to the alternate maps, or as they suggest drawing new ones, planners would revise the maps to display what's being described.

At the end of the meeting—or series of meetings, if more than one is necessary to hear all interested citizens' views—a single map would be determined, depicting agreement about where future land uses should be located. Most city plans include such a final map portraying a city's future physical development. But what distinguishes the Projections for the Future map contained in a Good City Plan is the highly organized and focused participatory process by which it was created. By preparing alternate maps of development patterns for public perusal and study, and by inviting citizens to criticize those maps and even to offer their own, planners can acquire more refined conclusions than by merely asking citizen-participants the more typical and haphazard question: Where do you think future growth should go?

Depending on the economic circumstances of any individual city, additional projections of future development might also be appropriate, and require additional maps for public discussion. Where voters have approved a bond issue to build a new stadium, separate maps might project foreseeable demands for using land adjacent to the stadium. Or in a city where the federal government has agreed to subsidize a new high-speed rail project, projections might include changes likely to arise near any designated station. Irrespective of the specific type of anticipated development, the plan will ultimately describe every projection and every alternate map created with the assistance of citizens whose goals and vision the plan will clearly embody.

At the conclusion of these public meetings, planners then write the Projections for the Future section. The contents summarize pertinent projections of economic and demographic change, describe foreseeable development that will likely accompany such change, and include a supportive map showing how citizens prefer future uses of land to be distributed throughout the city. Again, the refined preparation and discussion that are integral to the Good City Plan model are in behalf of the users of the plan who will open it, seeking guidance for their own efforts to engage the planning process long after the plan is written and adopted.

SIXTEEN

Formulating Good City Plans
Citizen's Guide to Land-Use Decisions

Unfortunately, despite the care that might go into devising any city plan, most cities do not develop precisely as their plans propose. Therefore, the third section of a model Good City Plan is imagined to help citizen-users of the plan cope with the fact of development proceeding differently from what even a Good City Plan has specified.

Land-use decisions enacted by city councils are the primary mechanism that causes cities to develop differently from how their plans envision. Yet it should be reiterated that most development in a city does not require city councils to make land-use decisions at all. Normally, the city's zoning ordinance—which is predicated on the city's existing plan—authorizes most uses that property owners propose and set in motion. New single-family houses, for example, are *allowed by the zoning ordinance* in all residential districts and require no new governmental decisions; new shops are also *allowed by ordinance* along all commercial thoroughfares. New industries are *allowed by the zoning ordinance* in industrial zones. Typically, no additional authorizing land-use decisions are made for such activities. All fall within existing land-use ordinances.

City councils, then, are typically asked to make new land-use decisions only when proposals are unique and unforeseen by an existing ordinance (a casino in downtown New Orleans, for example), or when an otherwise allowable land use is proposed in a heretofore unauthorized location (an apartment building on the site of a hot-sauce factory). In each case, before the new use can proceed, elected leaders are required by law to review it to determine if the new use would be beneficial to the city. If leaders find the proposal beneficial, they generally authorize it. If not, they generally don't.

Landowners propose previously unauthorized uses (or uses in previously unauthorized locations) primarily because they are convinced there is a defensible rationale for what they propose. One such rationale might be that an unperceived demand for the new use is now perceived. Another rationale might be that if a city doesn't authorize a particular proposed land use, businessmen will take their business to another city, or to the suburbs. Because both city plans and zoning ordinances only reflect the state of the city at the time of their adoption, it is not unusual that these documents would lag behind more up-to-date changes in citizens' real needs and desires, and that landowners' rationales for unauthorized uses would become defensible and find their way to the city council.

A series of events in New Orleans will serve as a case in point. As the city's economy began to recover from the oil-bust years of the 1980s, young professionals moved to town, many of them choosing to rent apartments in the French Quarter. The number of French Quarter vacancies then decreased and landlords there—noting a shortage—increased their rents. Watchful developers soon saw a new market for converting obsolete industrial buildings located *near* the French Quarter into apartments. And since neither the city's plan nor its zoning ordinance had foreseen such uses, new land-use decisions to authorize these evidently beneficial conversions became necessary.

The chain of events that culminates in all unplanned land-use decisions begins when a landowner submits an application obtained from the city planning office—an application that requests approval of an activity not currently authorized. When city planners receive such an application they institute a public legal notification stating that it is received. In pursuance of this notification, planners then send letters to property owners whose land is near the newly proposed use, and publish this same notice in the city's newspaper. Planners then assess the application to determine how the newly proposed activity might affect the adjacent properties and how it is consonant or not consonant with the vision of the city's future as expressed in the city's plan, after which they write a report of their assessment and publish their findings.

Next, the planning commission undertakes consideration of the application, and also of planners' conclusions about the proposed use. The commission convenes a public meeting where it listens first to the applicant's description of his proposed development, and then to any observations concerned citizens express about the proposal. After consideration, the commission makes its recommendation to the city council for how it should vote on the application. Eventually, the city council reviews the planning commission's recommendation, holds its own public hearing, and then votes to approve, deny, or modify what the landowner has proposed. The protocol for all these procedures is customarily described in a city's land-use regulatory documents (such as the zoning ordinance).

However, the description of these procedures as found in the zoning ordinance typically offers no information to an interested citizen seeking to learn the standards that a land-use proposal would or would not be required to meet for a city council to authorize it. Having no information about such standards, citizens with an interest in a proposed land use are routinely in the dark about how properly to frame pertinent arguments for or against a particular application, and are often prevented from full participation in the planning process. For these reasons citizens are routinely in jeopardy of being baffled and alienated by decisions of a city council.

The Citizen's Guide section seeks to remedy this crucial lack of information. A user of a Good City Plan would find in this section a clear rehearsal of the standards that proposed land uses are required to meet, and that citizens can understand and usefully apply in advancing and framing a point of view. "Standards that proposed land uses must meet" is a planner's expression, best rephrased in the ordinary language of a citizen as: "What we should know about a proposed land use before agreeing that it should be authorized." The Citizen's Guide contains clear language and clear guidance for any citizen who wishes to oppose or support an unplanned-for land use. This guidance takes the form of specific questions devised by planners and provided to citizens to be used in the event that planners or elected leaders fail to ask them. Thus, users of the guide always have an opportunity to insist on answers during public hearings before city councils reach a decision about new development proposals.

In writing the Citizen's Guide, planners prepare a group of questions that draw directly on concerns now familiarly expressed in the State of the City and Projections for the Future sections of the Good City Plan. These questions for citizens' use relate to how a proposed development will affect the human environment: namely, will the new development affect a city's valued attributes? Will it solve problems that need solution? And will it bring about improvements a citizenry desires? Other questions pertain to the location of a proposed land use: will the new use lie where the map of future land use (in the Projections section) designates such development should occur? If not, then why is the proposed use appropriate to a location different from where the plan has suggested?

As noted earlier, reiterating these questions and concerns throughout the plan establishes coherence and a clear continuity among all three sections of the Good City Plan, and in so doing creates an internally consistent and ultimately more intelligible document for citizens to use in appraising unexpected land-use proposals.

Finally, users of the Citizen's Guide will find several questions that seek to disclose the possible effects that unanticipated land uses might exert on their proximate surroundings. These questions must be formulated by using the Good City Plan model of public discussion—the model used to write the State of the City and Projections for the Future sections—and as such require citizen participation.

In preparing for public discussion, planners rely on their professional training. They of course are aware of the more generalized textbook ways by which various uses of land produce adverse effects. Planners can, for instance, accurately predict the amount of increased traffic a new commercial enterprise will occasion, and can calculate in advance the air and water pollution caused by new industrial plants. They can also estimate how much parking will be necessary to accommodate tenants of new condominiums.[1]

Planners also know several techniques of visualization that depict a proposed land use in three dimensions, thereby allowing citizens to "see" how a new building or a new subdivision will look in the context of its environs. And planners know that new land uses can cause fiscal effects in cities—bring on additional tax revenue, but also elevate the cost of providing municipal services.

Based on their professional knowledge, planners drafting the Citizen's Guide devise an array of questions with which users can glean the effects an unforeseen land-use proposal will cause. For example, one question would propose an applicant "show" the appearance of his proposed development among its neighbors. Another question would ask an applicant to estimate the tax revenues his project will add to the city's budget, and also estimate how much the city will be required to pay for providing municipal services such as fire protection and garbage collection.

Planners will next convene a public meeting to consider questions that will ultimately be installed in the Citizen's Guide—again, questions citizens will use in public forums such as city council meetings where land-use decisions are made. Planners will discuss the questions they have drafted one by one with citizens in a meeting convened for this very purpose. Planners can expect to justify each question they propose. Citizens might dispute the need to ask a prospective store owner to provide a projected daily schedule of deliveries. Planners would answer that the purpose of the question is to prevent delivery trucks from arriving at times when children who live nearby would be walking to and from school. Through the course of these public meetings by which the Citizen's Guide is written, planners might successfully advocate their questions—or else amend them. If questions don't seem worthwhile to citizens who are participating in writing the plan, those questions would be deleted.

In addition, planners will add questions that the public thinks are missing. Citizens are almost always keenly aware of how one land use can affect its neighbors adversely. From having lived with the consequences of various land uses, citizens know about the poor air quality near interstate highways, as well as the expedient and disruptive routes delivery trucks take through residential areas. In addition, citizens often fear the outward appearance of any new use—whether it will dwarf adjacent buildings or somehow compromise the traditional symmetry they perceive in an existing neighborhood. Finally, from the combined intelligence expressed in the public meeting—what planners know and what citizens know—a final set of questions can be agreed to, and planners can install them as the Citizen's Guide section of a Good City Plan.

Thus, writing the three principal sections of a Good City Plan would be complete. A citizen who opens the State of the City section of the plan will find descriptions of the current conditions in a city, the attributes its citizenry values, as well as the problems that need solution and the improvements the citizenry desires. In the Projections for the Future section, a citizen will find a description of the nature of land-use decisions likely to arise, and a description of where new land uses should be located. Finally, in the Citizen's Guide section, the user will find the pertinent questions a city and its residents should ask about future development proposals *before* those uses are authorized. By drawing on intelligence and questions from the previous two sections of the Good City Plan, the Citizen's Guide integrates the entire plan into a coherent and highly useful document.

SEVENTEEN

Activating Good City Plans

Of course, the good intentions of any plan—whether a Good City Plan or a conventional plan—must be activated for a city's future to be as assured and made as intelligible as humans can make it.[1] Planners' most usual and frequently used strategy for activating a city's plan following its adoption is to revise the local zoning ordinance so that it reflects the vision of the new plan and assures that individual parcels of land will be developed in accordance. The revised zoning ordinance is, in effect, planners' principal instrument whereby a city plan is executed. In the specific case of a Good City Plan, this strategy for execution means amending the zoning ordinance so that it matches the map of future land uses depicted in the Projections for the Future section.

No matter what sort of plan a revised zoning ordinance seeks to execute, most landowners develop their parcels according to—not in opposition to—how they are zoned. Thus, most new development is fundamentally influenced and directed by the zoning ordinance, and as a result most new uses of land match what a plan and its zoning ordinance portray as a citizenry's vision of the future. The significance of a Good City Plan is best appreciated by noticing how useful it becomes when landowners seek to develop their property differently from those ways authorized by the plan and the zoning ordinance.

All state constitutions require that cities provide citizens a means of arguing for legal authorization of their intended land uses. To comply, cities design application forms for individuals seeking such authorization. The application form officially initiates the process of consideration whereby a proposed development is authorized or not authorized. And this authorization most commonly seeks a change in the zoning ordinance—in ways that have previously been discussed.[2] As unlikely as it may seem, then, the second significant mechanism for "executing" a plan (after revising the zoning ordinance) is the design of the application form property owners complete when they seek to change the zoning ordinance so it allows a previously unauthorized use of their land. The application form is commonly represented in the zoning ordinance itself, but is a publicly obtainable document. Designing this form might seem a prosaic task, but it is a highly consequential duty of city planners. Indeed, the design of the application form—and the form's subsequent use by citizens—distinguishes Good City Plans from conventional plans.

A city evolves, in part, as individual landowners seek to develop their small parcels of land. Typically, most urban landholders own title to parcels that are but a few hundred square feet in area, or at most a few acres, and as such these holdings compose only a tiny portion of the large amount of land that makes up a city. Yet if owners' use of their relatively small holdings could be precisely restricted to what the plan deems appropriate—as expressed in a zoning ordinance—eventually a city will be built as the plan has forecast. However, the possibility that people can—and *do*—imagine inventive and beneficial (and unauthorized) uses for their land can often make for a livelier city. For this reason, attempting to restrict all uses of land to what a plan has foreseen at the time of its adoption—and that the zoning ordinance formally stipulates—would suppress potentially desirable and dynamic responses citizens make to urban life. It would also likely be impossible to achieve.

A Good City Plan acknowledges that what enlivens any city is frequently a product of the unexpected. And in that vein, an application form to allow a heretofore unanticipated land use becomes an instrument by which property owners can prove that their proposed new uses of land will indeed contribute to the future betterment a citizenry desires. Again, it must be noted that planners design application forms for zoning ordinance changes in most all city plans. But the reimagined application form devised for a Good City Plan allows property owners a greater opportunity to argue in behalf of authorizing their proposed uses. The newly conceived form achieves this by relying on concerns expressed in the three principal sections of the plan: the State of the City, the Projections for the Future, and the Citizen's Guide to Future Land-Use Decisions.

All application forms for land-use decisions ask an applicant to describe his proposed development by providing details about how it will be constructed on a parcel of land. Such details include, for example, disclosing the distance a proposed building will be from structures on adjacent parcels of land, revealing where necessary parking will be provided, noting whether any landscaping will shield the proposed use from its neighbors. These construction details are regulated by provisions of the zoning ordinance, and serve to advance the goals of conventional plans as well as Good City Plans.

The distinguishing feature of an application form designed to activate a Good City Plan is that in addition to asking applicants to provide descriptive details of their proposed uses of land, the form also affords applicants an opportunity to justify their request for zoning changes in the terms specific to the plan itself. As described previously, the Projections for the Future section of the plan denotes those locations where citizens have agreed different types of land uses should be located in the future, and designates those locations on a map of the city. The first opportunity the new form provides whereby applicants can justify their proposed land use originates in this section of the plan. The application form specifically asks whether applicants' proposed land uses lie within an area designated on the map as suitable for their type of development. And if that is not the case, the form allows applicants to put in writing—on the form itself—explanations for why their individual proposals should be approved, despite being contrary to the plan and the zoning ordinance.

Applicants are also offered the chance to answer questions—again, on the application form—that originate in the concerns of the State of the City section of a Good City Plan. For example, an applicant can justify his proposed development in terms of how this use will affect each item included on the three lists of civic goods the plan has projected will result from future development. As described earlier, the first list identifies the features of a city that citizens value and want to preserve; the second list names the problems that exist because of the way land has been developed in the past, and that a citizenry wants solved. The third list is of improvements that citizens desire future developments to provide. These three lists of civic goods—components of the plan's vision—are attached directly to the application form, and applicants are asked to describe how their proposed uses of land will affect the items on each list.

Finally, the application form offers applicants an opportunity to respond in advance to objections citizens might voice regarding the proposed developments. The Citizen's Guide section of a Good City Plan contains questions whose answers determine whether a proposed use of land will adversely affect adjacent, already existing land uses. Some questions pertain to traffic a proposed use might create; other questions pertain to whether the proposed use will "fit in" with the neighborhood. By knowing the questions that citizens will pose, an applicant can design his development so that the questions are answered affirmatively.

In a city that has adopted a Good City Plan, a copy of all questions from the Citizen's Guide is attached to the application form, and applicants are directed to answer only those that pertain to the particular land uses they envision. Obviously, more questions and answers would be required to prove that an industrial enterprise would fit in with its neighbors than would be needed to prove that a multiplex movie theater would not harm the operations of a nearby shopping center. Proposing a small apartment building among one- and two-family houses would require answers to even fewer questions to prove its compatibility with the surrounding neighborhood. By posing these questions and citing these civic goods, the application form derived from a Good City Plan invokes and integrates the entire plan and makes it a forum for public deliberation regarding unforeseen land uses, and in this way helps activate the plan itself.

No plan contemplates all citizens being satisfied by all land-use decisions. Not only can every effect of new development not be foreseen (that is, *planned* for), but each and every decision a city council makes regarding the use of land means that improvement occurs in some neighborhoods but not in others, that some problems are solved while others aren't. Therefore—and inevitably—each and every land-use decision a city makes will disappoint some set of citizens and please others. A Good City Plan contemplates what *is* possible—that citizens can determine, on balance, how well their leaders' land-use decisions have served them, and can participate by returning to office only those leaders whose decisions have generally complied with the city's adopted plan.

Though a Good City Plan can be understood and consulted by citizens whenever the city is called upon to make a land-use decision, the premise of such plans does not contemplate the impossible situation of all citizens being satisfied by all land-use decisions. However, when citizens enter the planning process by basing their arguments and observations specifically on such a plan, elected leaders will then feel pressure to take greater account of those very citizens—and of the plan itself. One could call this an indirect method of convincing elected officials to use their city's adopted plan. But there are more direct methods that planners could employ when convincing elected leaders, and such methods are a worthy topic of discussion.

EIGHTEEN

How Good City Plans
Influence Elected Leaders

In early autumn 1994, a few months after New Orleans' new mayor took office, he and I were invited to address an association of retailers whose stores resided on Canal Street—the city's principal downtown shopping district. Canal Street had once been provided with fashionable department stores, fine luggage shops, a renowned music store, and distinctive jewelry merchants known throughout the South. But by the early 1990s, tennis-shoe emporiums, pawnshops, and discount gold jewelry bazaars were now strewn among the remnants of the old thoroughfare's bygone mercantile elegance. The historic jewelry store—New Orleans' version of Tiffany's—still operated at its original location but was by then in the shadow of the city's new casino, still under construction a few blocks away. "What City Hall Can Do to Bring Business Back Downtown" was the topic this group of local boosters wanted to hear the mayor and the director of city planning discuss.

Before our speeches, the mayor took me aside to tell me that before each biweekly meeting of the planning commission, several of its members (my bosses) routinely called him to ask whether he wanted them to approve or deny any items listed on their agenda. Time and again, the mayor said, he'd encouraged the commissioners to decide planning dockets only on the merits of each case rather than on his say-so. And yet they continued to call him every two weeks. He was late this very morning, he said, because several planning commissioners again had called to ask how to vote at their meeting scheduled for later in the day. I said I would explain to the commission the ethical perils its members were tempting by such phone calls, after which the mayor and I finally turned to address the Canal Street shop owners—encouraging them to participate in the new land-use plan that I would explain during my portion of the morning's program.

At that afternoon's meeting of the planning commission, I brought up the subject of ethics, and reviewed the state's constitutional provisions for planning boards, summarizing several relevant judicial rulings. I concluded by saying to the commissioners that land-use decisions should not be made during the course of private conversations, no matter who the conversations were with. Commissioners asking the mayor how he wanted them to vote, for instance, bespoke political manipulation and for that reason was unethical, even in Louisiana. All the commissioners nodded, and assured me they subscribed to the gist of my overlong lecture—that the public's business had to be conducted in public.

Months later the mayor told me that the phone calls from planning commissioners had never ceased, nor was he surprised that they hadn't. I realized that what he'd said to me before the Canal Street speech hadn't been a complaint. Instead, it was a confidence, meant to reassure me that he wouldn't interfere with how the planning commission voted. In the subsequent eight years that I worked for this mayor, he was good to his word.

Of course, this mayor's lack of surprise about the continuing calls from planning commissioners is itself not surprising. Both he and I knew that previous mayors' practice had been to speak to commissioners individually whenever important issues arrived on the planning commission's agenda—such as approving the downtown casino, or denying a competing riverboat gambling enterprise, or considering a proposed site for a necessary new landfill. These issues are the large, albeit rare, planning subjects that mayors take an interest in. Smaller planning matters such as zoning changes to allow Albertsons in an uptown neighborhood or the Preserve Apartments in a defunct hot-sauce factory simply don't rise to the level of mayoral concern.

As a consequence, planning commissioners typically have little contact with a mayor once he's appointed them. And perhaps because some of my commissioners had expected a closer intimacy with the mayor, they—in later conversations—told me they felt "in the thick" of government only when the mayor pressured their votes. Indeed, they believed that calling the mayor was nothing more than showing their support for the administration's new policies. He hadn't told them how to vote, they continued, and therefore in their view no ethical violation had occurred. Furthermore, by eliciting the mayor's view on particular decisions, the commissioners felt they would help make his new administration as efficient as he'd promised it would be during his mayoral campaign. Ethics weren't involved, they said. Streamlined governance was.

You might say that these commissioners had an unusual take on the standard concept of good government. But wherever planning boards and commissions exist, it is typical for members to improperly rationalize constitutionally prohibited behavior in the name of doing service to good government. As a recent *Planning Commissioners Journal* reported, having the opportunity to be a part of good government is the primary reason that planning board members agree to serve their communities.[1]

The American financier J. P. Morgan was the first civic leader on record to imagine the practical utility of citizen advisory boards.[2] Morgan's ideas about citizens' boards were in anticipation of his interest in New York City's Metropolitan Museum of Art. Morgan wanted to encourage the New York moneyed class to make large gifts to the Metropolitan. He determined that if he named the wives of wealthy donors to an advisory board at the museum, he would accord these women the prestige and social standing he believed they liked, which would then encourage the husbands to keep making donations. He had no expectation that these female board members would know anything about art, or about what made museums successful. Morgan's idea was proved correct, and the museum went on with the donors' contributions to purchase many of the important masterpieces that have secured its international renown in the art world.

You might say that an unintentional consequence of Morgan's strategizing was that the function of advisory boards has grown far from its origins and has taken hold in all manner of institutions, including governmental ones. Today, citizens (and not just women) are named to serve on a seemingly infinite variety of public boards, including planning boards. And they do so for a range of reasons, which may include attaining social prominence, allaying personal boredom, satisfying a sense of duty, feeling "in the thick" of public affairs, being a part of good government reform, and doing the board's proper business.

Planning boards (also commonly known as planning commissions) were first constituted in America when the idea of a planning profession itself took hold during the Reform Era of the early twentieth century. Mayors typically chose influential civic leaders to serve as board members on the theory that these leaders could persuade their peers that planning (something reform mayors by the time wanted) was a worthy activity of good government. In New Orleans, for example, housewives seated on the city's earliest planning commissions were identified as "civic ladies"—meaning, one can suppose, that they had a wide circle of influential citizen friends who might take an interest in talking up the virtues of city planning and good government. The male commissioners, as it happened, were mostly real estate agents known locally for being knowledgeable about real property and land values, which made them credible when they talked about planning to hard-to-convince citizen landowners.

In the 1920s, most state legislatures adopted what is known as "enabling legislation" to authorize planning as a function of local government. Typically, a state's enabling legislation stipulated that citizen boards were responsible for planning—that is, for adopting a city's plan, following which city councils could adopt land-use regulations such as zoning ordinances to carry the plan out. Thereafter, landowners would be able to undertake only such activities as the city plan and the zoning ordinance allowed. The reasoning that led most states to enable municipal planning was a belief that more stable neighborhoods—those not threatened by such discordant land uses as dressmaking factories located near fancy shops on Fifth Avenue in New York, for instance—would result in increased property values.

A justification for limiting the uses land could be put to, of course, was no easy matter to argue successfully in the United States, where a sense of civic stability was based on the rights of property owners to use their land as they saw fit—not as the government saw fit. Therefore, to be certain that the goals of planning were met, most individuals appointed to early planning boards were not recalcitrant property-rights advocates, but were citizens who had similar backgrounds to those in New Orleans—less tendentious civic ladies and realtors chosen because they could champion planning before audiences of those very citizens certain that they and they alone should determine how their land was used.

Partly because of the efforts of these early planning commissions, and partly because of crucial decisions by the U.S. Supreme Court and thereafter by all other courts in the American judicial system, most cities now have planning boards which operate on the assumption that it is prudent to restrict property owners' use of their land to bring about the underlying goals of planning itself. City plans and land-use regulations have become so widely accepted in America that the city of Houston is all but unique in *not* having such restrictions. Land-use regulation has become such a routine function of American city government that skill in persuading influential friends and property owners about the virtues of planning is no longer a valued requisite for membership on planning commissions.

Though neither is knowledge about the first principles of city planning a prerequisite for planning commission membership. Indeed, there are no requirements except that members reside in the city. This means that commissioners from time to time take idiosyncratic or surprisingly un-orthodox or logically insupportable positions on the land-use matters that come before these boards. In my experience, commissioners can often be persuaded in their decisions by the personality of an applicant. Or they may be moved by how beautifully a proposed project has been rendered by a draftsman. Or they may be persuaded by how many people speak publicly against (or for) a new land-use proposal. Or they may simply want to comply with what a mayor has told them he'd like them to decide. In any of these instances, it would be fair to say the influence of a city's legally adopted plan has receded from deliberations.

As demonstrated by those planning commissioners in New Orleans who consulted the mayor before their meetings, the plain truth is that modern members of citizen boards almost always understand that they have been chosen for their posts because they're likely to vote consistently with an administration's policies. Because this mayor was newly installed in office, some planning commissioners might have been uncertain of what he preferred, and therefore decided to call and find out. The telephone calls—those that the mayor had confided in me—were no more than the predictable legacy of J. P. Morgan's insight about populating citizens' advisory boards.

The only truly surprising aspect of the mayor sharing a confidence about the commissioners was that he did it at all, since—as any planning director knows—mayors rarely confide in them. In institutional terms this is because planning directors are not hired by mayors and typically do not serve at their pleasure, which to a large extent explains the typically distant working relationship between the two.

Most city planning directors are hired by and work for citizen planning boards—a chain of command that has endured since the planning profession was founded circa 1910. At that time, political machines governed most big American cities and policies were decided among politicians without the aid of public discussion. And because city planning—even at its inception—relied on a *public* process that entailed introducing citizens' viewpoints when land-use decisions were made, this new governmental function posed a significant threat to the powers of elected politicians. Progressive reformers could foresee that politicians like those then thriving in Tammany Hall in New York City would insist that planners hired by the city cooperate with what had been predetermined by the machine, or face loss of employment. More important, planners' failure to cooperate endangered the entire basis of city planning itself.

To avoid such a bad outcome—politically influenced land-use decisions or the termination of planning as a function of city government—states wrote enabling legislation for city planning functions which provided that a citizens' board would hire and oversee the work of all city planners, thereby, it was hoped, shielding their work from politics and politicians. The citizens' board—the planning commission—was itself legislatively protected from politics by an additional enabling stipulation that its members could not be removed from their posts based on decisions they made or on the work of the planners they appointed.

Reliant on these protective devices, planning commissions have endured for nearly a century, although the duties they perform have been transformed by changes in American society and governance. Among these changes are that land-use regulations and city plans are now both usual and required by law; citizens have achieved greater knowledge about government—including city planning—because of open-meeting laws and modern requirements that give the public access to official documents and proceedings. More citizens indeed can vote, and more have learned how to organize for political action. Furthermore, most city planners are members of a civil service, and are appointed to their jobs through competitive examinations and are evaluated according to standard tests. As a result of these dramatic changes, the planning function in American cities is reasonably secure, and thus planning commissions' duties have evolved away from eliciting popular support and shielding planners from political influence.

Modern planning commissions now practice city planning by conducting public hearings and deliberating over controversial land-use decisions, although they continue to discharge one of their original duties: hiring a city's planning director (and assistant director). These two individuals—who are usually not members of the civil service—serve at the pleasure of the planning commission rather than of elected officials. And presumably a director's professional work is protected from political pressure just as the commission is. However, and as most planning directors have learned from experience, planning boards have never protected them as textbooks and city charters and good-government organizations prescribe. In practical political terms, most planning directors are not hired without the explicit assent of the city's mayor—and a director may lose his or her job the instant this assent is withdrawn.

Furthermore, because the great portion of any planning director's work concerns land-use decisions made by the city council, directors can also be fired (in effect) by displeased council members who persuade the planning board of "conflicts" requiring the director to be replaced. These are the well-established terms of employment that all planning directors agree to when they assume their position in city hall. But what directors know, or soon learn, is that because they are institutionally "distanced" from council members, these leaders rarely seek planning directors' advice before they decide how to vote on a land-use matter.

To render their advice more persuasive and to gain an audience with policy makers, planning directors are left to find ways of working around the sometimes unwieldy fact that they are not employed by the elected leaders—mayors and city councils—who make land-use decisions. In the course of my career, whenever a city has had to consider crucial development proposals, I've been forced to imagine how to forge a better working relationship with several very different mayors and many different city council members. But my successes—and my failures, too—always depended on the individual personalities of the elected leaders as well as my own personality.[3] In addition, even when I worked well with individual mayors, I did not routinely gain an audience. Only, in fact, when large issues such as a casino arose did our paths seem naturally to cross. As a consequence, I never felt I achieved the close working relationship that, for instance, a public works director or a city's financial officer had with the mayor, who appointed each of them, and who met with them routinely because city business required it.

Nor did I find a particularly close working relationship with city council members, even though their semi-monthly meetings (where I was assuredly present) were primarily devoted to land-use decisions. With these leaders too, my counsel was never *presumed* to be valid or necessary—as the police superintendent's might have been when he advised that his budget should increase to allow additional foot patrols in dangerous neighborhoods. Though some council members looked favorably on the advice I gave, as often as not their indulgence resulted from some agreeable conjunction of our personalities and the particulars of the land-use decision under consideration. In the ways we worked together, nothing was institutionalized or became routine.

The planning profession at large, of course, is well aware of the typically poor working relationships among planning commissions, planning directors, mayors, and city councils. A few cities have adopted a "cutting-the-knot" solution whereby planning directors are chosen by, and work for, elected leaders. Currently, for example, New York City's mayor appoints the planning director, and the director both oversees the professional planning staff and chairs the planning commission. But the success of such an arrangement necessarily relies on the personal attributes of a single leader (one who's willing to hear his director's advice) and a single director (one who knows how to persuade the mayor). This it would seem is a thoroughly idiosyncratic pairing—one that's difficult to replicate or generalize from. In addition, a suitably skeptical observer of city politics might wonder if a director could give objective advice to a mayor for whom she or he directly works. Therefore in most cities the Reform-era tradition continues: planning directors are chosen by and work for a board composed of citizens.

Nonetheless, the practice of planning has seemingly become as secure a governmental function as any other in city hall. But contemporary planning directors still need to overcome their lack of influence on mayors. This lack in good part results from the historical—some would say, vestigial—stratagem of directors working for planning commissions. This book proposes that Good City Plans offer alternate strategies by which modern planning directors can effectively influence elected politicians, whether particular individuals have a positive working relationship—or not.

In our American democracy, the most direct influence on elected politicians comes from voters—who must decide to return or not return a candidate to office. As described earlier, a Good City Plan offers voters an improved— more efficient and more direct—way to assess how well a mayor or city council member has been able to guide growth and new development in the cities they govern, and subsequently to determine as well whether an elected leader has solved the problems or brought about the improvements listed in the State of the City section. And finally, such a plan encourages voters to assess whether the leader's land-use decisions have diminished the qualities of the city valued by its residents. Constituents can also de- termine whether their council members have insisted that developers give satisfactory answers to the questions that appear in the Citizen's Guide section.

Because constituents can evaluate elected leaders' performance by referring to sections of a Good City Plan, council members might be en- couraged to consult the plan before rendering a land-use decision. The plan can also guide a mayor's choice of policy initiatives to be undertaken while in office. Newly elected leaders are diverse. Some come to office with a well-thought-through set of policy ideas conceptualized far in advance of obtaining office. Other leaders have only a vague notion of what poli- cies they might undertake. But for all the diverse levels of preparedness that exist among newly elected leaders, a Good City Plan offers specific direction. The State of the City section includes lists of the improvements a citizenry would like the city to make, as well as a listing of the problems the citizenry would like solved. For example, a desired improvement may be new swimming pools in all neighborhoods, and the mayor might initiate a bond issue to build them. Or a new councilman may initiate a program to tow away the many abandoned cars that litter residential streets, a problem constituents listed in the State of the City section. Still other elected politi- cians may undertake such large matters as fortifying neighborhoods likely to flood. By these means, elected leaders could better justify voters' trust by showing how citizens' aspirations as expressed in the plan have been brought to fruition over the course of a term. In effect, a Good City Plan can influence the policies pursued by a variety of elected leaders, and the city can eventually change as the plan has intended.

A final attribute of Good City Plans is that they require regular evaluation by city planners, who would prepare, say, a five-year report summarizing land-use decisions made over that period and comparing them with what the plan intended. Planners would determine whether new development occurred according to the map shown in the Projections for the Future section. If not, did developers give creditable reasons for locating their projects where the map would have prohibited them? In another example, planners would consider whether new development solved any of the problems—or bring about any of the improvements—listed in the State of the City section. Did new development create new land-use conflicts? Planners would review the questions in the Citizen's Guide section and analyze whether, for example, specific questions asked of prospective developers made development over the five-year period consistent with the plan's vision. When evaluating these questions, planners would review such decisions as were made in the case cited earlier—in which a developer had to provide a virtual tour of the neighborhood where his small apartment building was to be built. Based on their professional skills, planners would figure out whether that requirement led to a beneficial land-use decision. Clearly, planners' judgment is involved, which is an appropriate use of their experience and knowledge. Of course, the specific aspects of the plan that will be evaluated—and how they will be evaluated—will differ from city to city, again depending on local circumstances.[4]

Planners will prepare reports that detail the results of their evaluation, and will conclude with a set of recommended amendments to the existing plan that would overcome any newly arrived weaknesses. Based on such a report, the planning commission—following its usual processes for considering land-use matters—would amend the current Good City Plan, which would then be in effect for another five years, at the end of which another evaluation and amendment would take place. By this legislative requirement of regularly occurring reviews, the plan's execution would be routinely evaluated and improved. Of course, if a city were to undergo substantial change—unusual population growth or unusual devastation such as that caused by a hurricane—its plan could be evaluated more frequently and stringently.

The first time a city goes through the process of creating a Good City Plan, all will seem unfamiliar. However, once the completed plan has been adopted, it becomes in essence permanent, subject only to revisions that improve its workability. For example, changes to the State of the City section might become necessary as some anticipated improvements are completed, as other improvements are desired, or as listed problems are solved and other problems identified. Or, upon review of the Citizen's Guide Section, planners might determine that some questions have not elicited good answers and for that reason should be rephrased. Irrespective of the particular changes suggested by regular review, the result will always be an amended plan, which stands alongside the valuable original Good City Plan. Over time, all these accumulated revised plans will constitute a reliable archive of how a city has changed and developed, and how a citizenry's desires have shifted and been responded to.

As I have conceived this notion of a Good City Plan, the plan is never discarded or completely replaced with another—as is the common practice of city planning throughout America. Citizens and their leaders, and city planners, too, can see where they've all come from and how well they all have improved their city. The plan is therefore a more robust and supple document than other plans, and it is rooted in history.

What city planners know is essential to great cities. Yet what planners know has not systematically influenced the land-use decisions that elected leaders make. This failure of influence—the trouble with city planning—includes three critical and defective aspects of planning practice that have led to this condition. First, city plans are used only by city planners; second, planners miss out on what citizens know; and finally, political leaders can ignore city plans when they make land-use decisions. A Good City Plan can correct these debilitating aspects of professional planners' practice. A Good City Plan is a document that citizens can understand and will use. Planners could provoke the intelligence—and creativity—of citizens when plans are formulated and then implemented through land-use decisions. Finally, city plans could influence the elected leaders who make land-use decisions. Making all of the suggested changes is obviously no small task. But the final short section of this book demonstrates that the effort will be worth the transforming effects it makes possible.

NINETEEN

Good City Plans and Great Cities

September 28, 2008. It is three years after Hurricane Katrina left 80 percent of New Orleans underwater, and only one year after the Unified Plan for rebuilding the city was adopted. Given the extent of reconstruction needed—and given the Unified Plan's forecast that rebuilding would take at least ten years—an interested observer might find it odd to learn that the city would replace the Unified Plan. Yet on this late-September morning the *Times-Picayune* ran a story reporting on the first of what were promised to be forty meetings, all scheduled by planning consultants hired to write another plan for the still devastated city. The first of these meetings had already been held at Xavier University, the historically black college famous for preparing minority students to find rewarding careers. Planners must have thought this would be an inspirational site.

The *Times-Picayune* further noted that the citizens attending the meeting were welcomed by Dr. Norman Francis, Xavier's president and a native of New Orleans, whose distinguished career had brought him a Medal of Freedom from President George W. Bush. Dr. Francis was reported to have said that he saw the meeting "as the beginning of the end of planning"—a perception enthusiastically applauded by his audience, many of whom were citizens who had participated in so many previous meetings that the term "planning fatigue" had achieved wide circulation.[1] However, their fatigue was probably less about the lost hours spent in meetings with planners and more about these citizens' realization that the meetings had not yet resulted in a plan to restore New Orleans.

Evidence of these previous plans' failure was all around the city. Two months after the meeting at Xavier, the *Times-Picayune* ran another story, this one alongside hopeful wire-service reports of President-elect Obama's energetic plans to recover the nation's beleaguered economy. Local prospects, the story said, were less hopeful. On the front page was a color photograph of a rebuilt two-story home in New Orleans—a large house on a corner, complete with an attached two-car garage, a freshly installed lawn, newly laid sidewalks, and saplings along the street front. This pretty house stood "like an island among empty lots," the caption read, and readers could see that its surroundings were the slab foundations from neighboring houses demolished after the storm. The paper said similar "islands" were scattered throughout the city, in every devastated neighborhood. New Orleans, the story suggested, was a long way from being restored. And still—after more than three years—the city did not yet have a reliable plan for its restoration.

The post-Katrina planning experience in New Orleans provoked my search for solutions to what I've called the trouble with city planning. What I have advanced is the idea of a Good City Plan, which would be useful for restoring New Orleans even now, five years after its devastation. But such a plan can also be useful to any city in which citizens are troubled by the results of their city's plan and disappointed by the effectiveness of city planning in general. The most important measure of a plan lies in the benefits that accrue to citizens, developers, planning commissions, and city councils as a city makes various land-use decisions that affect a city's future. There are a number of real benefits for a city that writes and executes a Good City Plan.

The first benefit is that the plan actively elicits from citizens the consequential character of living in a city. As previous chapters have shown, an underrealized power of a citizenry is its ability to observe how land is used all around itself. Citizens notice how different land uses affect their daily lives, and they routinely think about how their neighborhoods might be made better. Yet planners often don't capture such informal—though empirically based—knowledge. Nor do planners routinely discover the creative solutions that citizens imagine for the problems that surround them. With the methods proposed here for encouraging active public deliberation, citizens' knowledge and creativity can be put to the service of a city's future.

A second benefit of a Good City Plan arises from its aim to provide specific protocols with which citizens can frame their support or opposition to particular land-use proposals. By relying on those explicit criteria which the plan puts forward as pertinent to land-use decisions, citizens can frame more persuasive and relevant arguments before their elected leaders. In addition, because the plan provides these protocols, it frames the terms for public discussions that precede all land-use decisions made by city councils. A Good City Plan recognizes that different people—citizens, city council members, planners—may have different and legitimate ways of understanding what constitutes development that is consistent with the plan's vision, and that a civic dialogue regarding a particular land-use proposal offers the occasion to reconcile those different interpretations. By being written to be understandable to both citizens and their leaders, the plan itself can focus public discussion on its vision and on consistency with that vision, and thus yield greater civic agreement among a citizenry—which is always a good thing in a democracy.

A third benefit results from developers and landowners being apprised *in advance* of the questions they'll be required to answer publicly before a city council will approve their proposed projects. The plan itself stipulates the nature of the information to be elicited. Because public meetings are held to draft those questions (as part of writing the plan), landowners and developers might well see an interest in participating in planning activities themselves. And *should* they participate, then the sphere of civic deliberation about a city's future would be widened and enriched. But even if landowners and developers elect not to attend public meetings involved in formulating a Good City Plan, the clarified and practical protocols of such plans might incline them to design projects with an aim to satisfying the questions in the Citizen's Guide.

By requiring developers to respond to concerns contained in the Citizen's Guide, the Good City Plan encourages a wider conversation about the city's future and spreads responsibility for bringing about what a citizenry desires beyond the purview of planners who analyze proposed developments in terms of a plan, as well as spreads the responsibility beyond the purview of elected leaders who often encounter arguments for or against land-use proposals expressed only in self-interested personal terms. Because developers can be induced by the plan to imagine their proposals in terms that accord with it, developers' efforts to justify their projects might provide new intelligence about how to solve civic problems or provide civic improvements—or how to enhance those qualities of a city that are precious to its residents. Innovative and beneficial ideas can occur even to individuals seeking land-use decisions, and the plan gives them the opportunity to advance such creative responses as they design and defend new development.

The premise of a Good City Plan is that growth and change are both natural and desirable in an existing city, but that new land uses must be consistent with what a citizenry expects about its civic future. Obviously, citizens' expectations about the future can themselves shift. A Good City Plan provides landowners and developers clear guidance and an explanation of a citizenry's expectations, and steers developers to imagine proposals that achieve positive answers to the questions included in the Citizen's Guide. This conception of a useful plan is illustrative and suggestive—by which I mean that to be widely useful in cities other than New Orleans, such plans must be tailored to the particular circumstances of individual cities, to their specific and perhaps unique underlying problems and their unique set of citizens.

City planning as conceived here signifies planning that is practiced in *existing* cities, where conflicts and "disruptive" land uses predate the current plan. The concept of planning presented here relies on understanding what constitutes a great city. Great cities are the result of plan, vigor, will, and application. But they are also the progeny of luck and error and intuition and even sudden inspiration—for which there is no predictor, and in the midst of which surprising things just happen. Great cities result from inventive development proposals, from creative ideas for solving long-standing problems, and from innovative solutions to seemingly unresolvable issues. The questions that are contained in the Citizen's Guide section encourage creativity wherever it might arise; but simultaneously those questions mean to mold creative ideas that do not disturb or dismantle or dishearten what citizens value in their city, but instead bring about improvements and solve existing problems.

Great cities also result from accident—from the unintended and certainly unplanned side effects of new land uses shouldering their way into an existing landscape. A New Yorker would recognize that such an accidental side effect was caused by the Seagram Building, set back dramatically from Park Avenue as no other building had been before. The Seagram Building was built to offer a broad plaza that separated it from the street, and New Yorkers—some, to their surprise—discovered that the plaza offered a welcome visual relief from the "canyon" of imposing buildings that lined Park Avenue. The setback created by the plaza was of course fully intentional, designed by the architect to make the building stand out from its surroundings. The accidental benefit of this innovative design was a citizenry's delight that the city's iconic landscape of skyscrapers could provide something more than the usual pleasures of window shopping. Because Good City Plans invite landowners to imagine new uses for their land—and also insist they provide satisfactory answers to questions in the Citizen's Guide—such plans are always susceptible to the beneficial side effects of imaginative development.

The effects of a plan as advanced in this book will accrue only gradually, as citizens, landowners and developers, elected leaders, and even city planners themselves realize the plan's possibilities. The simple explanation of such gradual accrual is that land-use decisions are almost always about small parcels of land, the development of which occurs randomly. And therefore, what any plan accomplishes is always hard to see in a short period of time. Citizens will only gradually—one decision by one decision—realize that the plan has helped them be persuasive when elected leaders make choices about future development. Citizens will only gradually notice that they can actually judge their leaders' performance based on the land-use decisions they make. Daniel Burnham wasn't wrong to say that plans should "stir men's blood" as his magnificent Plan of Chicago did. Good City Plans will stir citizens' blood, but for a different reason: they give citizens a significant voice in how their city grows and changes. Burnham made plans *for* citizens. Good City Plans are made *with* citizens, and are meant to be used *by* them.

Property owners and developers will gradually realize that proposals for new land uses are more likely to be approved if the proposals are designed according to the stipulations of a plan rather than designed simply to secure a majority of votes on a city council. And for their part, elected leaders will very gradually realize that by fixing the trouble with city planning in the ways this book suggests, they can take better advantage of what planners know. Despite nearly a hundred years of considering city planning a remote and inconsequential part of municipal government, city councils and mayors will come to realize that they can use city planners as a virtual in-house think tank when undertaking new policies. Furthermore, elected leaders will gradually realize that solving problems listed in a Good City Plan will provide them a good and measurable record when they stand for reelection.

Finally, and perhaps less gradually, planners themselves can be transformed. The process of creating a Good City Plan draws on planners' training and experience and knowledge about how cities work. And elected leaders will be encouraged—when they undertake policy initiatives—to draw on the considerable abilities of city planners. By fixing the trouble with city planning as this book suggests, professional planners will find that more of their abilities will be put in the service of guiding a city's future. That feeling alone, the feeling that their training and experience is consequential, can inspire planners' own inventiveness in creating great cities.

Lewis Mumford was once asked about how he viewed the future of cities. "Optimistic about the possibilities," he said, "but pessimistic about the probabilities." I take a similar view about fixing the various troubles with city planning. I don't suppose that what I've suggested will work in all cities, or possibly *any* city, precisely as I've conceived it. At best, I expect that many other people—planners and laymen interested in planning—will modify the ideas suggested here to make them applicable. Any city planner would be optimistic only that *some version* of what she suggests is put to use.

In 1718, Sieur Bienville—the French king's designated explorer—returned to a particular sweeping arc of the Mississippi River, a site he'd first visited nearly twenty years earlier. Supposedly pointing his sword at the site of what we now know as the French Quarter in New Orleans, Bienville is said to have declared: "Here. Here will arise a great city." His prophecy took a long time to be realized, but no American doubts that it happened. Despite the destruction caused by Hurricane Katrina, New Orleans has not lost its stature as a great city. It has only suffered a setback.

Of course, New Orleans did not become a great city because of city planning—even though its earliest foundation was a plan drawn by French military engineers. Nor will New Orleans retain its stature because of planning. Like all great cities, New Orleans is sustained by the people who live there and by how these citizens conduct their lives. However, New Orleans would be a better city for its citizenry to live in—and rebuild in—if it were served by a Good City Plan. Such a plan will put an end to plans that only planners can use, an end to plans that do not extract what is on a citizenry's mind, and an end to plans that elected leaders can ignore when they make land-use decisions. Good City Plans are my vision of a hopeful future for New Orleans and for every other city where citizens choose to see plans—as I do—as a path to a better life.

APPENDIX
Plans to Rebuild New Orleans

Elected leadership in New Orleans sponsored five phases of planning efforts to rebuild the city after Hurricane Katrina. Many other plans were written for specific neighborhoods and for specific local organizations, but those plans—good as many of them are—lie outside the scope of this book.

Although the two plans that were ultimately adopted to guide rebuilding New Orleans are easily found on the city's website, the other officially-sponsored plans are difficult to find. This appendix is meant to be useful for a reader who wants to learn more about any plans created during each phase of planning—and about who wrote them.

Planning Phase Number 1
Mayor Nagin's Bring New Orleans Back Commission

The mayor's commission developed a plan in concert with a panel of specialists in urban and post-disaster development, who represented the Urban Land Institute (known as ULI, located in Washington, D.C.). The plan was presented to the public on January 11, 2006, but was never adopted.

Principal planning consultant: Wallace, Roberts & Todd (commonly referred to as WRT, and located in Philadelphia) served as the principal planner, working with several local firms and individuals to write the Bring New Orleans Back Action Plan.

Planning Phase Number 2
Mayor Nagin's Laissez-Faire "Plan"

The mayor's second planning effort was to allow "the market to decide" how New Orleans would be rebuilt. "We chose to go forward with a market-driven recovery effort," he said. "I believe citizens can make intelligent decisions about where to live. It is my position that government investment will follow citizen investment."[1] There is no official document from this planning phase, nor is there a planning consultant associated with it.

Planning Phase Number 3
"New Orleans Neighborhoods Rebuilding Plan"

The city council of New Orleans sponsored this plan to rebuild fifty neighborhoods that had been badly damaged by the effects of Hurricane Katrina. The plan was not adopted.

Managing principal planner: Paul Lambert (Lambert Advisory, located in Miami).

Managing planners: Lonnie Hewitt (Hewitt and Washington, New Orleans) and Alfredo Sanchez (Bermello Ajamil & Partners, Miami).

Other members of the planning team: Billes Architecture (New Orleans), Byron Stewart Architects (New Orleans), Cliff James (New Orleans, member of the American Institute of Architects), Dr. Silas Lee & Associates (New Orleans), Sheila Danzey/SHEDO (New Orleans), St. Martin Brown & Associates (New Orleans), Stull & Lee Architects (Boston), and Zyscovich (Miami/Fort Lauderdale).

Planning Phase Number 4
Mayor Nagin's "Unified New Orleans Plan"

This effort, paid for by the Rockefeller Foundation, was inaugurated in July 2006 and adopted about a year later.

Principal planning coordinator: Steven Bingler (Concordia, LLC, based in New Orleans). Fifteen other planning teams—composed of "internationally renowned" professional consultants, some from New Orleans—were chosen from more than sixty applicants who expressed interest in working on the Unified Plan. These teams included: H3 Studio (St. Louis), Goody Clancy (Boston), Frederic Schwartz Architects (New York), EDSA (Columbia, Maryland), EDAW (San Francisco), E. Eean McNaughton Architects (New Orleans), Burk-Kleinpeter (New Orleans), Williams Architects (New Orleans), HDR and HOK (Tampa and St. Louis), KL&M/CH Planning (New Orleans and Philadelphia), now (New Orleans, Boston, Charlottesville, Virginia), Davis Brody Bond (New York), Torre Design Consortium (New Orleans), Villavaso/Henry Citywide Recovery Planning Team (New Orleans).

Planning Phase Number 5

Three plans were developed concurrently with Planning Phase Number 4.

A. Re-inventing the Crescent

The mayor found expert consultants—planners and internationally renowned "starchitects" to create a plan that would transform neighborhoods in New Orleans that lay along the Mississippi River. This plan was adopted by the New Orleans Building Corporation, an agency of the city.

Lead design consultant: Eskew+Dumez+Ripple (New Orleans).

Other design consultants: Adjaye Associates (London); Hargreaves Associates (Cambridge); Michael Maltzan Architecture (Los Angeles).

B. Target Area Development Plan

The mayor's recovery director created this plan, which identified seventeen areas within the city where reconstruction would be concentrated. The city council used this plan to authorize the recovery director to spend the first $117 million of federal rebuilding funds received by the city.[2]

C. Master Plan

Inaugurated—and ultimately adopted—by the City Planning Commission, this document was described as New Orleans' "blueprint for the next 20 years" that would lead to "the development of a new, user-friendly Comprehensive Zoning Ordinance."[3]

Lead planning consultant: Goody Clancy & Associates.

Other consulting teams: Camiros, Ltd. (Chicago), Concordia (New Orleans), Creative Industry (New Orleans), Mark Davis (New Orleans, Tulane University Institute on Water Resources Law and Policy), EJP Consulting Group (Shoreline, Washington), Fernandez Plans (New Orleans), Julien Engineering (New Orleans), Kittleson & Associates (Portland, Oregon), Mt. Auburn Associates (Somerville, Massachusetts), Perez APC (New Orleans), Villavaso & Associates (New Orleans), W-ZHA (Annapolis), Zimmerman/Volk Associates (Clinton, New Jersey).

NOTES

INTRODUCTION

1. Nelson, *Planner's Estimating Guide*, 2.

CHAPTER 1. CITIES AS PLANNERS SEE THEM

1. Platt, *Land Use and Society*, 177.
2. Early maps of New Orleans sketched a "river-to-lake" canal, which historians contend suggests the canal was "vastly important to New Orleans and its hinterland." Campanella, *Time and Place*, 167.
3. Construction of Louisiana's extension to the Intracoastal Waterway started in 1958, although plans for this second alteration to New Orleans' navigable waterways officially began in 1944, when the Louisiana legislature empowered the state's governor "to aid and assist the Federal Government in obtaining and completing" a tidewater channel to the sea. Accordingly, in 1948, Governor Jimmie Davis wrote a letter of support for such a channel, asserting that it would "permit rapid development . . . and great additional benefits to the Port of New Orleans." U.S. Army Corps of Engineers, *Mississippi River Gulf Outlet*, ii.
4. The average annual cost of maintaining the Mississippi River–Gulf Outlet was $12.5 million (in 2000 dollars), although in the wake of hurricanes and tropical storms, supplemental expenditures were routinely required. U.S. Army Corps of Engineers, *Mississippi River Gulf Outlet*, 4.

    Throughout the 1980s and 1990s, when there was very little barge traffic using MRGO, the Army Corps of Engineers and the shipping industry discussed the wisdom of closing the channel by ceasing dredging operations there and letting it "silt-in." It wasn't until Hurricane Katrina forced water upstream on MRGO, flooding St. Bernard Parish and Orleans Parish, that action was finally taken. When the Corps of Engineers submitted the Final De-Authorization report in June 2008, MRGO was officially closed; simultaneously, construction of a "rock closure structure" was authorized. In July 2009, the "closure structure" was completed, and MRGO was no longer a shipping route to the Port of New Orleans. U.S. Army Corps of Engineers, "MRGO Navigation Channel Closure," *MRGO: Mississippi River Gulf Outlet,* www.mrgo .gov/MRGO_Closure.aspx.

5. A full—and highly readable—account of the development of New Orleans East can be found in Magill, "Rushing into the East."

CHAPTER 2. INTIMATIONS OF TROUBLE

1. Leading the effort to craft the Bring New Orleans Back plan was the Philadelphia-based consulting firm Wallace, Roberts & Todd (often referred to as WRT), which had written a variety of plans for New Orleans over a period lasting more than thirty years—starting with the 1974 Growth Management Program that created the "downtown development district," one of America's first special improvement districts. The firm was co-founded by Ian McHarg, the venerable planner who wrote *Design with Nature.* In that seminal book, McHarg argued that plans should take natural geographic circumstances into account rather than try to overcome them. Professional planners would easily find McHarg's guidance in the Bring New Orleans Back plan, wherein low-lying areas were designated as parkland (rather than as residential areas) so as to provide places where floods from future hurricanes and heavy rainstorms would naturally flow without destroying residential neighborhoods. The experience of planning for the Bring New Orleans Back Commission is recounted in "On the Ground in New Orleans," a conversation with the principal planners from WRT, John Beckman, Richard Bartholomew, and Paul Rookwood, in *Planning* magazine.

2. A search of articles that appeared in the months following Hurricane Katrina yields a large array of advice that New Orleans should be made *smaller:* from urban planners at work throughout America and in foreign countries, professors in various disciplines, and esteemed urban scholars. One could only characterize their advice as impassioned and pertinent, wherever it appeared: in the *Wall Street Journal,* the *Detroit News,* the *Washington Post,* the *Los Angeles Times,* the *New York Times,* the *New Yorker,* and online publications such as *Slate.*

3. A member of the mayor's Bring New Orleans Back Commission—the co-chairman of the commission's Urban Planning Committee—was said to have told the *Wall Street Journal,* "Those who want to see this city rebuilt want to see it done in a completely different way, demographically, geographically and politically." While some residents understood his meaning as hopeful, most New Orleanians—particularly those who'd been displaced by the storm—found his words ominous: that the city would have fewer poor people, would be reduced in physi-

cal extent, and would vote into office a different set of leaders from those who'd been elected in recent years. A detailed account of the reaction to comments by members of the Bring New Orleans Back Commission is found in Davis, "Who Is Killing New Orleans?" 11–20.

4. Yolanda Rodriguez, Executive Director, New Orleans City Planning Commission, interview by the author, April 2007. The necessity of "rebuilding the city's 'planning infrastructure'" in the early months after Hurricane Katrina is described in Lewis, "Next Steps in New Orleans," December 2005.

5. As it happened, most of the businesses that reopened in this early time period were small owner-operated enterprises. The larger national firms held back, and one could only assume they waited to see how promising the recovery of New Orleans was. Campanella, "Street Survey," 1.

6. Individual homeowners were promised compensation from a program known as "The Road Home," which provided up to $150,000 for losses to property. The program did not work smoothly—as accounts in every newspaper along Louisiana's Gulf Coast reported.

7. The grave facts about the cost of renting a place to live were so well established that political leaders beyond Louisiana knew them. Nancy Pelosi, Speaker of the House of Representatives, and Harry Reid, majority leader of the Senate, wrote in a letter to President George W. Bush on December 14, 2007: "The shortage of housing has pushed rents in the City [of New Orleans], and surrounding metropolitan area, well above their normal levels, with rents rising 45 percent since the storm."

8. The number of neighborhoods said to be included in the city council's plan (informally known as the Lambert Plan) varied according to which article one read: sometimes forty-nine neighborhoods, and sometimes fifty. For the sake of simplicity, I've used fifty.

9. The agency bearing the news to Mayor Nagin that a citywide plan would be necessary was the Louisiana Recovery Authority, created by the federal government and charged with distributing federal aid to hurricane-devastated parishes. The federal funds at stake were those that the city itself could use to rebuild infrastructure and public buildings. As noted earlier, "The Road Home" provided federal funds to individuals for reconstructing their damaged property.

10. The mayor's vision for transforming the Mississippi riverbank was described in a letter to "Stakeholders" written by one of the architects chosen to oversee the new waterfront plan.

11. The fears fostered by the 1927 flood were not paranoid delusions, but based on historical fact, as exhaustively—and rivetingly—recounted by

John M. Barry in *Rising Tide: The Great Mississippi Flood of 1927 and How It Changed America.*

CHAPTER 3. WHAT ARE CITY PLANS?

1. In a useful little document entitled *Planning ABC's,* the American Planning Association uses the metaphor common among planners of "a cabinet full of plans" to describe a community's comprehensive plan. Most planners employ similar metaphors—bookshelf is another—to help laymen understand that a comprehensive plan is a more complicated matter than it might seem, though admittedly such metaphors suggest only that there's *a lot* of material, not that the substance of the material is important.

2. A useful summary of reformers' views is attributed to Daniel Burnham, the famed architect-planner of the time. Burnham is said to have longed "for a city with clean air and neat, straight streets; for a city that was beautiful to look at, with Paris' pleasing symmetry and graceful parks; above all, for a city that was orderly and dignified. Achieve these goals, he believed, and people will be inspired to lead noble, productive lives." Lois Wille, review of *The Plan of Chicago: Daniel Burnham and the Remaking of the American City,* by Carl Smith, *Chicago Tribune,* November 12, 2006.

3. This sentence is my extrapolation (using a New Orleanian's predilection for parades to mark any occasion) of Mumford's remark that "Our imperial architecture is an architecture of compensation: It provides grandiloquent stones for people who have been deprived of bread and sunlight." Mumford, *Sticks and Stones,* 147.

4. *The Plan of Chicago* was written by Daniel Burnham and Edward Bennett, although as shorthand reference, the document is often ascribed to the more lastingly famous member of the team—and thus is often called "Burnham's plan."

5. Although planners agree that the quotation sounds like something Burnham might have said, there is no record of his uttering this famous advice.

6. In New Orleans, I wrote a "Blueprint for a Master Plan" in 1999, a document that would guide the task of completing the city's comprehensive plan. There were to be eighteen elements of this plan, ranging from housing to transportation, capital projects to economic development; a central element was the land-use plan. All eighteen elements took up the subject of the components of a modern, thriving city that planning—and land-use regulations—can affect.

7. There is, of course, no single way to distribute new housing, new commercial districts, new parks, and so on, among the different neighbor-

hoods in a city. Therefore, planners rely on their professional abilities and creativity and discretion to decide what is the most important factor in devising a city's future development—and expressing it on the map included in a land-use plan.

As recounted earlier, several recovery plans were written for New Orleans—each of which had a land-use plan as an element and each of which was quite different from the others. One can read each plan to decipher what the planning consultants who wrote it had thought was most important for the city's future. The planning consultants hired by the Bring New Orleans Back Commission thought the best expression of citizens' needs and development projections was to provide space where floodwaters from future hurricanes could go without harming a future citizenry. Mayor Nagin's notion of a plan that "let the market decide" relied on actions by independent property owners to rebuild the city. The Unified Plan consultants concluded from their evidence that it was important to get money into the hands of residents so they could rebuild their neighborhoods as they once had been, and proposed a plan that did just that.

CHAPTER 4. WHAT CITY PLANNERS DO AND WHY THEY DO IT THAT WAY

1. An excellent account of the hard road away from home that most successful New Orleans musicians follow is told by Mac Rebennack—Dr. John—in *Under a Hoodoo Moon*.
2. Frederick Law Olmsted, Jr., followed in the footsteps of his father, America's most gifted amateur, whose many accomplishments—beyond, say, designing Central Park in New York—are recounted in *A Clearing in the Distance*.
3. As explained earlier in this chapter, from the property tax revenue cities collect, they provide police and fire protection, public schools, recreational activities, sewage and water systems, local roads.

CHAPTER 5. HOW PLANNERS INTERACT WITH CITIZENS

1. This geographical designation is likely to confound anyone trying to understand the city using cardinal points, because the so-called West Bank actually lies directly *east* of the French Quarter. However, if one were to straighten the Mississippi River's meanders so that it flowed from north to south, it'd become clear that the West Bank lies on the western side of the river's course.

CHAPTER 6. THE AMERICAN EVOLUTION OF PLANS

1. Belson, "In Success of 'Smart Growth.'" For readers interested in knowing more about the intellectual origins—and actual outcomes— of Garden Cities (including Radburn), an excellent source is Hall, *Cities of Tomorrow,* in the highly readable chapter titled "The City in the Garden." Hall's central argument is that the original theories of city planning were ahead of the times—and thus cities weren't built as the theories would have counseled. Instead, as the planning theories were "belatedly [translated] into reality, there occurred a rather monstrous perversion of history," in which developers seized upon individual ideas contained in a theoretical scheme for planning a city, but discarded the overall concept (p. 3). Thus, it's possible to see a city as accumulated shards of old planning theories that appealed to a landowner as he decided how to design, say, the winding pathways of Lake Vista in New Orleans. But that landowner—the Orleans Levee District—did not construct a Garden City as it was originally conceived, and instead built an "ornament."

2. The ideas about planning New York City that Robert Moses had—and carried out—are wonderfully, if relentlessly, told in *The Power Broker,* a book that anyone interested in city planning must read. His ideas were gargantuan, as any New Yorker or visitor to New York can see at the Panorama of the City of New York, a nine-thousand-square-foot scale model of every building constructed before 1992 in all five boroughs. The model, housed in the Queens Museum of Art, was commissioned by Moses for the 1964 World's Fair, and in March 2009 the museum announced that it would update the panorama regularly. No planner can see this panorama without wanting one for her own city to help citizens visualize the effect of proposed development, but few planners have the finances that Robert Moses did.

3. The Chicago Department of Cultural Affairs marked the centennial of Burnham's Plan of Chicago with an exhibit of photographs taken in Manila in 2008. Burnham had drawn plans to modernize the capital of the Philippine Islands two years before he created the Plan of Chicago, and this exhibit—photographs taken by the photographer Tim Long— show that Burnham's design legacy has endured.

4. The most sweeping critique of the consequences of the federal urban renewal program, and not incidentally, a critique of city planning itself, is found in the masterpiece written by Jane Jacobs, *The Death and Life of Great American Cities.* The human face of people who were moved out of so-called slums by municipal dreams of "renewal" is hauntingly

described in Fried, "Grieving for a Lost Home." Both works are necessary reading for being informed about the practice of city planning.

5. Between 1954 and 1980, the federal government spent more than a billion dollars to assist suburban towns in preparing land-use plans, and later in this period to assist efforts to create regional plans (i.e., plans that encompassed more than one municipality). Nelson, "Leadership in a New Era."

CHAPTER 7. HOW PLANS TAKE EFFECT

1. Duncan, "Three-Star Celebrity."
2. Charles, "Using Stamford's Master Plan."
3. In most states, including Louisiana, only an elected legislative body can vote to regulate property. City planners advise legislators about the appropriate regulations, but have no legal authority to adopt them.
4. The legal action that makes a plat a permanent legal document is referred to as "recording"; it is the responsibility of a designated local official to keep records of these documents. In New Orleans, this designated official is known as the recorder. In the Recorder's Office there are plats dating back to the early 1700s, and it is possible to find the name of each individual who ever had an interest in a piece of property, and also to follow how any piece of land in the municipality was divided and sold, over the past three hundred years.
5. The early history of suburbs—and of early American commuting patterns—is recounted in Sam Bass Warner's classic study of Boston, *Streetcar Suburbs.* The percentage of Americans who lived in suburban areas increased from 27 percent in 1950 to 52 percent in 2000. Nelson, "Leadership in a New Era."
6. Any planner could list the contemporary problems associated with explosive growth of subdivisions—traffic tie-ups, underfunded school districts and libraries and emergency medical services, inadequate hospitals, insufficient sewerage systems, and more.
7. Quotation from the majority opinion in *Euclid v. Ambler,* as reprinted in Platt, *Land Use and Society,* 299.
8. The City of Irvine's website offers this explanation of the city's planning provenance: "Irvine's noteworthy, present-day status didn't evolve from happenstance. It's the outcome of mastermind planners, and those engaged to institute the plan. Each day, the Irvine City leaders and staff work diligently to ensure a quality environment for the City's future." City of Irvine, "History of the City," www.cityofirvine.org/about/history.asp.

9. In the zoning ordinances of most cities—large and small—undeveloped land is designated as suitable for single-family houses, on the implicit theory that such a use is "normal" and "expected" and, if the designated land is in fact developed as single-family houses, the municipality will endure fewer problems than if developed any other way. The implicit theory is rarely questioned, as planning board members across the nation could attest.

10. As described in Chapter 4, this sequence of steps is what planners are required by law to follow when advising a city council on land-use decisions that come before the council.

CHAPTER 8. CITY PLANNING IN ACTION

1. All cities prefer individual enterprises to be located on a single lot because assessing the value of each enterprise is uncomplicated by property lines that divide it, and also because it is uncomplicated to send out tax bills to an owner—and to receive what is owed. From this simple, commonsense explanation, the reader can see that efficient tax collection is the primary motivation for subdivision regulations.

   In addition, cities are motivated to enact subdivision regulations to ensure that new development is adequate to municipal standards—that streets are properly laid, that drainage is properly engineered—so that the city does not have to pay for improving what a subdivider left inadequate.

2. Planners have access to professional reference material that tells them, for example, the national standard for the number of parking spaces required by a variety of land uses.

3. Many studies of urban grocery stores show that residents of poor neighborhoods pay extravagantly high prices for substandard products. The *American Journal of Preventative Medicine* often reports such pertinent research as "Neighborhood Environments: Disparities in Access to Healthy Foods in the U.S.," and "You Are Where You Shop: Grocery Store Locations, Weight, and Neighborhoods." The subject is also a common feature of daily newspapers, appearing under such titles as "The High Cost of Poverty: Why the Poor Pay More" (from Washington, D.C.) and "A Plan to Add Supermarkets to Poor Areas, with Healthy Results" (from New York).

4. City budgets routinely include a line item—called "emergency" or "contingency" funds—as a reserve fund for unexpected but necessary expenditures.

CHAPTER 9. PLANS THAT ONLY PLANNERS USE

1. Stamford defined "affordable apartments" as dwelling units that were offered at a price families who earned less than the city's median income could afford.

2. In the interest of readability, the events that follow have been simplified. However, the important facts—and the outcome—are faithful to what transpired. And, as noted earlier, the trivial complications—who said what, and when—can distract from the consequential themes of public policy events such as these events describe.

3. This procedure is a combination of statutory and constitutional requirements, mixed in with custom and the idiosyncracy of a particular set of planning commissioners.

4. The three labels I've listed here—self-sustaining cities, green suburbs, and smart growth—are slogans meant to imply some commonsense *and obvious* meaning. Cities that are "self-sustaining" *obviously* do not require the infusion of outside assistance to thrive: they can pay their bills, offer their citizens all necessary public services. Suburbs that are "green" *obviously* do not create pollution or draw down unreplenishable resources. Development—i.e., growth—that is "smart" *obviously* does not create unwanted or unforeseen bad effects that, presumably, "dumb" growth would occasion. One has to grant the inspiring qualities of these labels—though with a little experience, one also has to acknowledge how poorly thought through the labels are. *How,* exactly, can a city be made self-sustaining? *How,* exactly, can a suburb be made "green"? And *how,* exactly, can a person determine what is "smart" growth? Good questions that the slogans actually work to leave unasked.

5. Danto, Introduction, xv.

CHAPTER 10. PLANS THAT DON'T INCLUDE WHAT CITIZENS KNOW

1. These meetings were held in each of New Orleans' thirteen planning districts, so that citizens from every part of the city could participate. The first of these meetings was the session in the Lower Ninth Ward described in Chapter 5.

2. Maine State Planning Office, "Visioning Handbook," 3.

3. Barbanel, "Remaking or Preserving," 1.

4. Louisiana Recovery Authority, "2007 Regional Vision Poll: Summary of Findings," 19.

CHAPTER 11. PLANS THAT ELECTED LEADERS IGNORE

1. Alternatively, the developer might pay for an option to buy the property once he secures a building permit for the hotel. In either case, money has changed hands, so the developer has a vested interest in seeing his project approved *as he imagined it,* because changing any aspect of the proposed development will cost him more money.
2. As described earlier, the New Orleans City Council had seven members. According to state statute, it took four votes to agree with a recommendation of the city planning commission, five votes to overturn the commission's recommendation. In the case of the casino, the planning commission had voted for *approval,* and therefore it would require only four members of the council to authorize the casino—while simultaneously removing any offending conditions suggested by the commission.

CHAPTER 12. CITY PLANS FOR CITIZENS

1. As in the number of neighborhoods said to be included in the city council's plan, the number of neighborhoods included in the Unified Plan was variously reported as seventy-two or seventy-three. However, in 1970 the New Orleans Planning Commission designated—and named—seventy-two neighborhoods in the city, so I will use that number as correct. *New Orleans 1999 Land Use Plan,* 8.
2. Eggler, "City Plan Gets Lukewarm Reviews."
3. The city council was—understandably, one might think—so eager to start rebuilding that it authorized the first $117 million of federal money for the recovery director to spend, without there having been a public discussion of *where* and *why* and *how* he would start rebuilding the city. Although the recovery director was a former professor of planning, he evidently did not feel a necessity to reveal his plans. *Times-Picayune* editorial, "Filling in the Picture."
4. Filosa, "Anger Hits Home for Housing Agency"; Ouroussoff, "History vs. Homogeneity in New Orleans Housing Fight."
5. Rogers, "City Indifferent to Residents' Ideas on Hospital."
6. The bibliography provides a set of references to "new" plans that members of the planning profession have devised in recent years—including the commonly referenced "New Urbanism" plans and "sustainability" plans.
7. *New Orleans 1999 Land Use Plan,* Appendix D.

CHAPTER 13. THE TROUBLE WITH MOST CITY PLANS

1. "Character" is a code word planners use to describe a cohesive quality of a neighborhood, although they try to give it some further meaning by employing adjectives. For example, the *New Orleans 1999 Land Use Plan* described the Lakeview neighborhood as having a "residential and recreational character" (127). Citizens, however, in discussions of proposed new development in their neighborhood often use the word "character" to describe some *unnamed* feature of where they live, which they do not want to change: that "nice" people live there, that life is peaceful. By implication, these qualities could be lost if the new land use under discussion were authorized.

2. Another, less apparent result of planners asking open-ended questions is that the discussion which follows often becomes dominated by citizens more "experienced" with what planners routinely ask, and who— because of their experience—believe they know the answers being sought. Citizens such as the representative of New Orleans' good government organization who came to the meeting in the Lower Ninth Ward "believe" (i.e., assume), for example, that speaking about abandoned property is "inappropriate" in discussions of the future because they believe the subject of abandoned properties is no more than a contemporaneous annoyance that administrators should solve. The casualties from discussions dominated by these "knowledgeable" citizens are the truly experienced voices—which are unfortunately left out.

3. Giving tax breaks is of course a form of investment, since it reduces the public funds that are available for line items in a city's budget. When leaders choose *not* to collect taxes on certain types of property, they reduce the revenue available for anything else they want to invest in.

CHAPTER 14. FORMULATING GOOD CITY PLANS: THE STATE OF THE CITY

1. As an example of statistical data about a city's physical environment, I've taken some information from tables found in *New Orleans 1999 Land Use Plan,* which described existing land uses. In 1999, single-family residential uses occupied 917 acres of the Lower Ninth Ward, which was 63.9 percent of the land in that neighborhood; parkland occupied 56 acres, or 3.9 percent. Such information is mostly useful for making comparisons with the city as a whole. Within the municipal boundaries of New Orleans, for example, 11.2 percent of all land was devoted to single-family housing, and 25 percent of the city was occupied by parkland. In other words, the percentage of land in the Lower Ninth Ward used for single-family houses was unusually high, and

land used for parkland was unusually low. *New Orleans 1999 Land Use Plan*, 23, 190.

2. *New Orleans 1999 Land Use Plan*, 22.

3. *New Orleans 1999 Land Use Plan*, 269, 270, 272.

CHAPTER 15. FORMULATING GOOD CITY PLANS: PROJECTIONS FOR THE FUTURE

1. The *New Orleans 1999 Land Use Plan* has a typical array of demographic facts that all city plans provide, including the number of citizens, number who are black, number younger than eighteen and older than sixty-four, the number of households in the city, the average number of persons in a household, and the average household income.

2. Planners have wide access to good ideas: the American Planning Association is a ready and willing resource, always able to recount new planning initiatives from across the country. In fact, the *New Orleans 1999 Land Use Plan* was devised after the city's planning staff had several conversations with the planning association about good models they might follow when writing a new plan. In addition, all planners have informal networks of advisers—fellow planners in other cities, professors they've studied under, knowledgeable citizens—who often provide good ideas from other cities, other planning experiences. Making use of all this information is one form of the background research planners complete before meeting with the public to discuss the Projections of the Future section of a Good City Plan.

CHAPTER 16. FORMULATING GOOD CITY PLANS: CITIZEN'S GUIDE TO LAND-USE DECISIONS

1. Planners have many professional reference books that tell them how much parking a restaurant will require, for example, or how large delivery bays must be for industrial uses.

CHAPTER 17. ACTIVATING GOOD CITY PLANS

1. One could say, of course, that a plan is "activated" whenever citizens use it—whether to decide how to develop property they own, or to learn how development might occur in the future. Such "activation" is random and informal, dependent on urges of single individuals. However, the subject of this chapter is what *planners* must do— formally—to activate Good City Plans.

2. Such changes include, for example, adding new uses to the list of what is authorized in a zoning district, or changing the boundaries of a zoning district, or changing the rules that land uses have to follow.

CHAPTER 18. HOW GOOD CITY PLANS INFLUENCE ELECTED LEADERS

1. Stephens, "Why Are You a Planning Commissioner?" 12. This article lists three broad categories of reasons that citizens serve on planning boards and commissions: professional development and self-actualization; personal and group special interests; and civic engagement and civil service. The author acknowledges that most planning commission members probably serve for some combination of these reasons.

2. Johnson, *A History of the American People*, 565–566.

3. What might be called a "personality issue" is the experience common to all planning directors. Norm Krumholz and Mayor Carl B. Stokes in Cleveland, or Amanda Burden and Mayor Michael Bloomberg in New York, are prime examples of personalities who work well together —but those examples do not serve as general guidance for other planners. Personality is a quixotic ingredient, with consequences that can't reliably be predicted.

4. Some cities might even adopt an Evaluation Appendix as part of the Good City Plan, which would spell out what aspects of the plan's execution are to be analyzed, and how.

CHAPTER 19. GOOD CITY PLANS AND GREAT CITIES

1. Reid, "Citywide Plan Starts Anew."

APPENDIX

1. Nossiter, "New Orleans Mayor Pleads for Patience in Meeting Goals."

2. *Times-Picayune* editorial, "Filling in the Picture."

3. "City Planning Commission of New Orleans," *City of New Orleans,* www.cityofno.com/pg-52-1-city-planning.aspx.

BIBLIOGRAPHY

REFERENCES CITED

Adams, Henry. *The Education of Henry Adams,* Modern Library Edition. New York: Random House, 1931.

Barbanel, Josh. "Remaking, or Preserving, the City's Face." *New York Times* (Real Estate Desk), January 18, 2004.

Barry, John M. *Rising Tide: The Great Mississippi Flood of 1927 and How It Changed America.* New York: Touchstone, 1998.

Belson, Ken. "In Success of 'Smart Growth,' New Jersey Feels Strain." *New York Times* (Metropolitan Desk), April 9, 2007.

Brown, DeNeen L. "The High Cost of Poverty: Why the Poor Pay More." *Washington Post,* May 18, 2009.

Burnham, Daniel H., and Edward H. Bennett, edited by Charles Moore, with a new introduction by Kristen Schaffer. *Plan of Chicago.* New York: Princeton Architectural Press, 1993. (Originally published by the Commercial Club of Chicago, 1908.)

Campanella, Richard. *Geographies of New Orleans.* Lafayette, La.: Center for Louisiana Studies, Louisiana State University, 2006.

Campanella, Richard. "Street Survey of Business Reopenings in Post-Katrina New Orleans." (Report on a study funded by the National Science Foundation.) New Orleans: Tulane University's Center for Bioenvironmental Research, January 2007.

Campanella, Richard. *Time and Place in New Orleans.* Gretna, La.: Pelican, 2002.

Cardwell, Diane. "A Plan to Add Supermarkets to Poor Areas, with Healthy Results." *New York Times,* September 23, 2009.

Caro, Robert. *The Power Broker: Robert Moses and the Fall of New York.* New York: Alfred A. Knopf, 1974.

Charles, Eleanor. "Using Stamford's Master Plan to Steer Development." *New York Times* (Real Estate Desk), November 2, 2003.

City of Irvine. "History of the City." www.cityofirvine.org/about/history.asp.

Danto, Arthur C. Introduction to *The Unknown Masterpiece,* by Honoré de

Balzac, translated by Richard Howard. New York: New York Review Books, 2001.

Davis, Mike. "Who Is Killing New Orleans?" *The Nation,* April 6, 2006.

Duncan, Jeff. "Three-Star Celebrity." *Times-Picayune,* September 19, 2005.

Eggler, Bruce. "City Plan Gets Lukewarm Reviews." *Times-Picayune,* May 22, 2007.

Eggler, Bruce. "Commission Approves N.O. Master Plan." *Times-Picayune,* January 27, 2010.

Eggler, Bruce. "Reclaiming the River." *Times-Picayune,* April 6, 2008.

Filosa, Gwen. "Anger Hits Home for Housing Agency." *Times-Picayune,* September 1, 2007.

Fried, Marc. "Grieving for a Lost Home." In *The Urban Condition,* L. J. Duhl, editor. New York: Basic, 1963.

Gerckens, Laurence C. *Planning ABC's.* Burlington, Vt.: Champlain Planning Press/Planning Commissioner's Journal, 2003.

Hall, Peter. *Cities of Tomorrow,* third edition. Malden, Mass.: Blackwell, 2002.

Inamagi, Sanae, Deborah A. Cohen, Brian Karl Finch, Steven M. Asch. "You Are Where You Shop: Grocery Store Locations, Weight, and Neighborhoods." *American Journal of Preventive Medicine,* July 2006.

Jacobs, Jane. *The Death and Life of Great American Cities.* New York: Random House, 1961.

Johnson, Paul. *A History of the American People.* New York: HarperCollins, 1998.

Larson, Nicole I., Mary T. Story, Melissa C. Nelson. "Neighborhood Environments: Disparities in Access to Healthy Foods in the U.S." *American Journal of Preventive Medicine,* November 2008.

Lemmon, Alfred E., John T. Magill, Jason R. Wiese, editors; John T. Hébert, consulting editor. *Charting Louisiana: Five Hundred Years of Maps.* New Orleans: The Historic New Orleans Collection, 2003.

Lewis, Sylvia. "Next Steps in New Orleans." *Planning* (a publication of the American Planning Association), December 2005.

Magill, John. "Rushing into the East." *Cultural Vistas,* Spring 2008. New Orleans: Louisiana Endowment for the Humanities.

Maine State Planning Office. *Community Visioning Handbook.* Augusta, Maine: State Planning Office, 2003.

Meitrodt, Jeffrey, and Frank Donze. "Plan Shrinks City Footprint." *Times-Picayune,* December 14, 2005.

Mumford, Lewis. *Sticks and Stones.* New York: Dover Books on Architecture edition; first published in 1924.

Nelson, Arthur C. "Leadership in a New Era (Federal Housing Act of 1954, Federal Water Pollution Control Act Amendments of 1972)." *Journal of the American Planning Association,* September 22, 2006.

Nelson, Arthur C. *Planner's Estimating Guide.* Chicago: Planners Press, American Planning Association, 2004.

New Orleans 1999 Land Use Plan. City Planning Commission of New Orleans, April 1999.

Nossiter, Adam. "New Orleans Mayor Pleads for Patience in Meeting Goals." *New York Times,* September 11, 2006.

"On the Ground in New Orleans." *Planning,* April 2006.

Ouroussoff, Nicolai. "History vs. Homogeneity in New Orleans Housing Fight." *New York Times,* February 22, 2007.

Platt, Rutherford H. *Land Use and Society,* revised edition. Washington, D.C.: Island, 2004.

Rebennack, Mac, with Jack Rummel. *Under a Hoodoo Moon: The Life of Dr. John the Night Tripper.* New York: St. Martins, 1994.

Reid, Molly. "Citywide Plan Starts Anew." *Times-Picayune,* September 28, 2008.

Riggs, Trisha. "Moving Beyond Recovery to Restoration and Rebirth." Press release from the Urban Land Institute (Washington, D.C.), November 18, 2005.

Rogers, Bobbi. "City Indifferent to Residents' Ideas on Hospital." *Times-Picayune* (letter to the editor), August 16, 2008.

Rybczynski, Witold. *A Clearing in the Distance: Frederick Law Olmsted and America in the Nineteenth Century.* New York: Scribner, 1999.

Stephens, Ric. "Why Are You a Planning Commissioner?" *Planning Commissioners Journal,* Spring 2007.

Times-Picayune editorial. "Filling in the Picture." *Times-Picayune,* September 19, 2007.

U.S. Army Corps of Engineers. *Mississippi River Gulf Outlet: Deep-Draft De-Authorization Interim Report to Congress.* Washington, D.C.: U.S. Army Corps of Engineers, December 2006.

Warner, Sam Bass, Jr. *Streetcar Suburbs: The Process of Growth in Boston, 1870–1900.* Boston: Harvard University Press/MIT Press, 1962.

Wille, Lois. Review of *The Plan of Chicago: Daniel Burnham and the Remaking of the American City,* by Carl Smith. *Chicago Tribune,* November 12, 2006.

FURTHER READING

What Planners Know About Cities

Alexander, Christopher. *The Timeless Way of Building.* New York: Oxford University Press, 1979.

Cronon, William. *Nature's Metropolis: Chicago and the Great West.* New York: W. W. Norton, 1991.

Cullingworth, Barry. *Planning in the USA: Policies, Issues, and Processes.* London: Routledge, 2000.

Fagin, Joe R., editor. *The Urban Scene: Myths and Realities.* New York: Random House, 1973.

Fainstein, Susan S., and Scott Campbell, editors. *Readings in Planning Theory: Studies in Urban and Social Change,* second edition. Boston: Wiley-Blackwell, 2003.

Girouard, Mark. *Cities and People: A Social and Architectural History.* New Haven: Yale University Press, 1985.

Hardin, Garrett. "The Tragedy of the Commons." *Science* 162 (December 13, 1968).

Jackson, John Brinckerhoff. *A Sense of Place, a Sense of Time.* New Haven: Yale University Press, 1994.

Lindblom, Charles. "The Science of Muddling Through." *Public Administration Review* 19 (1959).

Lynch, Kevin. *City Sense and City Design,* edited by Tridib Banerjee and Michael Southworth. Cambridge: MIT Press, 1990.

McHarg, Ian. *Design with Nature.* New York: Natural History Press for the American Museum of Natural History, 1969.

Mandelker, Daniel R., editor. *Planning Reform in the New Century.* Chicago: Planners Press, American Planning Association, 2005.

Mumford, Lewis. *The City in History: Its Origins, Its Transformations, and Its Prospects.* New York: Harcourt, Brace & World, a Harbinger Book, 1961.

Mumford, Lewis. *The Culture of Cities.* New York: Harcourt Brace Jovanovich, 1970.

Stilgoe, John. *Outside Lies Magic: Regaining History and Awareness in Everyday Places.* New York: Walker, 1999.

Professional Practice of Planning, Including "New" Theories in the Profession

Arendt, Randall. *Conservation Design for Subdivisions.* Washington, D.C.: Island, 1996.

Bunnell, Gene. *Making Places Special: Stories of Real Places Made Better by Planning.* Chicago: Planners Press, American Planning Association, 2002.

Daniels, Tom, and Katherine Daniels. *Environmental Planning Handbook.* Chicago: Planners Press, American Planning Association, 2003.

Duany, Andres, Elizabeth Plater-Zyberk, and Jeff Speck. *Suburban Nation: The Rise of Sprawl and the Decline of the American Dream.* New York: North Point, 2000.

France, Robert. *Handbook of Water Sensitive Planning and Design.* Boca Raton, Fla.: Lewis, 2002.

Hoch, Charles. *What Planners Do: Power, Politics, and Persuasion.* Chicago: Planners Press, American Planning Association, 1994.

Johnson, William C. *Urban Planning and Politics.* Chicago: Planners Press, American Planning Association, 1997.

Meck, Stuart. *Growing Smart Legislative Guidebook 3: Model Statutes for Planning and the Management of Change.* Chicago: Planners Press, American Planning Association, 2002.

Rybczynski, Witold. *Last Harvest—How a Cornfield Became New Daleville: Real Estate Development in America from George Washington to the Builders of the Twenty-first Century, and Why We Live in Houses Anyway.* New York: Scribner, 2007.

New Orleans and Louisiana

Brinkley, Doug. *The Great Deluge: Hurricane Katrina, New Orleans, and the Mississippi Gulf Coast.* New York: William Morrow, 2006.

Colton, Craig. *An Unnatural Metropolis: Wresting New Orleans from Nature.* Baton Rouge: Louisiana State University Press, 2006.

Eggers, Dave. *Zeitoun.* San Francisco: McSweeney's, 2009.

Lewis, Peirce F. *New Orleans: The Making of an Urban Landscape.* Santa Fe, N.M.: The Center for American Places, 2003.

Liebling, A. J. *The Earl of Louisiana: Profile of an Eccentric.* New York: Simon and Schuster, 1961.

Steinberg, Ted. *Acts of God: The Unnatural History of Natural Disaster in America,* second edition. New York: Oxford University Press, 2006.

Williams, T. Harry. *Huey Long.* New York: Alfred A. Knopf, 1970.

ACKNOWLEDGMENTS

Many people have influenced my professional life as a planner, although no influence has been as consequential and enduring and sweetly rigorous as that of Richard Ford, starting with my years at graduate school, continuing with my service in Missoula and New Orleans, and culminating with this book—which exists primarily because Richard encouraged and contributed to every step of its being written. He even insisted that my writing problems were the same problems he had—a wondrous conception that finally *was* encouraging.

When I was a student, Al Feldt and John Nystuen opened the challenging possibilities of being a city planner, and by simple good fortune I began my career working for great men—Dick Netzer, Chester Rapkin, and George Sternlieb, who were charismatic examples of impassioned intellectual and professional devotion. Mayor Sidney Barthelemy gave me the opportunity to lead New Orleans city planning in 1992 and to learn from his savvy adviser, former professor Al Stokes, about the political world within which a planner must make her way. In 1994, Mayor Marc H. Morial started transforming the city from its oil-bust dereliction, and included city planning in nearly all his administration's deliberations. Those eight years were significant to the origins of this book, and many ideas that I've advanced benefited from the insight of Mayor Morial, Tony Mumphrey, and Marlin Gusman.

From the first day on the job in New Orleans to the last, my happy realization was the fine quality of the staff in the city planning office. Two irresistible presidents of the New Orleans city council, Dorothy Mae Taylor and Jim Singleton, were true to their early promise to work with me as planning director, and both presidents defended planners' work when it bumped against individual developers and citizens.

Amanda Urban, Ileene Smith, Rae Zimmerman, and Inge Feltrinelli championed this book from the first, and their enthusiasm helped carry it through to completion. Joanne Sealy's talent for timely irreverence contributed both to my persevering as planning director and then writing about it. Lake Douglas, ardent researcher with a flair for finding subtle, elegant solutions to public policy problems was—and is—a stalwart friend no matter how stormy the political weather might prove to be. Dot Wilson, a jazz-singing force who's kept young people in school and a neighborhood intact, encouraged me by her example of a well-lived life of service. Bill Foster, dean of the Muskie School of Public Service, generously encouraged this book by giving me time to work on it while I was teaching. Donna Robertson and Alan Plattus read the manuscript in an early version, and their provocative insights made the final version more useful. At Yale University Press, Sarah Miller and Philip King were indispensable: Sarah shepherded the book through complicated publication processes, and Phil copy-edited the manuscript trying to raise it to his exacting standards and to save me from inadvertent gaffes.

This acknowledgment ends by once again mentioning Richard Ford's influence. As he took me to city hall for my first day at work in New Orleans, he said, "You must keep a notebook about your days here, and someday write about this job. Otherwise the day-to-day will sweep it out of your brain. And what you'll learn is too valuable to lose." I was lucky to hear his suggestion and then also to take it by keeping track of the fitful and equivocal and even successful dramas that constitute city planning. The best acknowledgment of Richard's influence is to extend it, to encourage all other members of my profession to keep notebooks . . . and someday to write about their experiences. City planning would benefit greatly from all such writing.

INDEX